Analyzing
Social Policy

Analyzing
Social Policy

Multiple Perspectives for Critically
Understanding and Evaluating Policy

Mary Katherine O'Connor
F. Ellen Netting

WILEY

John Wiley & Sons, Inc.

Copyright © 2011 by John Wiley & Sons, Inc. All rights reserved.

Published by John Wiley & Sons, Inc., Hoboken, New Jersey.
Published simultaneously in Canada.

For general information on our other products and services please contact our Customer Care Department within the U.S. at (800) 762-2974, outside the United States at (317) 572-3993 or fax (317) 572-4002.

Wiley also publishes its books in a variety of electronic formats. Some content that appears in print may not be available in electronic books. For more information about Wiley products, visit our website at www.wiley.com.

Library of Congress Cataloging-in-Publication Data

O'Connor, Mary Katherine.
 Analyzing social policy : multiple perspectives for critically understanding and evaluating policy / Mary Katherine O'Connor and F. Ellen Netting.
  p. cm.
 Includes index.
 Summary: "This unique volume outlines the different frameworks of policy analysis and explains how readers can use research and critical thinking skills to understand the different models from their formation and development to implementation. Approaching the topic from an analytical and research-based perspective, the authors help readers make better, informed choices for successfully dealing with the complexities of social policy. Social workers, public administrators, nonprofit managers and upper level students of these fields will find the tools necessary for understanding how social policies are analyzed, conceived, and ultimately applied."– Provided by publisher.
 ISBN 978-0-470-45203-5 (pbk.)
 1. Social policy. I. Netting, F. Ellen. II. Title.
 HN17.5.O26 2010
 320.6—dc22

2010019083

Printed in the United States of America

10 9 8 7 6 5 4 3 2 1

This text is dedicated to Donald E. Chambers and Peter M. Kettner, who were our early collaborators. They gave us roots so we could use our wings.

Contents

Foreword

I KNOW WHAT you're thinking; you're wondering if someone like you who believes they don't have any policy research skills can begin to do policy research. You're probably wondering what policy even has to do with practice and why it's so important. Okay, so maybe those thoughts ran through my brain when confronted with the task of policy research and how pertinent it is to have a better understanding of the relationship between policy and practice. Through my journey in a child and family policy course, I came to realize that policy is absolutely related to practice and the two have a symbiotic relationship. Furthermore, I also discovered that not only can investigating policy be considered research, but that I was able to do the research. I, a self-labeled practitioner who cringed any time the word "policy" was mentioned, actually realized the importance of doing policy research and ended up enjoying it.

MY EXPERIENCE

My experience began in a course that focused on the examination of local, state, and national policies related to children, adolescents, and families. As a clinical practitioner, I thought learning more about policies related to children and families would be both pertinent and beneficial to my education. Policy was something I viewed as a mundane phenomenon that was only remotely related to practice with families and children. My perspective on policy was mostly apathetic, yet I felt acquiring more knowledge about policies could help in my practice with children and families in need.

At the beginning of the child and family policy course, the class was presented with the challenge of using a policy research framework to explore a policy. We were to form groups and then pick a topic and a policy we felt needed further exploration. At the end, a final presentation and paper would be completed for the course instructor as well as for two individuals from the Commonwealth of Virginia's Department of Social Services. Well, this initially seemed like an extremely daunting task. I didn't feel as though I knew enough about policy, let alone policy research and the policies that accompany that research, to accomplish this task with which I was presented. And then to present this to people who directly affect policy for the Commonwealth? I was more than intimidated and felt completely ill-equipped to handle the assignment. Little did I know that I had more potential and capability than I originally supposed.

After choosing an area my group wished to explore, we decided the best way to analyze and explore the policy was by using an interpretive policy research approach (don't worry, you'll learn more about this shortly). This perspective allowed us some freedom in deciding how to approach the process of analyzing the policy we chose in order to better understand the mechanisms and structures related to the policy. The process I encountered was one of consensus building so that all members within my group were on the "same page" as to how the policy was being analyzed. It was through the process of consensus building that I realized I was actually doing policy research. I, along with my group, guided by a particular policy analytic framework, was exploring the relevant issues associated with the topic we chose and the policy related to it—how the policy was initiated, how it was implemented, how it was disseminated, and how it affected children and families in the Commonwealth. I was doing policy research, and I understood what I was doing. And maybe even more importantly, I understood why we were using the approach we were to analyze the policy we chose.

All of my apprehension, my reluctant thoughts, and my feelings of intimidation were gone, because I knew I was able to do policy analysis and I was able to understand why I was doing it. The tools were all there, both internal and external, which provided what I needed in order to examine and research policies. Now I know you are wondering what happened at the presentation. I can honestly say the outcome was very rewarding. The presentation regarding the policy analysis we conducted was well received by the individuals from the Commonwealth's Department of Social Services, which will hopefully lead to changes in policy for oppressed children and families.

CHALLENGES AND CAPACITIES

While I now truly appreciate policy analysis as research, I can't say that I didn't encounter struggles throughout my process. One of the first hardships I had to deal with was simply believing that I was capable of conducting policy research. Analyzing policies was a novel concept for me. I was someone who studied children and families in order to better serve individuals with whom I worked. What I previously failed to recognize until taking the course was that policies directly impact the day-to-day existence of children and family. Not to consider policies, or at least have a sincere appreciation for them, is, on some level, to be negligent of those systemic structures that impact so many lives. I realized—while working in a group—that the policy analysis we were engaged in was not overwhelming but was something practical and pertinent. The unfamiliar and intimidating became familiar and thrilling once I accepted that I was more than capable of participating in the process.

Another challenge I encountered was allowing myself to go "outside the box." What I mean by that is allowing myself to think about and examine a policy from a different philosophical stance. In this book you will be presented with several ways in which people think about things. It will be suggested that there are numerous policy research approaches that correspond to those ways of thinking. Various policy analysis approaches are applicable, depending on how one wishes to examine a policy. At first this can appear to be baffling, but in all honesty it's nothing more than considering research from a variety of viewpoints and choosing the policy analysis approach that is best for answering the question you have. I realized that choosing what I might be most comfortable with may not necessarily be the best for me to use. And while that was challenging for me, I realized it wasn't my comfort that was important, but researching the policy in the best possible way. Eventually, I became comfortable with considering something from a different point of view, which I believe helped to increase my capacity for researching policies.

What you are about to learn is probably going to be as new for you as it was for me. The most challenging aspect of the process I encountered was letting go and allowing myself to learn something new. It sounds rather easy when you think about it, but for someone like me who is used to working with people and not policies, letting go and allowing myself to make mistakes and learn from them was essential. The process in which you are about to embark may at times be challenging, but you will learn skills that will help you think critically and process and examine and analyze in a variety of pertinent ways. I learned to appreciate the relevance of policy research while taking that course, and that appreciation continues to this day.

CONCLUSION

Hopefully, you, too, will allow yourself to experience something new by letting go of what "is" and considering what "could be." For me it was necessary to let go in order to consider that policy goes hand in hand with practice. I had to walk out of my comfort zone to get to the point where it was okay to simply try. It was a challenge, but it has been extremely beneficial to my learning. Policy analysis is research, and just like any type of research, doing more of it leads to proficiency. I'm on my way and still need practice, but that hasn't changed my perception of how useful policy research can be. It was through recognizing the connection between policy research and practice that I realized the potential for change that can lead to increased social justice. Ultimately, in my opinion, effective policy analysis should always have social justice as one of its goals. So now it's time to start your journey, one that will bring challenges, learning, and, hopefully, change, if you let it. And remember, if I can do this, you can do it as well. You just have to put some trust in letting go.

Nathan Perkins, MSW
Richmond, Virginia

Preface

THIS IS A book that neither of us expected to write. For the many years of our collaboration, we have focused on the organization and community context of practice. We were quite content to work through our ideas of multiple ways of knowing and doing at the organization and the community levels, until we realized the conflict between where we had come related to multiple ways of planning and practicing and what we were teaching in our policy classes. It became clear to us that if Gibson Burrell (1997) is right about his description of pandemonium in organizing and organizations, those dealing with the policies that impact practices within them will soon need much more sophisticated conceptualizations to explore policy. Thus, this book was written to help policy advocates at whatever level to be political, strategic, and critical in their work.

This text is based on years of teaching social policy courses in which we have introduced students to multiple policy analysis frameworks. Typically, students warm to certain frameworks more than others and have even been heard to say "this is my favorite policy analysis model." This statement exemplifies the reason we are writing this book. First of all, a model by definition is prescriptive and reductionist, yet there are other approaches that are expansive and emergent. Thus, having a "favorite" model or approach can be limiting if the questions one needs to ask require different approaches. Our intent, then, is to introduce critical thinking into how one approaches policy analysis by envisioning policy analysis as a form of research designed for understanding social policy from formulation to implementation in our complex postmodern global society.

In this envisioning, policy analysis frameworks (models or approaches) are tools from which to carefully select, depending on what one wants to know. In the chapters that follow, policy analysis is compared to doing research; there are multiple units of analysis, and the selection of an appropriate tool requires that the purpose of the analysis must fit with the intended use of the selected instrument. Policy frameworks characteristically address policy process, content, and performance. Some tools are multifunctional, and others are specific to one unit of analysis. In addition, policy frameworks are based on different world-views, with embedded assumptions, often having deep philosophical roots that are positivist/rational, interpretive/nonrational, or critical. We hope to provide sufficient information and explanation to quell the cacophony that occurs when most students are challenged to engage in deeper analysis than simply a description of a complicated social policy, no matter what the level.

In the pages that follow, we use multiparadigmatic perspectives informed by the work of Egon Guba (1990) and Burrell and Morgan (1979). Their work takes our attention to multiple perspectives in understanding, analysis, and evaluation and applies that to the policy process. It is intended to extend the domain of the study of social policy by explicating the dimensions of traditional, interpretive, and radical approaches to policy analysis. The focus is the interrogation of frameworks for policy analysis drawn from social work, political science, sociology, public administration, and the philosophy of science.

To extend the idea of multiple perspectives in policy practice and analysis, the three major sections of the text outline different types of policy analyses built on different assumptions about what constitutes policy reality and how one can understand it and use the results in other aspects of policy practice. Our position is that the choice of an analytic framework in policy is analogous to the choice of a particular statistic in quantitative research. From this standpoint, not only are there embedded assumptions in every policy analysis framework, but each framework will produce different findings. This constitutes a multilayered approach to an exploration of social policy.

Our investigation of the literature suggests that with most analytic frameworks, neither the underlying assumptions nor the analytic focus are made explicit. Consequently, a conscious choice, based on those elements, is not possible without further interrogation of the framework. Having a "favorite" model may not provide needed policy analysis results, because no single approach can fit all situations. What we have found are criticisms, sometimes from quite different perspectives, lodged against most theories, models, or frameworks used in policy work. The literature is quite confusing to those new to policy analysis.

We think that the tendency to choose a favorite model has indicated a desire to reduce complexity. We fear that this tendency toward reductionism is occurring just at a time when social issues and concerns are most complex. We believe that by approaching policy analysis as research we can help the reader make better informed choices for dealing with social policy complexity more successfully. In this book, we offer methods to systematically question the underlying assumptions and values of policy analysis in general and specific approaches to analysis in particular.

Since many other texts have spoken to the policy-making process and the political and analytic skills necessary to effect policy change, this text focuses on providing readers with a set of tools that can be used to enhance their understanding of what constitutes policy and acceptable standards for critical analysis of policy. In this case, Guba's (1984) policy-in-intent, policy-in-implementation, and policy-in-experience are used to help to make policy relevant to the day-to-day activities of practitioners active in various disciplines in the human services. In addition, Gilbert and Terrell's (2010) perspective of policy types— process, product, and performance—will aid readers in understanding the importance of the focus of analysis. Finally, to give a full picture of how policy is formulated, developed, and implemented, the currently influential multiple paradigmatic and ideological perspectives are interrogated. Readers should receive a complex yet holistic picture, along with tools for understanding how policies are conceived and analyzed in response to a recognized social problem.

UNDERLYING ASSUMPTIONS

A number of assumptions have guided us in terms of what we have included (and not included) in our book, and we want to be transparent about what they are. First, there are many excellent sources that describe and provide historical perspectives on social welfare policies and trends with which the reader may be familiar (e.g., Blau, 2007; Dolgoff & Feldstein, 2009; Karger & Stoesz, 2009; Popple & Leighninger, 2008). In this book, we refer to specific policies as examples without attempting to describe their historical development or content in detail, because that information is available elsewhere. Second, there are many skill sets needed by policy practitioners. For example, Jansson (2008) suggests that policy practitioners need four types of skills: analytical, political, interactional, and value-clarifying (p. 86). We agree that all are critically important, especially for human services professionals. Here, our focus is on the analytical skills that are needed to understand policy at any stage of development, recognizing that without those skills the practitioner has little hope of figuring out the most appropriate political, interactional, or value-clarifying approaches to take. In other words, without analytical skills the practitioner is unable to advise others or to take action. This does not mean that analysis is a "step" or that it stops when one arrives at the middle of a policy process. Analysis is ongoing, and when continuing analysis reveals new insights, policy practitioners may need to alter what they are doing or to advocate for changes in policies.

In Chapter 1, we provide an overview of social policy analysis and define the terms needed to move the reader through the remainder of the book. We begin with a case example of how policy and practice are interconnected when a clinician faces the possibility of involuntarily committing her client for mental health inpatient treatment. We then focus on different forms of policy and multiple policy levels (local, state, national, and international), recognizing that these levels may be public or private and that lines across sectors are often blurred. We examine ways in which policy analysis can be conceptualized, including conceptual frameworks and theories of policy process, as well as the differences between policy models and approaches. We do this in order to make sense of the primary ways used to analyze policy, thus preparing for our position regarding policy analysis as research, the subject of Chapter 2.

In Chapter 2, we begin by briefly looking at the traditional role of research in guiding policy analysis and the limitations of focusing only on this role. The dimensions of research are defined in order to illustrate how a well-designed policy analysis contains the same dimensions. Approaching policy analysis as research expands the analyst's capacity for using existing tools to focus the analysis on formulation, product, implementation, or performance relevant to understanding policy; these foci are elaborated in this chapter. Chapter 2 also introduces a conceptual framework that informs the remainder of the book. In subsequent chapters, we locate policy analysis tools within this framework to make it clear that these tools share the same philosophical and methodological perspectives as other research-based means of knowledge building. We continue to use the involuntary commitment example presented in Chapter 1 to illustrate basic concepts introduced in this chapter.

At the end of Chapter 2 is a case example called "Service, Engagement, and Volunteerism: What's the Policy All About?" This case becomes an exemplar that is used throughout the remaining chapters and allows the reader to dig deeply into a real-world social policy—the Edward M. Kennedy Serve America Act enacted on April 21, 2009. The reader will follow Madeline, a director of volunteer programs, as she raises questions that require different approaches to policy analysis. We have developed this case knowing that it may not exactly reflect the practice arena or client population of interest to the reader, but knowing that in almost any human service context volunteers represent a vital resource that is influenced by policy at many levels.

Chapter 3 is the first of two chapters in which we explore the themes, assumptions, and major theories that undergird rational models of policy analysis. Note that we are using the word "model" when it is paired with "rational," because these approaches are prescriptive, fitting the definition of "model" as a predetermined approach. We begin with the themes of rational thought and linear reasoning by providing a short history of logical positivism and logical empiricism, the basis of positivism and postpositivism. Demonstrating how certain purposes of policy analysis lend themselves to rational approaches, we detail what should be contained in a well-constructed rational policy analysis. Examples of rational policy analysis aimed at differing units of analysis built on a brief overview of theories that inform rational approaches illustrate how these exemplars are both rational and compatible with the type of rigor expected in positivist or postpositivist systematic knowledge building. We close this chapter by presenting ways to determine whether a policy analysis approach is, indeed, rational, along with a thorough discussion of what is gained and what is lost in applying this type of model.

Chapter 4 is paired with Chapter 3, in that we use models previously introduced in Chapter 3 to demonstrate how to select and apply models of policy analysis when the policy research or analysis goal is one of sustaining and strengthening existing social and policy structures. We use the case to illustrate major points, as well as to demonstrate that how one looks at the case will differ as various sets of assumptions are used. How rational approaches can be applied in a systematic manner is the primary focus of this chapter. Starting with identifying the purpose of the policy analysis also determines the paradigmatic perspective for the research aspect of the process, Chapter 4 takes the reader through a decision-making process that results in the determination of an appropriate rational approach for use in analysis. Based on this chapter, the reader should be able to identify or construct a policy research question that fits within the positivist/postpositivist perspective. Anchored in the identification of the purpose of the research, you will be able to identify rational policy-analysis strategies and defend the use of those strategies to answer the policy research question.

Through determining the form, level (and scope), and focus of the social policy, you should be able to select and defend the selection of a particular rational approach to policy analysis along with some general ideas about what information might be necessary to apply each of the models discussed. The chapter ends with what rational approaches can and cannot offer when undertaking policy analysis.

Chapter 5 takes a different perspective, exploring nonrational themes, assumptions, and major theories that inform nonrational approaches and nontraditional strategies for understanding policy. The research aspect of nontraditional approaches to policy analysis also begins with determination of the reason for or the goals of the analysis. In this chapter, we continue the discussion of the history of the development of science, with a focus on the basis of the criticism of positivism and postpositivism and the limits of rational thought and linear reasoning. We demonstrate how certain purposes of policy analysis lend themselves to particular analytical approaches—this time to nonrational analysis. We detail what is contained in a well-constructed nonrational approach to policy analysis and continue with various examples of nonrational approaches aimed at differing units of analysis. These exemplars are compatible with more interpretive goals of developing policy through diverse participation based on recognition and management of power and politics. We close this chapter with ways to determine whether an approach is nonrational, followed by a discussion of what is gained and what is given up in applying this alternative. We then turn to Chapter 6 in which we demonstrate how to apply selected nonrational approaches to policy analysis.

The focus of Chapter 6 is on the "doing" of nonrational policy analysis as a type of research. Starting with identifying the purpose of the policy analysis, which also determines the paradigmatic perspective for the research aspect of the process, this chapter takes the reader through a critical thinking process that results in the determination of an appropriate nonrational approach. Based on this chapter, you should be able to identify or construct a policy research question that fits within the interpretive/constructivist perspective. Anchored in the identification of the purpose of the analysis, you will be able to identify nonrational policy analysis strategies and defend the use of those strategies to answer the policy research question. By determining the form, level (and scope), and focus of the social policy, you should be able to select and defend the selection of a particular nonrational approach to policy analysis. This chapter shows the reader how to engage in various types of nonrational policy analysis through the application of several nonrational approaches. The chapter ends with a discussion of what nonrational approaches can and cannot offer when undertaking policy analysis, and what is gained and what is given up when one engages in interpretive/constructivist policy analysis research.

The focus in Chapter 7 is on the critical paradigm, based on a worldview that is one of mass oppression that can be changed only through transformational class-level conflict aimed at rearranging or restructuring the social order. This paradigm also includes a worldview of individual oppression and limitation wherein the social goal is one of individual liberation in service of individual potentiality. This postmodern view is generally seen to be more radical than the other two paradigms previously introduced. In this chapter the reader is exposed to radical views that can be either progressive or conservative in attempting to replace the current social order with an alternative order more congruent with a particular ideology. Regardless of its location on a political ideology spectrum, a more radical approach to policy is introduced in this chapter, anchored in the assumption that policy analysis leads to policy change intended to be transformative, producing structural change with implications at the collective or individual levels. This chapter and Chapter 8 set forth the implications of an ideologically driven analysis process that uses both rational and nonrational approaches to policy analysis.

In Chapter 8, the focus is on the "doing" of critical policy analysis as a type of research. As with the other application chapters, we start with identifying the purpose of the policy analysis, which also determines the critical paradigmatic perspective for the research aspect of the process. In this case justice, power, and conflict play a part in the application of the approaches. This chapter takes you through another analytic process that results in the determination of an appropriate critical approach. Given the real and imagined risks involved in pushing policy analysis to a critical, revolutionary point, the discussion focuses on the systematic aspects of considering this research as well as the implications of critical research as a consciousness-raising intervention. In this chapter, you will learn how to engage in various types of critical policy analysis through the application of several critical approaches. More importantly, you will develop the type of critical judgment necessary to determine when and where the risks related to this more radical positioning might outweigh the opportunities that this sort of systematic consciousness raising might produce.

The text concludes with an epilogue containing some integrating messages from us as well as a challenge to the reader to independently engage in an integrated policy analysis project contained therein.

In summary, a first section, composed of two introductory chapters, gives definitions of what constitutes policies and provides details about approaching the analysis of policy as research. Three sections of two chapters each focus on (1) positivist policy analysis frameworks, (2) interpretive policy analysis frameworks, and (3) critical policy analysis frameworks. Each section details the approaches that can be used to guide each type of policy analysis in a chapter that focuses on understanding the policy's primary intent and the assumptions that underlie the three perspectives. The frameworks used in these chapters are drawn from multiple fields; they remain current in that they pose questions that are not time limited. In each section, a conceptual chapter is immediately succeeded by a chapter on the use of policy analysis frameworks from that perspective, followed by discussion questions to aid in understanding and knowledge acquisition. The text concludes with an epilogue consisting of integrating remarks in which the reader is challenged to apply a policy analysis approach from each of the frameworks outlined to one policy in order to get a sense of what is possible with comparative analysis using the three frameworks.

It is our hope that this book will provide insight into why we see policy analysis as research and that you will feel challenged and empowered as you read. We believe that if policy analysis tools can be seen as helpful devices for asking questions about various aspects of policies, readers will then have an assortment of powerful tools and possibilities for change at their fingertips.

Mary Katherine O'Connor
F. Ellen Netting

Acknowledgments

As with all of our writing about large systems practice, we are grateful to our students and community colleagues who have wrestled with us about the ideas contained in this text. If the ideas are relevant and useful it is because of our students' and colleagues' deep thinking and commitment to helping us make our work better. We are particularly indebted to three doctoral students who worked with us. Jason Sawyers, our graduate research assistant on this project, located numerous references and tracked down copyright permissions. Linda Love contributed case material on involuntary commitment in the introductory chapters. And Nathan Perkins provided a foreword to student readers. Thanks to Dr. M. Lori Thomas for helping us conceptualize and fashion the figures that guide this approach to policy as research. We are thankful to our former MSW student Amy Ernest, who was interested enough to be an early reader of the manuscript. We are also particularly indebted to our policy students with whom we tried these approaches, and especially to Jessica Jagger, who was courageous enough to use this material in shaping her dissertation research. We would like to express our thanks to our acting Dean, collaborator, and friend, Dr. Ann Nichols-Casebolt, who identified a very useful resource for us in the form of the Lejano text, and to Dr. Beverly McPhail, who pointed us in an appropriate radical direction through her insightful work.

Thank you to reviewers Ira Colby, Robert Hawkins, Richard Hoefer, and Elizabeth "Liz" Segal, who helped to make the text both clearer and better targeted. Their insights and suggestions were intellectually stimulating and extremely helpful. We are also grateful to the editorial staff at John Wiley & Sons, Inc., especially to Rachel Livsey, our editor, who has continued to be responsive and helpful to us in every aspect of this project. We are particularly grateful to the late Lisa Gebo, who inspired us to develop this book as part of a series of macro textbooks, all of which pushed the critical thinking envelope. May she rest in peace.

We wish to acknowledge and thank the *Journal of Social Work Education*, its editorial board, and in particular its former editor, Colleen Galambos, for their recognition of the manuscript upon which this book is built as the best conceptual article of 2009. That recognition let us know that we were on to something and gave us affirmation at a time when we were scrambling to finalize the book manuscript.

Finally, we acknowledge all the scholars whose models and approaches serve as the foundation of this book. Without their work, this could not have been written.

Analyzing
Social Policy

CHAPTER 1

An Overview of Social Policy Analysis

I N THIS CHAPTER, we provide background information and define terms needed for the reader to move through and understand the content of this book. We begin with what we think is necessary groundwork to the understanding of our approach, followed by a case example of how policy and practice are interconnected. We then examine what constitutes a policy, especially what are called *social policies*. We will look at different forms of policy and then at multiple policy levels (i.e., local, state, national, and international), recognizing that these levels may be public or private and that the lines across sectors are often blurred. We will examine ways in which policy analysis may be conceptualized, including conceptual frameworks and theories of policy process, as well as the differences between policy models and approaches. We do this in order to make sense of the primary ways used to analyze policy, thereby preparing for our position regarding policy analysis as research, the conceptualization of which is laid out in Chapter 2.

Our focus is on *social policy analysis*, not public (government) policy analysis in its most general form. There are hundreds of books on public policy analysis in general (e.g., Gupta, 2001; Heineman, Bluhm, Peterson, & Kearny, 2002; Lejano, 2006; Patton & Sawicki, 1993; Sabatier, 2007) to which the reader can be referred. Popple and Leighninger (2008) discuss just how broad the term policy analysis can be, referring to writers who have described policy analysis as a "babel of tongues" or a "slippery slope"; one could learn how to do it but could never fully define it. They adapt a definition by the Canadian political scientist Leslie Pal that is inclusive of a range of approaches:

"policy analysis is the disciplined application of intellect to the study of collective responses to public [in our case social welfare] problems" (Popple and Leighninger, p. 43).

This is why this book is being written—analytical skills are needed to determine the usefulness of a particular policy response. A social problem, then, *is* the context for social policy analysis, and since most policies do not include a full analysis of why they are being proposed, or even a statement of the problem they are designed to address, having the skill to analyze the underlying social problem is vitally important. Blau (2007) points out that most practitioners encounter situations in which they "must live and work according to the definition of social problems as other, more powerful people construct them. That is not always easy, because the definition of a social problem shapes the social policy designed to address it" (p. 8).

We are defining social policy analysis as *a systematic study of chosen courses of action within unique contexts with goals of preventing and addressing social problems.* Unpacking this definition reveals that

- Policy analysis, like research, is systematic and intentional.
- Policies (as courses of action) can be made in a vast array of contexts through public (governmental) and private (nonprofit and for profit) auspices.
- These unique contexts include any level of decision making (as broad as the U.S. Congress and as narrow as a local agency).
- Our focus is on problems that influence quality of care or quality of life for individuals and groups.

The policy practitioners who would be involved in analyzing policies are those who are involved in or concerned about the human service delivery system across a broad scope of arenas and contexts.

NECESSARY GROUNDWORK

In this section, our focus is on the analytical skills that are needed to understand policy at any stage of development, recognizing that without those skills the practitioner has little hope of figuring out what political, interactional, or value-clarifying approaches to take. In other words, without analytical skills the practitioner is disempowered to advise others or to take action. This does not mean that analysis is a "step" or that it stops when one gets in the middle of a policy process. Analysis is ongoing, and when continuing analysis reveals new

[handwritten annotations in top margin: "analyzing", "understanding social problem — social policy", "policy = collection of response — public problem"]

insights, policy practitioners may need to alter what they are doing or advocate for changes in policies. They can do this when the analysis is based on two important elements of knowledge and skills: critical thinking and political philosophy.

CRITICAL THINKING

No rigorous or even-handed policy analysis is possible without the basic building block of critical thinking. Paul and Elder (2009) suggest that critical thinking is an art for "analyzing and evaluating thinking with a view to improving it" (p. 2). When critical thinking is called an art it might be rejected as not sufficiently rigorous for the purposes of research and analysis. On the contrary, we see the process as intensely rigorous and complex. Critical thinking is a set of activities, a frame of mind, and a set of attitudes that allows for the examination of assumptions, goals, questions, and evidence. These are all basic to the creation of a social policy. To thoroughly understand a social policy, one needs to use reasonable and reflective thinking focused on what to believe and what not to believe through the self-conscious monitoring of strategies (in this case, policy analysis approaches and models) being applied to the problem or policy that is the focus of analysis.

For us and for others (see Rehner, 1994), critical thinking is part of problem solving, not just an assessment of claims or arguments. This means that it is not focused solely on discovering mistakes in thinking such as those identified by Gambrill and Gibbs (2009)—for example, *ad homonym arguments*, where the person rather than the argument is criticized; *begging the question*, where certainty is alleged based on illogical reasoning, unfounded generalizations, trick questions or ignoring the issue; *sweeping generalizations*, where the unique or the specific becomes the rule; *straw person arguments*, where the point is misrepresented in order to refute it; or *psychological persuasion*, where pressure from tactics such as pleasing, liking, fearing, threats, or labels are used to persuade. Our understanding of critical thinking is broadened to allow for a deep understanding of issues through a dialogic process that requires reflective or analytic listening, active and independent pursuit of clarity of expression, and a search for evidence and reasons with the certain inclusion of alternative points of view.

To employ the type of policy analysis we are proposing here, the analyst must engage in the process with fair-mindedness, seeing the interplay between various beliefs and ideologies and having the capacity to test those beliefs. That sort of testing requires a good deal of self-knowledge about personal strengths and limitations regarding reasoning and decision-making capacity as well as the courage to be an independent thinker, fully capable of questioning what others accept. Basically, this type of critical thinking requires the ability to depart when necessary from the perspectives of the "experts" in order to generate and assess multiple perspectives. It also requires the nimbleness required for shifting one's own patterns of thinking when needed.

Rehner (1994) has extended critical thinking to include critical reading and critical writing, both of which are essential to powerful policy analysis. Critical reading is not a passive pursuit of simple descriptive understanding. Rather it is a process of meaning making through an interaction with the written word based on recognition of personal experience aimed at discovery of patterns in order to build relationships among the ideas—a process that considers the situation, the ideology, the culture, history, and the time in which the text was written. Critical reading of the sort needed to address a written policy requires going beyond one's personal reaction to what is written based on personal preferences to critical judgment of the text. This critical judgment requires identifying the author's purpose. In the case of policy, it would involve identifying the intent of the policy. Critical judgment also includes identifying the reader's purpose, which in this case would be the goal of the policy analysis. Then, for full critical reading, there needs to be a shared meaning between the reader and the text about what words are saying. This requires attention to word choice, connotations, patterns, figures of speech, tone, biases, or methods of persuasion. What is both present and absent are needed to identify shades of meaning for the analytic process.

The activist policy analyst will also engage in critical writing. This involves a nonlinear recursive moving forward and backward in the writing process so that the writing itself becomes a tool for organizing and clarifying thinking. Moving backward and forward rather than starting at the beginning and establishing a middle and then an end in a linear fashion allows the opportunity for more learning. That type of learning establishes the potential for more persuasiveness; the final product is clear because the writer is clear. The recursive process allows the writer to recognize and clearly and strategically articulate (or not) assumptions because the writer is clear about what he or she is attempting to accomplish, about personal and professional attitudes, and about what the writer wants to convince the reader.

POLITICAL PHILOSOPHY

In the policy arena, a deep understanding of the history and intellectual basis of different political and ideological belief systems is also necessary. Thus using critical thinking in combination with knowledge of political philosophy may help the reader to engage in the work that follows.

For hundreds of years, philosophers have examined the role of government within various societal contexts. As far back as 378 BC, Plato asked how an ideal society would be governed in order to meet the needs of its vulnerable citizens. Aristotle, Plato's student, analyzed society as though he were a physician, prescribing remedies through a hierarchical, aristocratic, and undemocratic form of government. In the seventeenth century, Thomas Hobbes focused on the social contract, the individual power given over to the ruler (or society) to oversee the actions and behaviors of people who were seen as depraved and self-interested by nature, but who agreed to be civil, based on the rules set down by the larger society to control them. John Locke continued this focus, examining governmental authority as depending on a contract of mutual consent between rulers and citizens, with government depending on law (not force) to maintain order. Years later John Stuart Mill, a severe critic of Locke's emphasis on majority rule, assumed a utilitarian view that the rightness of any action should be determined by its consequences. Mill thought that majority rule should be limited and sometimes trumped by minority interests, and that government should not intrude in the private lives of citizens These early philosophers raised many of the questions policy analysts ask today regarding the role of government, where power belongs, what structures should be formed to oversee the formulation and implementation of policy, how minority interests are viewed, and how to address social problems (Reamer, 1993).

No mention of political philosophy would be complete without referencing the work of Karl Marx. Marx's criticism of capitalism focused on how human labor had been transformed from a creative activity to a unit of production, replacing the worth of a human being with the abstract concept of human work. Marx questioned a worldview that commodified labor from human worth to monetary value (Marx, 1887). This was a radical notion that is discussed in Chapter 7, which focuses on critical theory. Other critical philosophers such as John Rawls (1971) stimulated a great deal of thought about distributive justice. Building on the concept of the social contract that establishes a just society, Rawls proposed that if individuals operated under a "veil of ignorance" in which they did not know who was advantaged and who was disadvantaged, they would create a moral principle that protected the disadvantaged; they would be benevolent. In a just society, Rawls argued, there could be some differences in wealth and assets, but only if those who are not as well off benefited in some way. Rawls reacted to utilitarian philosophers who assumed that a just society is concerned with equity of distribution according to maximizing the total of a group's utility, satisfaction, or happiness. He viewed as unfair any approach that benefited the greatest number of people but still did harm to citizens who were not in the majority. Rawls's work has served as a starting point for other philosophers to counter some of his arguments and look for new ways to envision the welfare state.

Thus, political philosophy is concerned with basic concepts and the systems of beliefs that inform the way in which one views the roles of various societal sectors in addressing the needs of people. Mullaly (2007) discusses four sets of views: neo-conservative, liberal, social democratic, and Marxist. Each view envisions human nature, society, the nation-state, social justice, and social change in a different way. A neo-conservative philosophy views human nature as self-interested, society as a series of individual interests, the nation-state as a necessary evil to maintain law and order, individuals as responsible for looking out for themselves, and social change as slow and evolutionary (p. 79). A liberal philosophy sees human nature as moral and rational, society as loosely collective, the nation-state as protective of natural rights, redistribution of resources as important to social justice and social reform as valuable as long as it does not fundamentally change the society (p. 97). A social democratic philosophy views human beings as social animals and communal by nature, the nation-state's role as balancing the interests of different groups with equality of conditions as a social goal, and social elements as transformative but in an evolutionary way (p. 123). Finally, a Marxist philosophy views human beings as communal, with production being the basis of the nature of society. The nation-state is viewed similarly to the social democratic view, but with social justice meaning a classless society and change being much more revolutionary than the other three views (p. 143).

Political philosophy influences how one views every aspect of policy. If one believes that the role of the nation-state is to control, then policies will be controlling and highly regulatory. If one believes that change must be kept to a minimum, then policies will limit how much change can occur. If one believes that society should be transformed in order to address the needs of vulnerable groups, then policies will be designed with transformation in mind. What is critically important is that multiple ways of viewing human nature, society, and the role of the state come together in the stew that we refer to as "politics." Furthermore, policy analysts must be savvy enough to recognize that the politics surrounding policy formulation and implementation are deeply rooted in diverse political philosophies, whether they are played out in an organization, in a community, or in a broader policy-making arena.

We are assuming that the reader is someone who wants to *understand* policy, not simply to jump into the fray, feeling the adrenaline rush of engaging in a political process, or merely moving with the tide. We also assume that the reader is someone who recognizes that policy affects every aspect of life, who is most likely a practitioner whose job description includes many more tasks than policy analysis, and who often feels the direct or indirect impact of policy decisions in daily practice. "If practitioners and beneficiaries, professionals and recipients, workers and clients apply the skills to analyze the processes whereby policy comes into being, they are empowered" (Flynn, 1992, p. 1). This is our purpose here—to offer relevant analytical tools for the empowerment of practitioners.

Practitioners who engage in clinical work are immersed in policy, yet most may not consider themselves "policy practitioners." Thus, we begin with a case example that illustrates just how immersed practitioners are. This example was contributed by one of our doctoral students who is a true pracademic (a practitioner who is also an academic) and has years of clinical experience. Immediately after presenting the case, we will focus on definitional concerns.

Initiating an Involuntary Commitment

Jayne is a 30-year-old woman who has been in therapy for two years with Constance. She has been diagnosed with major depression and post-traumatic stress disorder. Jayne and Constance have a solid working relationship, and Jayne has made progress in disclosing her history of abuse and in forming a trusting relationship. Jayne's social support is minimal in that she has no family in

(*continued*)

(*continued*)
the state and she has only two close friends who are currently out of town. She recently lost her job.

Jayne had previously been hospitalized for attempting to commit suicide by overdosing on prescription medications. Earlier in the year, she changed her medications from name brands to generic brands and over the last few weeks her depression has worsened. She has just confessed to having stopped taking some of her medications due to the cost. Since she is now unemployed, she simply cannot afford them.

During her session, Jayne verbalizes suicidal ideation with a plan to overdose on medications. When Constance further explores her feelings and plans, Jayne expresses ambivalence about following through on the plan, but she is unable to commit to a contract for safety. Constance explores the risk factors present, which include the availability of medications that she could use in the suicide plan, the lack of her support systems in the area, the loss of her employment, the change in her medications, and her inability to contract for safety. The use of hospitalization is discussed, yet Jayne is unwilling to voluntarily admit herself.

Due to these risk factors, Constance feels ethically bound to initiate an involuntary commitment order. She is aware that the first step is to contact the police, who will come to her office and monitor the situation through the use of a temporary detention order (TDO). The police will then initiate an emergency custody order, allowing Constance to contact the area hospitals and locate an available bed for Jayne. In addition, Constance knows she must contact the treating psychiatrist and the area Community Services Board for the next steps in the process.

When Constance contacts the police, she is met with a series of questions that appear to assess the need for police involvement prior to an on-site evaluation. Is your client physically aggressive? Are there any family members who could transport her to the hospital? Would your client be willing to have you as her therapist and transport her to the hospital? Would your client be willing to drive herself and have you follow her to the hospital?

This process consumes 30 minutes, during which Jayne becomes more agitated, verbalizing a desire to leave and not "be such a problem." Given that Jayne is noncombative, the police state that they will not be coming. Constance's job becomes one of containing

Jayne and simultaneously arranging transportation to the hospital or the area Community Services Board for the initial assessment.

Constance is painfully aware of the implications of what she is planning to do in getting Jayne to the hospital. She is a resident of a state in which the involuntary commitment legislation has been altered after a mass shooting at Virginia Tech University by a lone gunman with a history of mental illness. The legislation surrounding involuntary commitment states:

> *That a person may be contained involuntarily if there is evidence readily available, including recommendation from physicians or clinical psychologist treating the person that the individual (i) has a mental illness and that there exists a substantial likelihood that, as a result of mental illness, the person will, in the near future, (a) cause serious physical harm to himself or others as evidenced by recent behavior causing, attempting, or threatening harm and other relevant information, if any, or (b) suffer serious harm due to his lack of capacity to protect himself from harm or to provide for his basic human needs, (ii) is in need of hospitalization or treatment, and (iii) is unwilling to volunteer or incapable of volunteering for hospitalization or treatment. (DMHMRSA, 2008)*

Constance knows that the mental health system is responsible for the "evaluation of the potential involuntary patient, the threshold decision as to whether the patient should be detained and long-term commitment sought, the patient's treatment, and the decision as to when to release the patient" (Appelbaum, 1992). She also knows that the justice system is responsible for providing safety to the client and the community during the decision-making process. This safety, seen frequently as containment, begins with transporting the client to an appropriate destination for evaluation by mental health professionals. According to the legislation, with an execution of a temporary detention order (TDO), Jayne will remain in law enforcement's custody until detained in a secure facility or custody accepted by appropriate personnel at a TDO facility. If Constance transports Jayne or has her transported, the therapeutic relationship will shift into an arena that has Constance assuming a different form of power and authority over Jayne. Once this process begins, their relationship will be forever affected.

(continued)

(continued)
   Constance asked for assistance by the police, which was denied. She was informed that the transportation was her responsibility. Should she transport Jayne or find someone else to take her? However Jayne is transported, Constance needs to be there with her for the assessment, for she has initiated a commitment process for her client. If Constance accompanies Jayne, what will happen with her next client in the waiting room? Constance might very well lose clients; her income base may be affected, her home life may be affected, and she may be responsible for Jayne for the next 6 to 10 hours. As a practitioner in private practice, there is a disincentive for her to initiate a TDO, given that the unintended consequences can be far-reaching at a professional and personal level. Yet, in her best clinical judgment, Constance sincerely believes that Jayne will do harm to herself. She has no choice but to begin this process and to follow the established protocols in the Commonwealth of Virginia.

This case was contributed by Linda E. Love, LCSW.

IDENTIFYING DEFINITIONS AND FORMS OF POLICY

Given that policy is such a broad concept and can be applied in so many settings, it comes as little surprise that there are so many definitions of policy in the literature. For example, Guba (1984, pp. 64–65) identified eight different definitions of policy: (1) an assertion of intents or goals, (2) the accumulated decisions of a governing body to guide that which is within its sphere of control, (3) a guide to discretionary action, (4) a strategy used to solve or ameliorate a problem, (5) sanctioned behavior approved either formally or informally, (6) a norm of conduct, (7) an output of the policy-making system, and (8) the effect of the policy-making and policy-implementing system. In the broadest sense, Guba's categorization suggests several levels of policy formality and several approaches to determine policy, each producing policies of different levels of complexity and type. As we move through this chapter, these levels, types, and complexities will be examined.

   Guba (1984, p. 65) points out that the first four definitions can be viewed as *policy-in-intention*, as having something to say about the purpose of a policy and why a particular policy may have been formulated in the first place. Items 5 through 7 are viewed by Guba as *policy-in-implementation*, including those actions, interactions, and behaviors that occur in the process of implementing the policy. And the final definition is viewed as *policy-in-experience*. Here Guba points out something very important that should never be lost—policy-in-experience is the *consumer's* actual experience (not the practitioner's experience, but the experience of the persons whose original needs were targeted in the first place).

In the case example of Constance and Jayne, policy-in-intention, policy-in-implementation, and policy-in-experience are all present. Intention is reflected in the newly amended involuntary commitment policy—no one wants another Virginia Tech episode ever to happen again. The intent is for practitioners to use their best judgments and to act as needed. The implementation, however, is never clear-cut, no matter how the policy is worded. Since the police do not feel that they need to come, the process comes back to Constance to figure out how best to carry out the next steps. And policy-in-experience speaks directly to the way in which both Constance and Jayne live the process that unfolds along with the unintended consequences of how the policy is carried out. Both their lives are about to change due to the intended and unintended consequences of a policy.

Given so many definitions of policy, Gilbert and Terrell (2010) take another approach. Acknowledging that an entire introductory text could be written on describing various approaches to defining policy, they say, "no single definition is universally, nor even broadly, accepted. . . . Skirting the conceptual swamp of social policy, public policy, and social welfare policy distinctions, we will focus instead on examining the functioning of those major institutions in society that structure and provide social welfare" (p. 2). At that point, they provide an overview of those institutions seen as providing the major activities of community life, including "kinship systems, religious organizations, workplace sites, economic markets, mutual assistance arrangements, and government organizations" (p. 2). Although they do not define policy or types of policy, they offer insight into the many contexts in which policy emerges. Context is particularly important in the way we define policy in this book.

Recognizing that there are multiple definitions and varied contexts, we are defining policy as *a chosen course of action within a particular context that is intended to achieve valued goals.* In this definition we see value-based judgments driving policy, because every choice (whether one admits it or not) is based on some value or valued set of principles or preferences. Otherwise, a chosen course of action would not be important enough to pursue in a social (often political) context composed of persons having different values or principles in mind. This means that more than one person (often many persons) will have to "buy into" a policy before the proposed course of action can be pursued.

Policy is a broad concept. Think about why. Consider that to get through all those decision-making points and to get as many people as possible to buy into a policy, it has to be broadly stated. For example, a number of years ago we were involved in what was called the National Health Care Campaign. The campaign was a movement across the country to get as many people engaged in advocating for policy change at the national level that would support health care coverage for persons who were employed but could not afford (or did not have options) to pay for health insurance. There was very little resistance to the goal of this proposed policy. Everyone from the American Medical Association to the National Association of Social Workers supported the policy in concept. As long as there were few details on how this policy would be implemented, everyone was on the bandwagon. As soon as there was dialogue about the specifics of how this would change a free-market system of health care into a more social democratic form, the national coalition fragmented across groups who held very different ideologies about what is a right and what is a privilege in this country. Interestingly, those ideologies are still part of the public discourse today.

Health care policies such as the one in this example and mental health policies such as the one in the involuntary commitment case have an impact on the lives of individuals and groups. They influence access to care and quality of care once services are provided. When policies are intended to make a difference in quality of life they can be included in a special type of policy—a social policy.

SOCIAL POLICIES AND SOCIAL PROBLEMS

We are not yet finished with defining policy. In this book, we are concerned with a subset of policies that are called *social policies*. This raises the question of what makes a policy "social," since policies typically involve many people in some ways. Aren't all policies some-what social? Similar to the health care example just provided, a social policy is concerned with problems of individuals or groups in relation to the social context of which they are a part.

Jansson (2008) defines social policies as "a collective strategy that prevents and addresses social problems" (p. 9). Building on Jansson's definition and our definition of policy, we are defining social policies as *"chosen courses of action within unique contexts with goals of preventing and addressing social problems."* In addition, social policies may contain or lead to principles and procedures that guide a course of action dealing with individual and aggregate relationships in organizations, communities, and societies.

So what are social problems? A social problem generally involves issues related to maintaining or achieving quality of life for groups of people. Depending on the context, these concerns can be the result of a wide consensus within members of an organization, community, state, or nation. The concern can also be voiced by the socially powerful or economically privileged. A problem, then, to be considered a social problem rather than an individual one, needs to be big enough (impacting numbers of individuals or groups), severe enough (representing sufficient concern, even danger), or important enough to be called a social problem by those who are powerful enough to name it as such. Thus, Jansson's distinction between "preventing and addressing" is decisively important, since prevention requires different strategies to alert people to potential impact or concern before the social problem has become so obvious to demand a reaction. In the United States, we tend to have trouble dealing with problems before they are defined.

Since most policies tend to be reactive (addressing rather than preventing), Chambers and Wedel (2009) suggest that a social problem usually is an aftereffect of first-order economic, business, technological, or environmental problems. Jansson (2008) also offers a word of caution in this regard, suggesting that there are not "rigid boundaries between social policies and other kinds of policies" (p. 12). He uses the example of tax policies, some of which are definitely social policies in that they impact individuals economically in certain ways that affect unemployment and poverty but others of which may be specific to large corporations in terms of how they depreciate their equipment or other properties. Similarly, policies intended for the oversight of water and sewer systems are not typically considered social policies until public health issues arise when a water system is compromised. Then those more general policies become critical to addressing the quality of life of individuals and communities.

In the United States, due to the incremental nature of our public policy-making process, it sometimes appears that almost every policy response results in unintended consequences that in themselves then become social problems requiring a policy response. For example, when national policy tried to eliminate segregation in housing based on race, segregation in housing based on economic status, was created because middle- and upper-class African Americans could move out of the inner city to the suburbs, leaving the inner city principally for the poor. These changes shifted tax bases and had implications for public education and other public services.

When these consequences are recognized as social problems they give rise to social policies, and the programs that are derived from the policies serve as corrective measures. This process represents a link between policies and practice. To truly understand a particular social policy and what it is intended to accomplish requires understanding the context of the social problem, the goals of the policy, and the response that is implemented as a result of that policy.

We now turn to the different forms of social policy that can be the focus of that analysis.

DIFFERENT FORMS OF SOCIAL POLICY

Whether a policy is being considered by a nonprofit board of directors in a local agency or in a proposed bill before the state legislature, many decisions must be made. Who should be involved in the process; who needs to be convinced to help move the process along; what should be included in the actual wording of the policy (and what should not); what approach should be used in presenting the policy to a decision-making body—these and numerous other decisions are central to the formation of a policy. As Blau (2007) points out, sometimes this means you will be involved in the policy formation process, but it is more likely that you may inherit policies constructed by decision makers in powerful positions, just as Constance did in our case example. What you inherit or what you might construct could appear in a multitude of forms.

Jansson (2008, pp. 12–14) identifies the following forms:

- *Statutes*—A public form enacted by some level of government.
- *Policy objectives*—Mission-type statements within statutes that shape actions and choices of persons implementing a policy.
- *Rules and regulations*—Specific directives intended to constrain what persons carrying out the policy can and cannot do.
- *Budgets*—Policies that determine the nature and amount of resources allocated to implementing policies.

- *Court rulings*—Judicial decisions that either enforce or rescind policies typically made by government.
- *Formal or written policies*—Those policies issued in writing by public (e.g., legislative, judicial) or private (e.g., standard-setting bodies, agencies, or interorganizational) groups.
- *Informal policies or unwritten policies*—Courses of action taken by persons and groups involved in implementing policy when the formal policy is not specific about how to proceed, thus requiring the use of discretion and judgment.

One more form can be added—standards. *Standards* are normally developed and approved by professional associations to guide ethical decision making as practitioners do their work. Standards guide action and could be viewed as professional policies often captured in the form of codes of ethics and practice approaches. Standards are usually regulated and overseen by public credentialing and licensing bodies. Their intent is to protect consumers from unscrupulous practice. They, too, can be understood as a type of social policy aimed at ensuring quality of care. Table 1.1 provides an overview of the various forms of social policy.

Regardless of what form a social policy takes, the choice to even begin a policy process most often involves a cluster of decisions governed by rules and regulations, budgetary concerns, court rulings, and standards. Although there may be hundreds of pages of written

Table 1.1
Forms of Social Policy

Form	Description
Statute	Enacted by federal or state government (public)
Policy objectives	Mission-type statements
Rules and regulations	Specific directives, often directing administrative aspects of policies
Budgets	Allocation of resources
Court rulings	Judicial decisions
Formal	Any policy that is in written form
Informal	Any policy that is unwritten but takes the form of practice
Standards	Professional policies such as codes of ethics, best practice protocols, and credentialing requirements

policy, some aspects may not be covered or may be left to the informal discretion of the practitioner tasked with implementation. There may be practice precedents such as informal procedures about how decision making should happen within a specific context that one needs to know which may not have been codified in written form. It is this complexity in policy forms that requires a good deal of savvy on the part of the student of policy.

Some statutory social policy (enacted by government) may be vaguely written, containing the hoped-for policy objectives in general terms, the identified targeted population of the policy, and the designation of which agency of government is responsible for implementation. In these cases, to aid policy enactment more specifically construed administrative rules will be issued to guide implementation of the policy, including standards and regulations, "that have the force of law developed subsequent to some enabling legislation. . . . Federal administrative procedures, legislation and the administrative procedures, acts of virtually every state requires a rather detailed and explicit set of routines for an administrative agency to follow in publishing proposed rules . . . in receiving and responding to input offered on the part of those affected and final legislative review prior to promulgation of the rules" (Flynn, 1992, p. 187). Other nonstatutorial social policies may contain more detail, essentially embedding rules and procedures within the initial policy. The norm for policy advocates though is to set the agenda for the policy without going into so much detail that the decision-making process bogs down because of different interpretations of details. But lack of detail at the agenda-setting level is not necessarily advantageous at the implementation level. Vague language that allows agreement on general principles rarely gives sufficient specific instructions needed to shape precise instructions at the implementation or programmatic level.

Most practitioners will feel the full weight of statutory policies when they work in settings mandated by enabling legislation. There they encounter huge volumes of administrative rules that have been promulgated to guide their work. As one will see throughout the text, policies in the form of rules are in constant tension between precision and vagueness, centralization and discretion, incentives and punishments, seriousness and blameworthiness of violations, or off-targeting of the consequences of the choice. In the United States, this push/pull tension of different positions and ideologies means that statutes and even the administrative rules and procedures derived from them are in constant flux. It is in the midst of this constant tension that policy analysis gains its meaning and its power. The process of analysis of the formal rules along with the interpretation of those rules can result in intended and unintended consequences. Thus, the most potential impact in shaping future policy choices may be what is learned in the implementation process.

In our case example, Constance and Jayne would certainly be aware of how the police interpreted their roles. Had Jayne been violent, they would have come. Yet, as long as Jayne appears passive, the transportation mandate is seen by the police as flexible. When they refuse to transport, this does not change the expectation for Constance to protect Jayne. While she is going to the effort to enact that protection, there are important unintended negative consequences to other clients and to the financial stability of her private practice.

COMPLIANCE AND POWER WITHIN POLICY

Policies as sets of rules operate as a form of social coordination. These rules induce compliance about something without invoking too many coercive sanctions for the actions of those governed by the rules. As such, policies derive power from legitimacy. They prescribe actions in particular situations or contexts. Rules are accepted based on the political choices that set the policy framing in motion. Since policies are political, they may include, exclude, unify, or divide by creating categories of those served or not served by the policy choice. Policies also create natural alliances of privilege and lack of privilege (those who receive the benefits of the policy and those who are not allowed to become beneficiaries or those who can avoid following the policy as compared to those who must comply with the policy). These alliances represent yet another aspect of how political and complex policies are.

Depending on the form that the enactment of the policy takes, there will always be formal and informal interactions between obligations and duties prescribed by the policy rules. There will always be some sort of mandated behavior both on the part of those enacting the policy and those who are targets of the policy. Thus, policy confers power on how the implementers of the policy must act. That power will be greater or less depending on the degree of consensus about what constitutes the chosen policy response. See if you can determine how that seems to have worked in our case example.

Good rules have precision, but policies are a result of compromise, so policies generally represent vague rules very much open to interpretation about meaning and expectations. Precise rules assure fairness so that cases that are alike are treated alike. Precise rules provide predictability and assure that people involved in the policy response are insulated from political or ideological interpretations (some say whims) of those enacting the policy. Equal treatment is thought to be possible with precise policies. However, precision in rules sometimes also allows different cases to be treated as if they were alike in the sense that unique situations are not considered in a "one size fits all" policy response. Equality may impede social justice. Precise policies also stifle creative responses to new situations. Vague rules, on the other hand, leave room for discretion. They allow for flexibility, interpretation, and sensitivity to differences. Vague policies may well allow for the expression of community ideals and values that are different from the ideals and values of the framers of the policy.

What is certain is that public debate about policy at any stage allows for the balancing of formal with informal power, precision with vagueness in the policy, discretionary power with control. The goal of the debate in democratic settings is to eliminate unnecessary discretionary power and to create precise rules that are also perfectly flexible, neutral, and enforceable. As you probably know, these goals are hardly possible in diverse organizational, community, and societal arenas, but there is a sense that the myth must be preserved because it is essential to the legitimacy of laws. In the United States, belief in the rule of law is persistent. So the myth must exist to counteract the natural libertarian or individualistic pressure for evasion or disobedience of the policy or law.

Recognizing the issues surrounding compliance and power is just the beginning in discovering the levels of complexity in policy. Policies and procedures will be developed at various levels of government and within the private sector that influence what practitioners do. All of these policies and procedures carry their own constraints beyond those already identified. Nested within these layers of public policy, and sometimes derived from them, will be administrative policies that have been approved by decision-making bodies responsible for overseeing what happens in organizational settings. Those policies will interface with internal policies that direct organizational activities, additional levels of power, and additional expectations regarding compliance. "The nested structure of rules within rules, within still further rules, is a particularly difficult problem to solve" (Ostrom, 2007, p. 24). Thus, with this additional complexity in mind, it is important to examine in detail different levels and scope of social policies that range from the grass roots to the highest echelons of government.

RECOGNIZING LEVELS AND SCOPE OF SOCIAL POLICIES

The narrowest level of social policy would be a personal or family policy. A personal policy that states that "I won't smoke cigarettes" or a family policy that mandates that "all family members must remove their shoes before entering the home" are examples of policies that apply only to a particular individual or to all members of a family. Technically, these would be social policies on the most grass-roots level. They would likely be informal in the sense that they are not written down, and they are "social" because they influence the quality of life of self and others and are adhered to only by particular groups of people. Knowing the effects of secondary smoke, an individual's decision to refrain from smoking has an impact on others' quality of life. This decision may be tested even more in the local community when a smoking ban in restaurants is enacted by the city and the "choice" not to smoke is no longer the individual's but the city council's. In short, what was originally an individual policy decision has become the choice of government exercising control over the individual.

The family's decision about taking off their shoes upon entering the house is an example of an unwritten policy. Note that this policy is very specific—one either takes off one's shoes or one doesn't. But what is the problem that makes this a social policy rather than simply a rule superimposed by a head of household over its members? If one assumes that the problem is that the house becomes dirty much faster when family members track in debris, so much so that no one can possibly maintain a clean living environment, then the actual policy goal (albeit unstated) may be that family members owe it to one another to pitch in as a unit and maintain the quality of their living space. In this situation, what sounds like a targeted policy is actually stated in the form of a "house rule" that does not fully articulate the reasoning behind it. It is a family social policy that can be simply described, but determining why people take off their shoes represents the beginning of a policy analysis.

Clearly, these personal or family policies might impact those around them, but they rarely are the source of generalized policies, nor are they the primary focus for this discussion other than to demonstrate that personal and family policies are value or preference driven, like other policies. Whatever consequences by way of coercion to comply or sanctions for lack of compliance are only within the individual or within the scope of how a family defines its members.

In summary, at the most local and familiar level, policies can be personal and familial. The decision not to smoke is an example of how one's personal policy can have an impact on others and illustrates how sometimes personal policies become the basis for broader social policies, such as banning smoking in restaurants in order to protect the public's health. A family's desire to share in the responsibility of keeping their immediate environment clean and healthy can actually trigger rules such as taking one's shoes off at the door.

As you can see, even these simple examples can have a certain level of complexity. They are useful, but for our purposes here we are primarily interested in the policies that are directly linked to the larger practice environment. Moving beyond the individual/family context, we now focus on organization/community, county/state, regional/ national, and international policies to illustrate just how diverse social policies can be.

ORGANIZATION/COMMUNITY LEVEL AND SCOPE

Organizations are the arena in which policies are most often imple- mented, because they are legal entities in which programs and services are carried out. They are also the context within which most practi- tioners feel the most impact of how policy at any level influences practice. This will be true regardless of the particular organizational culture or organizational type, ranging from large public bureaucracies to small grass-roots associations and including everything in between (O'Connor & Netting, 2009). All organizations, regardless of size or culture, along with their employees must comply with federal, state, and local policies that pertain to their activities, whether that compli- ance relates to employment policies or policies governing how an organization can care for other people's children. Thus, an agency or association setting is one in which practitioners experience the intermixing of policies from various sources that impact what they can and cannot do.

In addition, other organizational or programmatic rules and proce- dures may exist as the result of organizational administrative choices, such as specifying appropriate work apparel or policies stated by board directives governing practice in such things as the budget or program design. Human service practitioners should note that ignorance of the policies governing practice has never been a legal excuse when prob- lems occur that land the worker and the agency in court. The message here is that the first level of responsible, professional practice is to be able to describe and understand the policies governing practice at whatever level practice occurs. It is also important to understand that remaining at the descriptive level (knowing what the policy is) is not sufficient. Analysis of social policies and their impacts are a central function (some would say an ethical expectation) of human service professionals. In order to engage in sophisticated social policy analysis, regardless of the policy source or level, a few more details regarding policies are needed.

Mancini and Lawson (2009) offer an example of policies that pertain to a mental health agency. They report the results of a study on consumer-based mental health services in which persons who have experienced mental health problems themselves are recruited to provide peer support to others who are in distress. The consumer-based movement represents a nationwide trend that began in the 1970s when grass-roots activist groups advocated for mental health rights. As this informal network grew, self-help groups emerged, with peers helping peers. Today, consumer-operated programs continue to advocate for consumers' rights and are a common component of many established community-based mental health service systems. As part of these programs, local level "peer providers" use what they have learned from their own psychiatric disabilities to help others deal with their unique challenges. One difficulty in designing a peer-provider support approach is that this is highly intensive emotional labor in which peers can quickly become overwhelmed by trying to help others.

When peer-providers are employed by formal mental health systems, they are often called "peer-employees or peer-specialists" and they "are embedded within larger non-peer organizations and have mostly non-peer coworkers and supervisors. . . . Unfortunately, without adequate organizational supports, negotiating the roles and demands of work in nonpeer organizations can lead to isolation, role-ambiguity, stigmatization, and emotional exhaustion" (Mancini & Lawson, 2009, p. 5). This study reveals how important it is for mental health providers that hire peer-specialists into their organizational cultures to be able to support these workers and to establish optimal job configurations that maximize the use of peer and professional staff in an interactional manner. The authors elaborate on the concept of emotional competence for peer-workers and for organizations to support their development through interventions such as practice "circles" in which peer and non–peer-providers can exchange information and provide mutual assistance and emotional support (p. 18).

It may seem that this is a direct service dilemma about how to integrate peer-workers into a mental health provider system, and in fact it is. But it is also riddled with policy considerations. No national or state agency is dictating to a local mental health agency that it must include peer-workers in its staffing pattern, so it is up to the agency's board of directors to debate the issue. If they move with the trend and incorporate peer-workers into their systems, the limited empirical evidence to date suggests that there must be supports in place to integrate these workers into the system. Before a decision is made to hire peer-workers, a good deal of debate must focus on the pros and cons of many important issues. Agencies will need to consider at a minimum how a new hiring policy will impact the current professional staff, the liability issues of having nonprofessional staff interface with consumers, and appropriate supervision and monitoring of the new workers. In the process of considering this decision, an analysis of the issues surrounding such a policy must occur. And should the board decide that peer-workers should be hired, the process of implementation should become an ongoing policy analysis of performance and impact for the good of the agency and the clients they serve.

In summary, the example of the problems associated with mental illness and the need for mentally ill persons to receive appropriate treatment shows that one can approach policy at the organizational level. How to respond to the social problem of persistent mental illness is often left to the discretion of mental health agencies that must make choices about how to intervene. A board of directors searching for options may consider policies different from those guiding standard programming. Many issues will be associated with whatever policy choice is made. Analyzing those issues and recognizing beforehand all the consequences—both intended and otherwise—will avoid unfortunate surprises or complications. In this example, what appears to be a simple and empirically based staffing choice will become more complicated as it interfaces with professional practice standards and credentialing requirements.

County/State Level and Scope

State and county policies apply only to people within the confines of that state or county. These rules also tend to apply to cities or localities as well. In most states, cities are part of county government structures. In the four commonwealths (Virginia, Kentucky, Pennsylvania, and

Massachusetts), cities are separate governmental entities with their own legal and policy structures separate from the counties that may be contiguous to them. At times this may be confusing because of paralleling political and administrative structures, but for the most part (including in the commonwealths), state, county, and city policies are made to conform with federal policies and guidelines and to each other. In all of these cases, various governmental entities, officials, and citizens interact on a policy level, and there is a great deal of diffusion. The policies specifically apply to people residing in a state, county, or city, but they apply also to those who may be passing through. For example, if someone from South Carolina was driving through Virginia, the Virginia state laws regarding speed limits, when driving lights should be on, and when it is okay to stay in the left lane of the highway would apply even if they differed from the laws under which the driver from South Carolina gained a driver's license. These rules would apply whether the driver were in a city or a county in Virginia. However, there might be specific policies in particular cities or counties for public parking, for example, that would not apply statewide, nor would they necessarily resemble what the South Carolina driver experienced at home.

Because there are so many areas in which social policy is made at the state level without the universal shaping mandated by some federal policies, there is great variation across states. For example, Mollica (2008) provides an overview of the way in which "assisted living" has gained increasing popularity as a balance between independent living and nursing home care in the United States. Since there is currently no federal legislation that oversees this burgeoning industry, there is no uniform definition of what constitutes "assisted living." State regulators use the term differently to include a range of residential facilities for older adults, such as what was previously known as residential care, adult care, personal care, or boarding homes. There is no consistency from state to state regarding what sort of services should be the target of regulations. Facility developers use the term "assisted living" for marketing purposes, but with no consistency in terms of what services are actually offered to older consumers.

Mollica provides background information on how the industry has grown since the late 1980s and early 1990s. By 2007, 41 states and the District of Columbia used the term "assisted living" in their regulatory policies (p. 68). Policy makers at the state level have to determine what the definition will be for that state's assisted living, resulting in different regulations in each state. Regulatory policy is continually being updated as new variations on the theme emerge and as the assisted living industry markets new products that do not always conform to state definitions. In short, the evolving industry is a moving target. "The frequent review and changes in state regulation help policy makers to keep pace with changes in consumer preferences and changing business models" (p. 68). According to Mollica, regulators across the United States have continuing concerns about residents' abilities and status, staff/resident ratios, and appropriate rates of occupancy at a time when state revenues are in decline, reducing the number of staff available to survey facilities and investigate complaints. Policy analysis is an ongoing process at the state regulatory level, just to keep up with developments.

Chambers and Wedel (2009) suggest that policy analysis is undertaken in order to understand how the social problem is defined and how and what another person or group thinks and believes about a given situation that is being described as a social problem. Only from an understanding of the problem that the policy has been designed to eliminate can one make judgments about policy effectiveness. In addition to the foregoing example, we could have mentioned a plethora of problems related to various age groups, about which a variety of people would have different definitions. For example, states struggle with how to define abuse and neglect both for child protective service workers and for adult protective service workers, just as states vary in how they define assisted living for the regulation of a section of the long-term care industry. In other words, even with model statutes circulating about a particular subject, context must be considered and state policies will overlap in some ways and diverge in others. The major point is not to forget the social problem that a social policy is trying to address.

In the assisted living example, the underlying problem is that the population is aging and as people age in place they may need supportive services beyond what they can receive in their own homes. They may not qualify for nursing home care, and most people do not aspire to be placed in a nursing facility, so assisted living is a marketed service to fill the gap in the continuum of care. But the difficulty that arises as one analyzes this situation is that left on their own, developers may build facilities with profit rather than care as the top priority. What policies, then, need to be in place to protect vulnerable consumers of service? Understanding this situation is necessary in order for any viable policy to be formulated, and that's where analysis comes into play.

In summary, as the context for policy becomes more complex and diverse, the need for analysis becomes both more important and more complicated. As the examples presented here have demonstrated, county- or state-level policy is particularly context dependent. What is preferred and accepted as appropriate policy will change from context to context, because what is defined as the problem that the social policy is developed to address tends to change to some degree from context to context. Because of the differences in interpretation, universal application of regulations and even universal methods of analysis may present great challenges.

REGIONAL/NATIONAL LEVEL AND SCOPE

At this level or scope, we are interested in the policies that are linked to the political and governmental structure of the United States. We include "regional" here because many federal agencies have regional offices that actually oversee the implementation of policies. For example, decisions that are made regarding whether or not state-level interpretations of federal expectations related to public child welfare practice are acceptable is not determined at the Children's Bureau in Washington, D.C., but at the various regional offices located throughout the country. Some of these offices are known to be more conservative in their interpretations, while others are known to be more liberal in their ability to accept state differences regarding implementation of federal policy. This means that even at the federal level, interpretation of policy and universal application of regulations is challenging.

Even with the existence of regional offices, federal-level policy has the widest scope. Federal policy applies to everyone within the boundaries of the United States and its protectorates. Federal policy is found in the public laws developed by the Congress and signed into law by the president. It is also found in the rules and procedures of the federal agencies charged with enacting the particular policy instrument or program that develops as a result of the policy choice. Finally, federal policy is found in the decisions of the Supreme Court, which is charged with monitoring legal findings for their congruence with the Constitution of the United States and its first 12 amendments, better known as the Bill of Rights.

There is probably no policy debate that recycles through the Congress more than what to do about access to and the cost of health care in the United States. In a policy analysis of health care systems worldwide, Tanner (2008) points out that most health care systems are struggling with concerns regarding access and rising costs and that it is somewhat of a myth that the United States has unique problems in this regard. Tanner points out that trend data suggest that health insurance does not mean universal access because many countries actually promise universality only to ration care and have long waiting lists; that costs are rising everywhere not just in the United States; that countries heavily weighted toward government control have access, rationing and physician choice issues; and that countries with the most effective national health care systems still incorporate market mechanisms into their systems. Using data from the United States, France, Canada, Norway, The Netherlands, Spain, and Japan, Tanner embarks on a comparative analysis that concludes with a recommendation that the United States learn from the successes and failures of other systems, which means increasing consumer incentives and control rather than "follow the road to government-run national health care" (p. 36). He concludes that the United States needs to be cautious about "heading down the road to national health care but [needs to learn] from the experiences of other countries, which demonstrate the failure of centralized command and control and the benefits of increasing consumer incentives and choice" (p. 1). Whether one agrees with Tanner's analysis or not, a thorough policy analysis at the national level requires comparing what is known about a problem in a global context when it comes to pressing needs such as health care.

In summary, then, at the federal level even more considerations are involved in any policy decision. For without careful consideration, policy makers would be operating without meaningful information on which to make critical decisions that affect the quality of care and quality of life of millions of people. Competent policy analyses are central to decision making. Hopefully, it is also becoming clear how political both the analysis and the decision making may become.

INTERNATIONAL LEVEL AND SCOPE

Although our focus is on policy within the United States, the previous example on health care illustrates how interconnected national policies are within an international arena. Therefore, we provide two examples of social problems that are currently on the international radar screen just to demonstrate how important it is to analyze these problems in a global context. The first deals with international adoptions, and the second deals with the consequences of establishing a national language.

The point is that international policy in many ways has local, family, and individual impacts that must be understood.

Roby and Shaw (2006) offer a set of policy quandaries in their analysis of the problems associated with international adoption, particularly in light of the number of orphans in Africa. Even though they focus on adoption in their analysis, they are careful to say that adoption is only one option for African children. Even setting boundaries around one option reveals a multitude of complex policy issues such as the lingering effects of American slavery, modern-day slavery and child trafficking, the identity and well-being of children, and the disproportionate number of African-American children in the U.S. foster care system. From a position of protecting the child in the adoption process, there are countless legal and procedural issues. What is revealing about Roby and Shaw's analysis is the complicated overlay of national, state, and private policies. For example, the United States may have in place all sorts of provisions stipulating how children may enter the country, but the country from which a child is coming may have conflicting, limited, and different policies with which to contend. Within the United States, state child welfare systems reflect a mixture of federal and state policies, just as within the country of origin nongovernmental and private organizations have their own policies. And on an international level, organizations such as UNICEF have position statements and standards for inter-country adoption. Further, the creation of the Hague Convention has established a baseline for acceptable practice for all nations that are signatories of the Convention. Understanding this complex set of interrelated (and often incongruent) policies challenges the most reflective practitioner and is essential to anyone whose practice involves intercountry adoptions.

As another example, Van Parijs (2000) has written a provocative analysis of native languages in a global world. There are approximately 6,000 living languages, out of which 2,000 have fewer than 1,000 living speakers and are thus dying out. That still leaves 4,000 languages surviving in the world. As various countries establish national languages, the expectation is that anyone entering that country will be able to communicate in the official language. For example, immigrants entering a country in which their native tongue is not spoken will find themselves in classes and their children in schools that teach the official language of that country. Since language is so important to culture, the impact of superimposing a linguistic requirement on persons who speak other languages is essentially a policy decision

Table 1.2
Levels of Social Policies and their Operationalization

Level	Operationalized Through
Personal and/or Familial	Members of domestic units
Organization and/or Community	Grass-roots associations and coalitions Health and human service agencies and their boards Community groups
County and/or State	Public agencies serving counties and states
Regional and/or National	Federal agencies
International	Public and private organizations and groups that have cross-national missions

with extremely significant consequences for the identities and well-being of individuals and entire groups, communities, and cultures.

In summary, as one moves among the levels just described there are proportionately more and more people affected by policies. See Table 1.2 for an overview of the levels just discussed. Just as it is important to know that there are levels of policy nested within one another that take different forms, it is equally helpful to know that there are different approaches for conceptualizing policy analysis.

CONCEPTUALIZING POLICY ANALYSIS

To be politically astute and effective, practitioners need to be able to see connections between social policies and direct organization and community practice. At this early stage it should be clear how complicated understanding policy and all its important connections can be. One engages in policy analysis to understand something about the policy and so that judgments can be made about its worth. Determining the appropriate focus for the analysis is essential so that the results have meaning and impact. This is the clue to sophisticated policy analysis. That focus will be influenced by whatever conceptual frameworks guide the analysis.

CONCEPTUAL FRAMEWORKS AND THEORIES OF POLICY PROCESS

Ostrom (2007) points out an important conceptual consideration when she defines frameworks, theories, and models. These terms are often used interchangeably or without specificity. A conceptual framework is the broadest of the three terms, helping the analyst "identify the elements and relationships among these elements that one needs to consider . . . they provide the most general list of variables that should be used" for analysis (p. 25). Often a practitioner knows what themes or areas are important to analyze, but does not have a theory about how they all fit together. The use of a conceptual framework is a reasonable starting point in approaching one's analysis. We define *conceptual framework* as "any intellectual structuring used to corral assumptions or related concepts into some form for understanding." Frameworks may be skeletal (just beginning) or complex. They may be broad or narrow, but practitioners should think architecturally when arriving at frameworks, because they are mechanisms for making ideas hang together in a sensible way. Sometimes these frameworks are tightly constructed enough to be considered theories.

Ostrom contends that "the development and use of theories enable the analyst to specify which elements of the framework are particularly relevant to certain kinds of questions and to make general working assumptions about these elements" (2007, p. 25). According to Mullaly (2007, p. 205), theories carry out four basic functions: description, explanation, prediction and control, and management of events or changes. In a traditional way, theories are sets of interrelated concepts that explain how and why something works or does not work for the purpose of enhancing understanding. For example, sociological theories describe how societies, institutions, communities, or organizations function. These *descriptive theories* assist in analyzing what is happening within these systems, but they do not provide the practitioner with methods to change a situation once it has been analyzed. Descriptive theories show how elements are held together. In contrast, *prescriptive theories* are intended to provide direction or guidance for persons wanting to change or intervene in a situation and are the underpinnings for practice models (Netting, Kettner, & McMurtry, 2008). Prescriptive theories provide avenues or directions to cause incremental change. Challenging traditional theories are *critical theories*, which are committed to change the world "in ways that can help 'emancipate' those at the margins of society by providing insights and intellectual tools they can use to empower themselves" (Mullaly, 2007, p. 215). Some critical theories provide prescriptions, much like prescriptive theories; however, the prescriptions are in the direction of transformative structural changes. Sometimes theories are used in policy analysis to identify the cause of the social problem; sometimes theories are used to predict the impact of the social policy when enacted. Theories, then, when used to guide one's policy analysis will influence the questions one asks and how descriptive, prescriptive or critical the analysis will be.

Sabatier (2007) identifies seven frameworks for analysis of the policy process, based on the following criteria: (1) concepts are relatively clear and there are causal relationships among variables, (2) the framework is viewed by policy scholars as viable to understanding the policy process, (3) each must be positive in that it seeks to explain much of the policy process, and (4) the framework must address aspects of policy-making process such as conflicting values and interests, how information flows, organizational relationships, and environmental variations. Sabatier views five of the frameworks "as focused on explaining policy change within a given political system or set of institutional arrangements (including efforts to change those arrangements)" (p. 10). As you read the bulleted list below, see if by their descriptions you can tell whether they are built on descriptive, prescriptive, or critical theories:

- *The stages heuristic*—Views the policy process as going through stages of development from formulation to evaluation.
- *Institutional rational choice*—A family of frameworks focusing on how self-interested individuals make choices within established relationships with specific sets of institutions.
- *Multiple-streams*—Developed by Kingdon (1984) and based on Cohen, March, and Olsen's (1972) garbage can model of organizational behavior, the policy process is viewed as three streams of actors and processes coming together. These streams are (1) problem (data and definitions of the problem), (2) policy (proponents of solutions), and (3) politics (elections and elected officials).
- *Punctuated-equilibrium framework (PE)*—Views U.S. policymaking as punctuated by brief periods of major policy change in a characteristically long period of incremental change.
- *The advocacy coalition framework (ACF)*—Proposes that policy change occurs when interaction occurs between advocacy coalitions (as subsets of the larger system), composed of activists with shared beliefs, and the larger political system.

Two additional theoretical frameworks "seek to provide explanations of variations across a large number of political systems" (Sabatier, 2007, p. 10). These are

- *The policy diffusion framework*—Explains adoption of specific policy innovations across a wide area (such as multiple localities or states), arguing that adoption emanates from both specific characteristics of political systems and various diffusion strategies.

- *The funnel of causality and other frameworks in Large-N comparative studies*—Focuses primarily on budgets to explain variations across large numbers of states and nations. (Sabatier, 2007, pp. 8–10).

Sabatier's listing of frameworks provides a sample of the richness and complexity of what is available as tools for the policy analyst.

MODELS AND APPROACHES

Models are more focused than either conceptual frameworks or theories, making "precise assumptions about a limited set of parameters and variables" (Ostrom, 2007, p. 26). Like frameworks, they are built around theories (whether broadly or narrowly construed or whether stated or implied). Models are prescriptive in that they tend to direct the analysis in a predetermined direction. Most dominant in the social policy field have been models built around what Sabatier calls "the stages heuristic" and "institutional rational choice" theoretical frameworks. These are called *rational models*.

Stages and rational choice frameworks create models of analysis that assume that there is a single truth—that is, one right answer. This single truth can be arrived at through a series of well-defined steps in a fixed, prescribed sequence. Rational models also assume that with defined steps, control can be exerted to assure certainty about the "rightness" of the findings of the analysis. This is possible because it is assumed that the social system within which social policies are constructed is a system in which individuals pursue their own welfare by exchanging things with others (i.e., a market economy). These models assume that self-interests drive policy making. Rational models also assume that policies are arrived at in a prescribed way by a collection of rational decision makers who choose the best policy response based on the most benefit for the least cost. Elsewhere (Fauri, Netting, & O'Connor, 2005) it is also suggested that the rational model of analysis is rather linear, built on "if/then" steps with prediction based on objectives, alternatives, and assessment of consequences such that decisions are made by selecting from alternatives and minimizing objections. Here, reason is the basic building block based on market assumptions where choices feature selection of that which will provide the "biggest bang for the buck." On the whole, this type of policy analysis is expert dominated, because only the expert knows the appropriate steps in the analysis and is able to make the determination that the policy choice actually provides the most benefit for the least cost.

The rational approach works well for policies that are theory driven, and where the problem is well defined and well accepted as defined. Unfortunately, based on our earlier discussion about diversity and complexity of policies and their interpretations when scope of the problem and the policy are at issue, most social problems and the social policies that are developed to address them are value laden. There is much dispute about the value(s) that should have precedence when either the problem is defined or the policy is selected as a response. Disputed values create a political forum where the costs and benefits of the problem and the policy response are also in dispute, because what is a problem to one group may well be a benefit to another. Further, it is essentially impossible to objectively judge conflicting or competing costs and values since weighting and even-handed comparison is difficult, even with the most advanced, computerized analytic techniques. Even if that were possible, it is generally impossible to predict with certainty what the intended and unintended consequences of policy alternatives will be. Cost/benefit analysis cannot simply be considered as part of the market economy; diverse social, economic, and political values must be recognized when assessing the policy choice and its impact.

A way to manage these challenges is through a *nonrational approach* to policy (Fauri, Netting, & O'Connor, 2005) which is based on assumptions of multiple and competing truths with no fixed sequence or analytical steps. Note that we are no longer using the word "model," which implies a predetermined, prescriptive process. Instead the word "approach" implies that there is not just one best way, but multiple ways. For example, the multiple-streams and advocacy coalition frameworks identified by Sabatier (2007) are more likely aligned with an "approach" rather than a "model" orientation in that they allow for uncertainty, given that groups of uncontrollable advocates intervene in the policy process in unpredictable ways. Without predictability and predetermined ends, these approaches are nonlinear and nonrational.

A nonrational approach to decision making includes multiple perspectives or understandings of the social problem and the policy response with decisions based on power and politics. It assumes that what goes on in organizations, communities, and societies is particularly political. It assumes that ideas are the medium of exchange rather than the cost and benefits of the market. Context and influence from diverse stakeholders influence what is seen as "good" and what should be avoided for being "bad" in the policy choice. The policy shaping is actually occurring through the participation of all with a

Table 1.3
Frameworks, Theories, Models, and Approaches

Concepts	Definitions
Frameworks	Any intellectual structuring used to corral assumptions or related concepts into some form for understanding.
Theories	Sets of interrelated concepts that may serve different functions: description, explanation, prediction, and control. Types of theories include *Descriptive*—Telling what is happening. *Prescriptive*—Providing direction about what to do about what is happening. *Critical*—Providing insights that empower one to change what is happening.
Models	An approach based on rational prescriptions having predetermined outcomes. Thus models are a type of approach.
Approaches	Possibilities that can take the form of models, but can also be based on nonrational and critical assumptions. Thus an approach is a broad concept that can be used in any paradigm.

stake in the issues making it part of a community dialogue. Shared meanings motivate people to action. This dialogue may turn dialectical when paradox and politics become such a part of the process of agenda setting and decision making. What is clear here is that political reasoning is very much a part of the process, which means that this sort of policy analysis is more value, ideology, or passion driven than the theoretically driven rational approach. This approach is more fluid and circular than linear. Table 1.3 provides an overview of frameworks, theories, models, and approaches.

From this perspective, policy is political, because the political system has the task of ordering and ranking values in order to make choices about which policy to select. Some, such as Stone (2002), would argue that the political system determines what is important and then persuades society's members to accept the ranking, perhaps manipulating the choices. The political system can reorder the ranking of preferences in accordance with the socio/cultural/economic environment. With changes in the ranking of preferences come changes in the structure of the chosen policy position. So in many ways policies represent changing goals, shifting problem definitions and shifting acceptable solutions at any given time in politics.

In summary, two principal perspectives or approaches seem to predominate the policy analysis field. Regardless of the details of the theory, the framework, or the focus of the analytic process, they are based on either rational or nonrational assumptions. Later it will become clear how both perspectives help to shape our arguments about policy analysis being research. Chapter 2 explains that it is possible to take a policy-analysis perspective that in fact combines both rational and nonrational (and sometimes irrational) assumptions in ways that do not set up impossible paradoxes.

CONCLUSION

This introductory chapter was intended to offer an overview of the major aspects of social policies and a preliminary understanding of the challenges that comprehending social policies represents. It provided an initial discussion about how to approach social policy in more than just a descriptive way. We hope we have set the stage for further enhancement of both critical thinking and leadership skills for human service practitioners in the social policy context. These skills are elemental for competent, ethical practice, because in most cases, human service practitioners are being called to a practice guided by policy at some level. It is essential for the professional practitioner to know more than just what the policy says about the expected practice. It is also important to competently assess the policy and, when necessary, advocate for alternative policy responses.

Returning to the involuntary commitment case presented early in this chapter, we suspect that Constance and Jayne are well aware of just how value laden policies can be. The stated policy seems so rational—call the police, transport to the hospital, assess the client, determine whether to admit. It reads like a critical pathway in a medical setting. But in this process, both Constance and Jayne recognize that this "approach" is far from a prescriptive model. Depending on the circumstances, each client's situation is unique, and when it comes to implementation, the process may look different. For anyone wanting to analyze this seemingly straightforward policy, how one interprets it would be based on the questions asked, and with each client there would be unique questions to ask.

As we move further into the material of this text, we hope that this first chapter has begun to establish the argument that in enacting policy analysis much critical thinking is necessary to select the appropriate tool for that analysis. Because of the complexity of the policy-making and policy-enacting process, it is impossible to rely on only one framework, theory, model, or approach to guide analysis. In the following chapters you will see that our guidance entails approaching policy analysis as research. In what follows we hope to provide you with a variety of resources and tools to create powerfully constructed, evenhanded approaches to understanding social policy, judging the worth of social policies, and establishing reasonable alternatives to policies requiring changes in order to assure that they address the social problems as defined.

DISCUSSION QUESTIONS

1. What assumptions do you bring to policy analysis? How did you develop these assumptions, and have they changed over time? How might they influence your work as a policy analyst?
2. In the involuntary commitment policy example, what would you have done if you had been Constance (the therapist)? What do you consider to be the pros and cons of allowing the therapist to transport a client?
3. We have defined social policies as a specific subset of public policies, but it is often difficult to distinguish when a policy is "social." Identify at least three policies being heavily debated in current political discourse. Would you describe these as social policies? Why or why not?
4. According to Guba, there are three categories of policies: intention, implementation, and experience. Using the same policies identified in item 3, dialogue about how you would categorize these policies and why. What form do these policies take?
5. In Table 1.1, we list a number of policy forms. In a substantive area with which you are familiar, come up with examples of each form. How do these policy forms interact within your substantive area? What are the places in which they work together and in which they conflict? Who has the power to address the places in which they conflict?
6. In Table 1.2, we list levels of social policies and their operationalization. Given your response to item 5, discuss how the forms you've identified fit with various levels and scopes.
7. Different writers use terms in different ways. Review Table 1.3 and how we are defining frameworks, theories, models, and approaches. How do these concepts work with what you have learned in other places? Are there ways in which you would use these terms differently? Why or why not?

CHAPTER 2

Thinking of Policy Analysis
as Research

I N CHAPTER 1, we defined policy analysis as a *systematic study of chosen courses of action within unique contexts with goals of preventing and addressing social problems.* Systematic study is what research is all about; thus, our first goal for this chapter is to emphasize how policy analysis *is* a type of research. We begin by briefly looking at the traditional role of research in guiding policy analysis and the limitations of focusing only on this role. Next, the dimensions of research are defined in order to illustrate how a well designed policy analysis contains the same dimensions. Approaching policy analysis as research expands the analyst's capacity in using existing tools to focus the analysis on formulation, product, implementation, or performance relevant to understanding policy. These foci are elaborated in this chapter.

Our second goal for this chapter is to introduce a conceptual framework that will guide the remainder of the book. We will locate policy analysis tools within this framework so that it will be clear that these tools share the same philosophical and methodological perspectives as other research-based means of knowledge building. In addition, we will continue to use the involuntary commitment example presented in Chapter 1 to illustrate basic concepts introduced in this chapter.

Much has been written across the disciplines concerned with understanding and shaping policy, especially social policy. Much of the literature focuses on the benefits or justification of a particular theoretical or practical approach to policy analysis, conveying a message that the justification of a policy analysis framework is often as political as the policy to be investigated. Rarely is it made clear what exactly the particular analytic approach overlooks or fails to capture. Rarely is sufficient explicit information provided for the consumer of the policy analysis framework to make judgments about the usefulness of the framework itself prior to its application. This is one of our concerns in writing this book. We think it is important for those who want to analyze a policy to know the strengths and limitations of the approaches they are using.

THE ROLE OF RESEARCH IN GUIDING POLICY ANALYSIS

Traditionally, research has often been seen as simply informing policy analysis. In this section, we hope to convey why this view may be limiting. Not only is research extremely helpful if used as background for understanding the social problems that policies are initiated to address, but the actual analyses of those policies are also relevant and useful research studies in their own right.

A TRADITIONAL VIEW

There is no question that the results of research are seen to be important resources for policy analysis and policy decision making. This position has been enhanced by the development of the evidence-based practice (EBP) movement that has influenced both micro and macro aspects of human service practice (Gambrill, 2005, 2006; Gibbs 2003; Hall, 2008). Indeed, regarding policy analysis, Jansson (2000) instructs that "an empirical approach forces analysts to structure their inquiry systematically" (p. 47). This position suggests that ideology and preferences are better enhanced with data.

It is beyond the scope of this chapter to go into details about the "ins" and "outs" of evidence-based practice or some of the controversies about what actually constitute evidence. There is a growing literature available to the reader who is eager to examine the macro implications of EBP (e.g., Netting & O'Connor, 2008). What is clear, however, is a general consensus that data should drive decision making about a policy. Certainly using what is known about a particular problem by way of recent studies, needs assessments, and evaluations of programs that result from policy developments is important for policy analysis and implementation—but there is more. Although Popple and Leighninger (2008, p. 43) acknowledge that policy analysis is comparable to research, little more is available to the policy practitioner to make the tactical connection between research and policy analysis. Without that connection, evidence-based practice remains almost spuriously connected to policy practice at the evidentiary level.

But recognizing the importance of research is only one way in which research and policy are interconnected. What data one collects depends on what questions one asks, and asking questions about problems and issues that lead to policy initiation is just the beginning. There are unlimited numbers of questions to ask about the policies themselves, from "who supported them and why?" to "did they make a difference in anyone's life?" Thus, a simple recognition of the role of research-produced evidence as support of a policy does not provide the grounding needed for the kind of sophisticated analysis that is necessary in a complex social world. For example, in formulating an involuntary commitment policy, it is important to know what has happened in the past to persons with mental illnesses and which situations have led to involuntary commitments. But it doesn't stop there. In analyzing different state policies, it is also important to be able to systematically contrast and compare different approaches to involuntary commitment so that the intent, implementation, and experience of these policies are studied. These policy analyses, then, become part of the research evidence that informs future policies, and they even help to evaluate current involuntary commitment policies.

To recap, although much emphasis has been placed in various disciplines on the role of research in policy analysis (see Bardach, 2005; Lennon & Corbett, 2003; Lincoln & Guba, 1986; O'Connor & Netting, 2008), the focus is principally on "the causes of specific social problems" (Jansson, 2000, p. 45). Although studying the causes of social problems is extremely important, policy analysis research is much more expansive. Policy analysis research includes understanding the social problem within its context, the goals of a particular policy and the forces that contributed to the selection of those goals, the decision-making process behind a particular policy response, the implementation process, the impact a policy has on various constituencies, and a host of other important elements. Thus, we hope to signal for the reader an unlimited number of opportunities for thinking of policy analysis as research.

THE UNDERSTANDABLE LIMITS OF TRADITIONAL POLICY ANALYSIS

Failure to be conscious of these necessary preliminary considerations prior to engaging in policy analysis will potentially lead the analyst to pose the wrong questions because the selected tool was not designed for the purpose for which it is being used. This is what happens when students are told to find a policy analysis model that they like. It also happens when a policy analyst uses only the one approach with which he or she has become comfortable. This way of proceeding speaks more about the cognitive framework or stakeholding position of the policy analyst than it does about the particular analysis tool. This approach has the potential of producing off-targeted information. At times and in different circumstances, what may be needed are not just the questions the analyst is comfortable asking but the questions that are necessary to truly interrogate the policy. The point is that without understanding what one wants to produce in the same way that one understands the requirement to have a research question prior to embarking on a research process; analysts tend to use tools that are comfortably congruent with how they see the world without regard to the rest of the questions necessary for systematic policy inquiry.

This is, of course, perfectly understandable in view of the developing information coming from brain science. One particularly informative book was written by Jill B. Taylor (2008), a brain scientist who suffered a serious stroke. From that experience came many useful insights that would suggest why one might choose one type of policy analysis tool over another. It may hinge on what part of the brain one tends to use most of the time.

If you mostly use your left brain, you will be thinking analytically and critically, looking for patterns, details, order. You will be developing rules and regulations to help maintain that order and shape information into what is manageable. Using mostly the left brain, you organize information by categorizing, describing, judging—a linear reasoning process. From pattern identification you identify boundaries and separations and draw conclusions to fill in the blanks on your quest for truth. This approach to the world will be much more congruent with linear models of decision making based on linear reasoning. Earlier we talked about rational and nonrational approaches, and in another text we have defined the difference between linear and circular reasoning (Netting, O'Connor, & Fauri, 2008). Here it is sufficient to understand that left brain users are particularly fond of reductionist thinking that takes a rather "if/then" approach. The policy analyst whose brain works like this would be more drawn to traditional models of policy analysis, the details of which will be the focus of much of what follows in this text under the title of rational thinking.

If, on the other hand, the policy analyst uses mostly the right hemisphere of his or her brain, then the world of ideas is what attracts. These people are sometimes known for having their "head in the clouds." What is certain is that those using the right brain welcome change. They keep in the present because they see the richness of the present. They are comfortable with a continuum of relativity and ambiguity because they are essentially optimistic and adventuresome based on a belief in abundance. For them the glass is half full rather than half empty. Those using the right brain are sensitive to nonverbal information and empathically able to decode emotions. They are intuitive and tend to be comfortable thinking outside the box and thus seem to be mostly open and creative. They are appreciative of chaos (or paradox) and slow to reduce information from the big picture.

If you are mostly right brained, then it makes sense that the newer, more emergent approaches to policy analysis that attend to context and politics or power in specific ways would make more sense and be more congruent with your analytic worldview. The right-brained policy analyst would be most comfortable leaving all options open, starting analysis where data are available, and trusting that in some way all the needed material will become identified and available. This is called trusting emergence. It requires living in an ambiguous way with the analytic process until the analyst "knows" the process has come full circle and the analysis is complete. This suggests working nonlinearly and nonrationally. Tools are available for policy analysis that allows an analyst to proceed in this way. But that nonlinear, more emergent and interpretive approach, no matter how attractive, may not be what is necessary for a particular analysis, regardless of how comfortable the analyst may be with the tool.

All of this is intended to show that there is no perfect policy analysis tool, just as there is no "perfect" way to come to "do" science, come to knowledge, or to use your brain. What you learn depends upon what you ask. What you ask depends on what you are comfortable with based on what you believe is important or what you think you know about how the world works. Sometimes one way of doing policy analysis is appropriate. At another time another approach to the analytic process is necessary to get what is needed. Sometimes the purpose of the analysis is so new or from such uncharted territory that there is no current policy analysis process capable of producing what is needed. In the rest of this text, we will help you to determine these differences. We will also show how one engages in differential policy analysis by using existing tools or developing one's own when necessary.

As we move through the chapter, it is important to recognize that there are different ways one can approach research, whether it is policy analysis research or some other type of research. Again, using the involuntary commitment example from Chapter 1, the questions one asks will lead to different ways of knowing about the policy. For example, if one asks "what is the outcome we want from involuntary commitment?" this question presumes a predetermined result in a rational world. There is no question that the policy should exist, but the question reflects a desire to tie down the specific intent and pull that intent through implementation. But if one asks "what is the value of having involuntary commitment?" more questions immediately emerge, such as "value for whom?" This more descriptive approach yields further questions rather than closing the questioning process down. And suppose one persists in a more critical way, asking "What are the implications of involuntary commitment for social justice?" The critical nature of this question poses a different stream of questioning that raises the possibility that involuntary commitment as a policy option may not be justifiable in a moral society.

Given the importance of the questions one poses, it should come as little surprise that one of the most challenging aspects of a thoughtful policy analysis is knowing where to start. Thus, we now turn to what actually constitutes research, beginning with a focus on asking research questions. We then take a close look at determining units of analysis, selecting research design and methods, and conducting data analysis.

WHAT CONSTITUTES RESEARCH?

When one engages in research, one is seeking answers to a question or wishes to find solutions to a problem. Research is conducted in various ways, but each way seeks specific information to answer the question or solve the problem. It can be a naturalistic questioning in one's environment, such as trying to understand why people behave the way they do. It can be library or electronic data–based such as finding out what has already been written about or collected about a particular subject. It can be conducted within a laboratory or other identified and controlled context, such as conducting a clinical trial to test a new medication. Research is more or less systematic. The more systematic it is, the more it is seen to be "scientific." Certainly, there is a great deal of controversy about what is necessary to make research science. Postmodern thought has helped us to move beyond the traditional scientific method into many ways of collecting, under-standing, and accepting information as solid answers or results.

The scientific method is a useful way to assure that objectivity is used to remove biases and values, or at least to make them explicit so that they have as little as possible influence on the process or the results of scientific inquiry. The early framers of the scientific method (see, for example, works by David Hume, Auguste Comte, the Vienna Circle of logical positivists, and Karl Popper) wanted to move away from magical thinking and religious or belief-based answers to the big questions about how the world worked. They developed an acceptable method about how to come to know that was based on empirical (measurable) information, rather than beliefs. The scientific method consists of applying mandates to collect data based on direct observa-tion, or operationalization when indirect measurement is undertaken, and to be systematic with procedures that are organized, methodical, public, recognizable, and replicable. The scientific method is determi-nistic in that it assumes that order can be discovered and that what is discovered is not simply due to chance. This also makes the discovery predictable. The scientific method views results as provisional; they are understood to be tentative conclusions subject to questioning and refutation, which are assumed to lead to a more accurate picture of reality.

Today, thanks to developments in the physical sciences, especially quantum physics, the scope of what is seen to be "scientific" and how one comes to know based on science has greatly expanded. Later we will demonstrate three very different perspectives on systematic know-ing. For now, let us continue to focus on the common elements of research designed in such a way that one can trust the information developed to answer a question or solve a problem.

ASKING RESEARCH QUESTIONS

Whether you are doing family genealogy, historical research, or re-search on a vaccine against swine flu, you are first and foremost guided by a question to be answered. In genealogy it might be "How are the Smiths connected to the Smithsons?" In historical research we have been guided by the question "What are lady boards of managers?" The swine flu question might be "What causes swine flu?" Notice that these are all different sorts of questions. The first is a question of association. The second is one aimed at identifying what constitutes the dimensions of a particular phenomenon. The last is a question about cause. In our practice example, a researchable question could be "What caused Jayne's mental illness?" All are legitimate arenas for systematic efforts of coming to know.

Similarly, one can pose a series of researchable policy questions. For example, "How are lobbyists influencing state legislators about a particular bill?" or "How does the governing board relate to the CEO?" These are associational questions, and they pertain to the strength of a relationship that may or may not be enough to propel a new policy through the legislative or board process. Many associational questions are asked when it comes to analyzing the politics and process through which a particular bill becomes law or the agency politics through which a new policy gains board approval. Another type of question might be "What is involuntary commitment?" This is a question about the content of a policy like the one in our example, including the dimensions of what constitutes the involuntary commitment procedure. There are many times when practitioners need to know the specifics that define a particular policy so that they can gain an understanding of what they must do to conform to its mandates. And there are questions about cause, such as "Why are practitioners advocating for health care reform?" This question seeks to get into the reasons behind advocacy actions and the causes that are driving such a strong motivation for change. In short, when a question or questions concern proposed, enacted, or implemented policies, one is poised on the threshold of policy analysis research.

DETERMINING UNITS OF ANALYSIS

For research to be useful, it is necessary to determine what unit of analysis will be most important in answering the question. For the genealogical question the unit could be the individual, the family, or even a region of the country. For the historical analysis the unit could be the organization, the board, or particular individuals. The unit of analysis for the flu could reflect public health interests at the community level or biological interests at the molecular level. "The setting that the analyst wants to examine and the questions that the analyst wants to address will determine the unit of analysis" (Schlager, 2007, p. 314).

"How are lobbyists influencing state legislators about a particular bill?" could be answered by interviewing state legislators and examining successful bills with strong lobbying support that made it through the legislative process. Both sources (legislators and bills) could be accessed, but the unit of analysis would be the bill. "How does the governing board relate to the CEO?" might require interviews with individuals, but the unit of analysis would be the governing board–CEO relationship. If multiple board–CEO relationships were studied in multiple agencies, a comparative analysis of these relationships could be undertaken. The unit of analysis for involuntary commitment may be the policy itself, and this policy could be approached in various ways. The appropriate unit of analysis will depend on the purpose of the research.

SELECTING RESEARCH DESIGN AND METHODS

Once a question has been identified and the purpose of the research is known, a study is designed to determine how to find the data to answer the question. The design can take many forms. It can be theoretically guided. For example, depending upon the research question, systems theory could be used to guide the identification of the variables needed to see how the Smiths and Smithsons are related, how lady boards of managers work, or how the H1N1(swine flu) virus lives within a host. Or in policy research, if one wants to know how lobbyists are influencing state legislators, what one knows about social exchange or social systems theories may be helpful starting points in determining how to develop an analytic plan.

In research, the chosen method may have a specific design that has already been developed by a particular discipline or group of methodologists. It can also emerge as the questioning process unfolds. Whether it is a prescriptive, predetermined research design or an emergent one, the research design can be articulated, and it includes all actions that go into collecting information (data or evidence) and analyzing it.

Approaching policy analysis as one would approach any research project will allow the beginning and advanced policy analyst to recognize a full set of useful policy analytic tools to be used differentially, depending on the policy analysis need or goal. Without this positioning it seems that one is left with a policy analysis process that starts in the middle of the analysis. We believe that the determination of the usefulness of the policy analysis framework can and should be undertaken before engaging in the policy analysis itself.

There are numerous policy analysis frameworks, and those frameworks or tools can serve the purpose of analysis with varying degrees of aptness. There is much confusion about what to use, but embedded in this confusion is the link between policy analysis and research. All these resources for analysis are potentially useful tools when they are used in an appropriately targeted way. But how does one know that a particular tool will provide the analytic results desired? This is a similar question to the previous one about whether or not the research design will serve the research purpose. Here, the answer comes from knowing the purpose for which the policy analysis is being undertaken.

In summary, policy analysis as research rests on one's understanding of the purpose of the analysis. Based on that purpose, one selects an analytic tool to "design" the policy analysis. One can then apply that tool almost as one uses a standardized instrument in human subjects research. Doing so makes clear that the analysis is intended to produce specific information and one should overlook other information based on how the tool has been constructed. In this way, each tool becomes an identifiably unique instrument for data collection.

CONDUCTING DATA ANALYSIS

Data analysis is another aspect of research. Once data in word or number form have been identified and collected, what has been collected must be made meaningful. In most instances the data must be reduced to a more manageable form in order to make sense out of them. Generally, that happens through statistical analysis of numerical data or content analysis of word data. What makes this process systematic research is that one is not allowed to pick and choose the information one wants to select as acceptable or useful results. One gets the results that the analytic plan produces. If the question or questions were well articulated, the design was appropriately related to the question, and the methods within the design were enacted systematically, the results should at least partially answer the research question. In many cases, the first results of a research process create more questions than answers, thus establishing the need for further inquiry; this is commonly known as creating a line of research.

In summary, then, for an information-gathering process to rise to the level of research that justifies the energy it takes to engage in the process, the following questions should be answered:

- What is the purpose of the research?
- Does the research question(s) fit that purpose?
- What is the unit of analysis to be studied?
- What research design will best serve the research purpose?
- Based on the design, what methods will be used?

- Does the research design demonstrate sufficient rigor that the results produced in the proposed process can be trusted?
- How will data be analyzed?
- Based on the results, what questions require further inquiry?

For policy analysis, we would add an element to replace the question, "What research design will best serve the research purpose?" with a similar question related to policy, "What policy analysis tool(s) will provide the analytic results desired?"

Further, to determine the appropriate tool for analysis, the complexity of macro systems must be recognized. If policy analysis is research, the analyst must determine what she or he wants to know and then determine the focus of analysis to be targeted. One's analytic focus will vary in this type of research, possibly even more than in traditionally constructed research. We now identify the potential foci in policy analysis research.

FOCUSING THE POLICY ANALYSIS

Many scholars have identified varying ways to distinguish the focus of a policy analysis, including identifying stages of policy development and types of policies, among other things, to create conceptual processes to focus the analysis. Because the "stages" and "types" discussion can become a bit confusing, we are combining all these concepts into a discussion of all the dimensions that need to be considered in determining the *focus of the analysis*. The focus must be determined before embarking on a meaningful or productive policy analysis; once one is focused, the unit of analysis can be more easily determined.

It is important to note that whatever focus is selected when starting the analysis, the analytic process may shift. For example, if the analyst wants to analyze a policy from formulation to impact, different questions will be asked at each stage of the policy process, because the focus of analysis has shifted from the policy goal to how enactment of the policy occurred and to what happened as a result of that enactment. The unit of analysis, however, could remain the same, depending on the purpose of the research. For example, in the involuntary commitment example in Chapter 1 about Constance transporting Jayne, the focus of one's analysis might begin with how practitioners were involved in this policy change, shift to how therapists are included as possible transporters in the content of the policy, move to looking at how therapists are implementing the policy, and end with how this policy change is impacting therapeutic relationships. The focus thus shifts, following the process of policy development over time, but the unit of analysis remains the practitioner. It is equally likely that as the focus shifts, so does the unit of analysis. For example, if one wants to know how this involuntary commitment policy was formulated and how the various stakeholders interacted, the unit of analysis may be the formulation process itself. Then if one wants to study the policy content that resulted, the unit of analysis may shift to the policy document. The point here is that practitioners must painstakingly think through what they want to know and for what purpose.

Another interesting challenge results from the incremental process of policy making in the United States. While it is rare that one can find revolutionary or fundamentally different policies being constructed or enacted, one does consistently see revisions to policies that are changed in increments. Social policies are not static elements; rather, policies go through the process of amendment and change over time, which also makes it necessary for the focus of analysis to shift.

In this section, we draw on Gilbert and Terrell (2010) who provide a way of thinking about policies and how to engage them analytically. Gilbert and Terrell (2010) identify three stages in policies: process, product, and performance (the three Ps). We build on their work to identify four foci of analysis: formulation, product, implementation, and performance. In our conceptualization, elements of Guba's (1984) intent, implementation/action and experience are also present. These are shown in Table 2.1.

Formulation: Policy Intent or Goal   Gilbert and Terrell (2010) suggest that if one is analyzing a policy to determine its original intent or goal, it is appropriate to use *process frameworks* that focus on agenda setting, problem identification, and policy formulation within a sociopolitical context. A process approach might examine the planning (or lack

Table 2.1
Four Foci of Analysis

Focus
Formulation: Policy intent or goal
Product: Policy instrument choice
Implementation: Policy action
Performance: Impact

thereof) of a policy or policies, and the decision-making and political processes involved in the formulation, development, and movement toward creating a policy product. In this way the focus is on the intent of the policy and on understanding the forces that came together to move the policy forward.

In using this formulation approach, we are referring to what Guba (1984) calls *policy-in-intention*. Guba emphasizes that when one is looking at the intent of policy, one is entering the domain of those persons who initiated the process, including decision makers such as organizational administrators and legislators. At the organizational level, policies may be initiated from practitioners or consumers—that is, anyone who calls attention to an opportunity or problem that needs to be addressed through the formulation of a policy. Sometimes this is called agenda setting (Jansson, 2008). The intent of the policy is the result of an agenda-setting process that is the precursor to the selected policy response aimed at ameliorating or eliminating the problem as it has been constructed. Policy-in-intention speaks to the goal of policy, and an analysis requires one to know what started the process rolling and the issues that emerged in that formulation process.

As an example, Martinson and Minkler (2006) critically analyze the formulation of federal policies based on the discourse surrounding civic engagement and older adults. Using a critical gerontology framework to guide their analysis, they draw from the rapidly growing research on volunteerism and aging to address the following questions: "What roles are older adults being encouraged to play in civic life? What meanings are implied by these roles? What political and economic forces underlie these roles? What types of civic engagement are left out of the conversation?" (p. 321). They interrogate the public discourse, the key writings in the field, and the numerous studies funded by advocates of the cause. Their systematic critical questioning raises the dangers in the civic engagement narrative that ignores "the diversity of the aging population, the ways in which society's structural and societal forces advance opportunities for some and limit them for others, and the economic and political incentives for utilizing older volunteers" (pp. 321–322). Their focus of analysis is policy formulation, and their critical study precedes the enactment of social policies such as the Edward M. Kennedy Serve America Act (H.R. 1388), signed into law on April 21, 2009, which reauthorizes and reforms the existing national service laws. In subsequent chapters we will return to this example in a more detailed case on civic engagement.

The involuntary commitment example from Chapter 1 is also helpful here. If the focus of one's analysis was on formulation or policy intent, one would have to ask what happened historically in the Commonwealth that led to involuntary commitment in the first place. Recognizing the factors that led to establishing this policy would reveal antecedent conditions that were in place when the original policy was formulated. But Constance, the therapist in this situation, would likely be focused on the formulation of the new policy change that allowed her as Jayne's therapist to provide transportation. Constance would be asking what factors led to this change, a change that she no doubt disagrees with and that has placed her in a challenging position. As long as transportation was mandated by police officers, it would be inappropriate for a therapist to transport her client. As Constance analyzes the new intent of the transportation policy, she may discover that cutbacks in public service in a strapped economy may have had something to do with the change. She may find that police officers were being called too often for clients who would willingly accompany others, raising a triaging possibility for therapists to transport clients who posed no violent threat. In other words, the focus of the analysis would be on the policy intent and how that came about.

Product: Policy Choice   Gilbert and Terrell (2010) suggest that there is merit in approaching the policy itself as a product containing a set of policy choices. "These choices may be framed in program proposals, laws and statutes, or standing plans that eventually are transformed into programs. The analytical focus of product studies is on issues of choice: What is the form and substance of the choices that make up the policy design? What options did these choices foreclose? What values, theories, and assumptions support these choices?" (p. 14). They see this approach to product as the least developed form of policy analysis. *Product frameworks* focus on the results of the planning process, complete with a set of policy choices that have been considered and then determined to be the best approach at this point within a certain context. This sort of analysis looks at the selected policy document. The policy document could be a cash grant, an administered contract, quality standards, in-kind transfers, a public promotion, a fine or price control, to name just a few. Product frameworks examine policy content and the issues embedded within the policy as the focus of analysis. The analysis is targeted at the ideology (why this over another) and the explicit elements of the selected policy document.

For the practitioner, the policy product is particularly important because this is what the practitioner inherits and has to figure out how to implement. Without understanding what choices this policy represents and what underlying assumptions supported those choices, one is disempowered to raise questions about how to approach implementation with a critical eye. The involuntary commitment example illustrates how Constance as a practitioner-therapist can inherit a policy without fully knowing what is behind its intent. Thus, in a way, Guba's *policy-in-intent* is reflected in the policy product as well as in the formulation process. Remember our discussion of how vague and generic some policies are? The product, then, is not transparent in revealing all the debate that went on in the process of formulation or what compromises were made. The policy rarely states the problem in much detail (if at all) but seeks to address that unstated problem. Thus, an approach to policy product may involve looking back at some of the process elements that Guba and Gilbert and Terrell identify, so that the person invested in understanding the product can gain insight into the original "intent" to understand the choices and the politics that made the policy become what it is.

An example of analyzing policy products is provided by Imhof and Kaskie (2008) who studied public policies designed to manage pain at the end of life. They reviewed federal and state policies, particularly in light of the factors that led to their formulation. In the process they reveal that the Institute of Medicine has "reported that many state prescribing laws, regulations and medical board guidelines are outdated and scientifically flawed relative to current medical knowledge about pain management" (p. 424). Imhof and Kaskie systematically examine the roles and relationships of public health policies, federal pain policies, the Supreme Court and the Executive Agency, as well as state pain policies including state legislatures, state courts, state executive agencies, state medical boards, and advocacy groups in the making of pain policy. The arguments for more or less restrictive policies in the use of pain-reducing medications are provided as a result of their study, adding insight into the thinking behind current policy content.

Another example comes from Nelson's (1984) study of how child abuse and neglect became a focus of policy. She reveals that there was never an intention of the policy framers at the federal level to add neglect to the legislation because, while they suspected the relationship between neglect and poverty, they also knew that the elimination of poverty could not be a goal of child protection. However, child advocates placed enormous pressure on the Congress and secured the inclusion of neglect in the initial national policies. It is noteworthy that this type of policy analysis is like opening a window on the issues, arguments, insensitivities, and frustrations that goes on behind the scenes in the formulation of policies that impact the lives of vulnerable consumers.

Implementation: Policy Action   Guba (1984) calls the implementation of a policy *policy-in-action*. This is the domain of those who carry out the delivery of the policy documents, the programs, treatments, or interventions that are undertaken as a result of the policy choice. It also can be understood as the operationalization of policy for it is in some sort of action that the policy is illuminated. It is at the action level that the theory regarding what is necessary to eliminate or ameliorate the problem actually becomes testable. In the involuntary commitment case, the new transportation policy is what Constance must figure out how to implement, and this action involves a great deal of angst that the formulators of the policy likely never fully understood.

Gilbert and Terrell's approach using *performance frameworks* is logical to use here, but there may also be elements of process frameworks that focus on the roles and relationships of various individuals and groups as they interact in the implementation process that are relevant as well. Here, policy analysis is very much akin to both formative and summative program evaluation, with action or delivery being process oriented and results being more outcome-focused. It is also here that great clarity is needed to be sure that the focus of analysis remains stable. If process is of interest to answer the analysis question, the analysis should not "slip" into outcome measures.

Thomas and Medina (2008) offer an example of conducting a policy analysis of implementation in a local temporary assistance to needy families (TANF) program. Using a social capital framework to guide their analysis, they studied the Working to Unite Families Project (WtUF), a demonstration project in Philadelphia designed to place mothers "who were at risk or had lost their children to formal or informal foster or kinship care" (p. 277) in care with their children. Interviewing the majority of an infrastructure committee tasked with implementing the program, they focused on the nature of the relationships among this cross-sector committee, the degree of trust, reciprocity, and collaboration. Thomas and Medina recognize that "the circumstances under which working partnerships between nonprofit and public sectors are made and maintained are rarely studied" (p. 287) and that funders, planners, and stakeholders "grossly underestimate the complexity, resources, and time required" (p. 287) for this type of implementation. This approach suggests that it is possible to find out a great deal about the nature of the complexity of policy implementation. Generally, this will also raise additional directions for future analysis, including tool development for accurate measurement of the next analytic focus.

Performance: Impact   The final test of the usefulness of a particular policy is in relation to what Guba (1984) calls *policy-in-experience*. Recall that Guba is mindful of the question of whose experience is important here—the client's or the policy practitioner's. Did the consumer benefit from what the policy produced? Was the implementation effective? Also, what was the cost at the personal, professional or institutional levels? Obviously, the policy at this level involves those who are both enacting the policy on which the program is built, as well as the policy/ program beneficiaries. It is with this focus of analysis that the actual results of policy can be examined. Was the policy fully enacted so that the expected impact was achieved? If so, at what cost to both the enactors and the beneficiaries? Were the beneficiaries actually carriers of the problem that the program was intended to address? Or was there off-targeting? If so, why?

This is where policy and program intersect. It is also where policy analysis and program evaluation become related, but not identical, since policy analysis is held to the investigation of the identified needs and their elimination as a result of policy or a series of related and prioritized policy options intended to eliminate an identified problem. Program evaluation usually results in a judgment about a program's worth as its end product. Policy analysis has a broader political scope.

So, then, *performance frameworks* focus on policy outcomes—what happens in the implementation and how the policy changes impact the situation. Here, the analysis is looking at the impact or result of the policy. The analysis of interest is at the experience level: First, of those carriers of the social problem that the social policy was designed to address or eliminate and second, of those implementing the policy, including the cost of achieving the outcome being evaluated. It is at this focal point that Constance and Jayne both become particularly important to the policy analysis because they will hold the clue as to the policy impact of the new involuntary commitment transportation policy.

Illustrating policy performance or impact, Estrada and Marksamer (2006) provide an analysis of the legal rights of lesbian, gay, bisexual, and transgender (LGBT) youth in welfare and juvenile justice settings. Although these youth have federal and state constitutional and statutory rights, there are regular violations in carrying out these policies. This is obviously a question of performance. Mandates may be in place, but it is in the daily experience of youth that reveal how these mandates do not always come to fruition. The role of the courts becomes evident in this analysis since law suits have been filed (and won) when juveniles were denied their rights. However, "these youth routinely are left unprotected to violence and harassment, subjected to differential treatment, or denied appropriate services" (p. 173). Estrada and Marksamer's analysis provides guidance for practitioners and advocates in reducing barriers to the adequate performance of these policies, indicating that it is the responsibility of agencies and facilities to educate their staff about the needs of LGBT youth and the scope of their civil rights. Their analysis takes into account issues of importance to both the enactors and recipients of the policy response.

In summary, determining the focus of analysis is essential when one is approaching a policy situation. The focus of analysis, whether it is at the formulation, product, implementation, or performance level should be conceptually clear prior to undertaking analysis. This is an important step in assuring congruence between analytic goals and basic assumptions in the universe of choices about tools for policy analysis.

AN EXPANSIVE VIEW OF POLICY ANALYSIS RESEARCH

Like research, policy analysis tools are also based on different sets of assumptions or ideologies, sometimes called paradigmatic perspectives. In other places we have discussed the importance of recognizing differing paradigms and their assumptions in making sense of and guiding practice (see O'Connor & Netting, 2009; O'Connor & Netting, 2008). One's perspective on what is real and how one comes to know it determines the expected level of rigor and to some extent also determines the type of data that will be acceptable for the analysis. Before selecting a tool with a particular focus, a critical task is to identify the tool's underlying worldview assumptions. This is needed in order to assure that the goals of the analysis are congruent with the general assumptions of the instrument or the approach taken so that the results of that analysis have the potential to make sense. Much more about this will be seen in later chapters.

Before we present an overview of this multiparadigmatic framework, it is important to recognize that we are using the words "tools" and "instruments" in a very general sense. Going back to the examples presented in the previous section, the policy analysts were using various research designs and approaches. Martinson and Minkler (2006) based their analysis theoretically on critical gerontology which poses nontraditional questions designed to deeply probe into the unintended consequences of popular policy causes. Their questions were generated to interrogate the concept of civic engagement, based on their critical philosophy. Because of their position, the use of a standardized or formal policy analysis tool would have been inappropriate. Imhof and Kaskie (2008) used a content analysis method, focusing on the words within the policies themselves and allowing themes to emerge in light of pain management. They were systematic in their approach, but they did not use a prescriptive policy tool. Nelson (1984) engaged in historical analysis. Thomas and Medina (2008) used a social capital framework to guide their analysis of the implementation of a TANF program designed to find employment for hard-to-place mothers. They were meticulous in listing contemporary definitions of social capital and intentionally used the concepts associated with social capital to guide their analysis. However, they ended by saying that a tool to evaluate social capital effectiveness is sorely needed. Thus, they were careful to use what was available to guide their analysis, but a formal tool was not yet in place. And last, Estrada and Marksamer (2006) analyzed the performance of statutory law for LGBT youth in foster care and juvenile detention settings. In all of these examples, no one used a specific policy analysis tool in the traditional sense of the word.

There are many policy analysis instruments and tools developed by professionals from various disciplines and professions. We will highlight many of them in forthcoming chapters. However, it is equally as likely that analysts will use theories, practice approaches, questions based on their own experiences, and the literature to interview individuals or interrogate documents. This is similar to what happens in clinical practice when a study is proposed and the search is on for a tool to measure self-esteem, locus of control, social networking, stress, and many other constructs. Policy analysis has tools designed to measure various aspects of policy, but they are rarely standardized in the same way that clinical tools are. As we move forward in presenting the framework that guides the remainder of this book, readers should know that there are certainly instruments available but they are less available when nontraditional ways of thinking about and studying policy are desired. There is definitely room for the development of new approaches and for policy analysts to critically think about what they need to know so that appropriate questions can be formulated when appropriate tools are not available.

We believe a useful structure for assessing policy tools (both formal and informal) can be created by adapting what was developed in an edited text by Egon Guba (1990). We chose Guba's approach for guidance, because it appears to capture both the practices and the rhetoric of the multiple perspectives in social science. Certainly there are other well respected ways that we have used in the past (see, for example, Burrell and Morgan, 1979; Lejano, 2006; Mullaly, 2007). In fact, regardless of the mechanism used to allow multiple perspectives, each provides for the orderly examination of the assumptions that inform various approaches to social science and disciplined inquiry such as policy analysis by focusing on ontological, epistemological, and methodological questions. Table 2.2 provides definitions of these important philosophical terms.

Determining the nature of what can be known (ontology), the nature of the relationship between the knower and that which is known

Table 2.2
Definitions and Descriptions of Philosophical Assumptions

Assumptions	Definitions and Description of Range
Ontology	The nature of being: An objectivist understanding of being is *realist*, positing a reality outside of the human mind. A subjectivist understanding of being is *nominalist*, or a product of the human mind.
Epistemology	The nature of knowing: An objectivist understanding of knowing is *positivist*, a belief that reality can be known. A subjectivist understanding of knowing is *antipositivist*, suggesting that only people's constructions of reality can be known.
Methodology	How one knows: An objectivist or *nomothetic* methodology uses the analytic tools of the natural bench sciences to deduce reality. A subjectivist or *ideographic* methodology attempts to inductively understand an individual or group's constructions of reality.

(epistemology), and how the inquirer should go about finding knowledge (rigor) are at the base of the different paradigms that give rise to differing frameworks for policy analysis. The different ways to answer these three questions are at the philosophical core of "how things really are" and "how things really work" (Guba, 1990, p. 19). These have created the realist and relativist ontologies, the objectivist and/or subjectivist epistemologies, and the order/control and radical ideologies that link policy analysis to research. A meta-framework constructed by the assumptions or beliefs of positivism and/or postpositivism, interpretivism and/or constructivism, and critical theory as articulated in Guba's *The Paradigm Dialog* create the philosophy of science underpinning for what we are calling (1) rational (linear), (2) nonrational (circular), and (3) critical (progressive) theories of policy analysis. Figure 2.1 provides an overview of these three perspectives.

These three perspectives in turn create the intellectual tradition that underpins the three paradigmatic approaches that constitute the conceptual framework to understand and engage in policy analysis as research. Figure 2.2 provides an overview of these three approaches along with their characteristics. As each is briefly discussed further along, we will be referring to both Figures 2.1 and 2.2.

RATIONAL (LINEAR) APPROACHES

Traditional rational perspectives on what is real and how we come to know are based on the philosophical positioning of positivism and postpositivism. The difference between the two is a matter of degree. Ontologically, positivism is realist and postpositivism is critically realist. In this perspective, reality exists "out there" and is not a function of one's mind. Epistemologically, both positivism and postpositivism are objectivist, with postpositivism taking a more critical stance regarding that reality. Positivism takes the position that there is a dualism between the individual and the external world. Postpositivism recognizes the role of subjectivity but seeks to maintain a position of modified objectivity. As with the positivist, objectivity remains the goal for the postpositivist, even if it is difficult to achieve. Truth is possible to achieve through controlled empirical means for positivism; while truth remains the goal for postpositivism, critical multiplism is acceptable. For both positivists and postpositivists, inquiry is undertaken in a prescribed, predictable manner, determined well in advance. Thus, the two are philosophically paired.

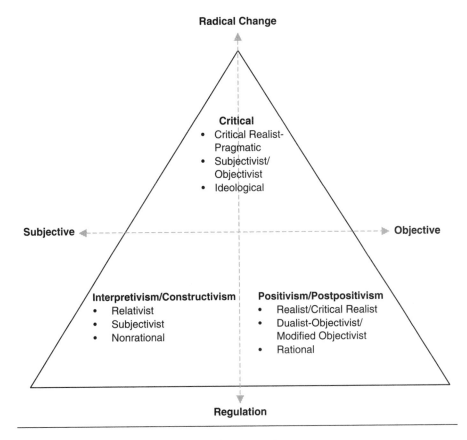

Figure 2.1 Guba's Paradigmatic Framework

Lejano (2006) supports our thinking about what we have named the classical, rational frameworks by suggesting that those within the positivist tradition "turn policy decisions into something like an objective exercise, where values only need to be measured for the different contributing factors and the cost of action that maximizes the total value chosen" (pp. 11–12).

Classical, rational approaches see policy analysis as a way of sustaining and strengthening existing social and policy structures. Policy analysis undertaken from this perspective will be pragmatic and problem oriented. Policy tools will apply linear reasoning using mostly traditional quantitative methods of natural sciences to accomplish analysis and decision making about policy (see Figure 2.2).

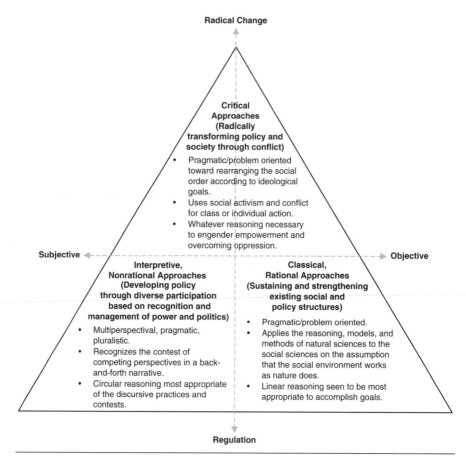

Figure 2.2   Framework for Understanding Policy Analysis Tools

NONRATIONAL (CIRCULAR) APPROACHES

The perspective known as either interpretivism or constructivism takes a relativistic ontological approach in that reality and truth are always context dependent. This is so because in both interpretivism and constructivism reality is socially constructed and a product of the minds of those involved in the construction. This means that episte-mologically this perspective is subjectivist. In essence, this position is based on the assumptions that reality is contextually driven, consisting of multiple truths resulting from an ongoing process of meaning making. Truth is never unitary, never static; it comprises a complex network of associations that are always emerging. Work is undertaken in context, and how it unfolds depends on who and what are involved in the context of the knowledge-building process. Benchmarks in the process may be known beforehand, but the details are known only in retrospect.

The interpretive, nonrational framework is also supported by Lejano (2006), who sees that the alternative to the traditional perspective on policy analysis "implies a greater willingness to consider subjective and interpretive elements of policy decisions as valid and, in fact, necessary. A more pragmatic, pluralist [policy analysis approach] portrays policy as crafted not out of some rational ethic, but out of the sheer contest of competing proposals" (p. 12). The interpretive, nonrational approach has the goal of developing policy through diverse participation based on recognition and management of power and politics. The analytic process is multiperspectival, pragmatic, and pluralist in service of the analytic goals. Policy analysis tools using this approach recognize the contest of competing perspectives in a back-and-forth narrative and apply circular reasoning as most appropriate for the analysis of the discursive and dialogic practices involved in policy analysis (see Figure 2.2).

CRITICAL APPROACHES

The assumptions of the critical perspective go beyond a critical theoretical perspective into a paradigmatic approach based on critical realism, pragmatism, and value-guided subjectivity, having a goal of dialogic transformation. Critique must lead to consciousness, which results in demands for fundamental, structural changes. This is the most radical of the perspectives with a post-modern bent of criticism, but criticism is not sufficient. Consciousness-raising resulting in large-scale fundamental change is expected. One truth can and should exist. Dialogical, conflict-embedded change leading to ideologically driven overall betterment is expected. This perspective is philosophically based as are the other perspectives, but because of the ideological nature of this philosophy, it can be either progressive or conservative.

Mullaly (2007) is very helpful in providing the intellectual support for the more radical approaches that work against the system and the status quo. The critical perspective aims to radically transform policy and society through conflict. This perspective is pragmatic and problem oriented but focused on rearranging the social order rather than on the incremental change sought in the other two perspectives. Policy analysis here is used to engender empowerment and overcome oppression. It is based on consciousness-raising moving towards social activism and, if necessary, conflict in order to demand and achieve change.

As you will see in great detail throughout the remainder of this text, one can place the various policy analysis tools within this multiparadigmatic framework based on the assumptions that were present in the construction of the particular policy analysis tool. We hope that as you move from chapter to chapter that the framework will be useful in clarifying the possible results of a policy analytical process—establishing the appropriateness of the tools, given their analytic goals and establishing standards of rigor to be used in the particular process. Selection of the best tool for a particular analytic process is made easier when the analyst is aware of the underlying assumptions of the particular tool. When tools are not already developed, using the framework should be helpful in guiding readers to discover what kinds of questions to ask in developing their own tools to interrogate policy.

A word of caution is in order. Analysts will have their preferences, just as you have yours. Look at the rational, nonrational, and critical approaches based on our earlier discussion of the brain and personal preferences based on personal cognitive processing. Without a thorough understanding of the assumptions of each of the perspectives upon which policy analysis tools are constructed, it is natural for the analyst to select the tool with which there is a sense of comfort because of worldview congruence. But this is not acceptable if one approaches policy analysis as research. Just as in direct or organization practice, the best response is not what the practitioner prefers but what is needed in the situation. Selection of a policy analysis tool must fit the situation rather than the analyst. Thus, being open to choosing which approach to take, based on the purpose of the policy research, is important, perhaps essential.

Still, more is needed to fully develop the idea of policy analysis as research. Aside from the worldview assumptions of the policy analysis tool, it is necessary to determine the part of policy on which the tool focuses. For us, the answer to that query determines the focus of analysis that can be interrogated by the policy analysis tool.

CONCLUSION

In the following three sections of this text, we will outline how all of these conceptual elements fit together to produce three very different ways of engaging in policy analysis based on different sets of assumptions or ideologies. We will provide ideas about ways to uncover the underlying assumptions on which a variety of policy analysis tools are built. We will detail how to apply differing tools to assure that the tool can answer the policy question that is being analyzed. With the material that follows, it is our hope that you will be able to avoid the challenges that occur when one fails to apply an appropriate tool, built on an appropriate set of paradigmatic assumptions and targeted at the necessary focus of analysis. Our goal is to arm you with the tools necessary to avoid off-target findings in policy analysis. And when there are few or limited tools to approach the policy analysis question your research poses, we will provide guidance in how to keep your analysis consistent with the perspective you are taking, by asking relevant questions that are congruent with your purpose.

DISCUSSION QUESTIONS

1. After reading this chapter, how do you think your challenges in working with policy analysis will be the same as or different from those that Nathan talked about in the Foreword? What might these similarities and differences mean to you as you work through the material in this text?
2. A traditional role for research is to provide resources and background information for understanding social problems that need to be addressed. Yet, there are many additional uses of research in policy analysis. Consider a contemporary social policy with which you are familiar and discuss how an expanded view of policy analysis as research might be useful in better understanding this policy.
3. Think about the policy issues that are being debated in the public discourse this week. What questions do you have about the policies being discussed? What might be the purpose of research designed to address those questions? How might you frame one of those questions as a research question? In order to address this question, what would be the unit of analysis to be studied? How might you design a study and how would you collect data?
4. Four areas of focus were discussed in this chapter: formulation, product, implementation, and performance. In any categorization there are strengths and limitations. Consider the strengths and limitations of this categorization and discuss how you might use (or change) these categories. Now take a policy with which you are

familiar and discuss the kinds of research questions that might be posed both within and across the four areas.

5. A framework was presented at the end of this chapter that will guide the remainder of the book. Talk about how this framework might be used in thinking about the policy discussed in item 3 in the foregoing list. Are there particular approaches (rational, non-rational, critical) that you feel most comfortable or uncomfortable using? Discuss the reasons for your answers.

Case Study

T HE FOLLOWING CASE has been constructed as an aid to application of the ideas that will follow in the remainder of the text. For some readers, this may be the first time that you have become so conscious of how policy impacts practice and practice impacts policy. The following story illustrates what direct work looks like when policy is a primary shaper of what the professional can and cannot do at work. As you read the case, you will find that there is much information provided that may at times feel confusing and complicated. We have constructed the case to reflect the real world of professional practice in human services where much information from lots of directions must be managed daily. It is our hope as you return to the case over and over again, through the examples that are provided in the chapters that follow, you will not only see the realities of policy practice but you will also develop a sense of your own competence in the policy arena.

SERVICE, ENGAGEMENT, AND VOLUNTEERISM:
WHAT'S THE POLICY ALL ABOUT?

She read the headlines several times: "Aging Boomers: Positive Health Outcomes Related to Civic Engagement." It was Sunday morning and she still received the *Times,* a relic of the past tossed in the driveway, *but there was something about holding a paper in your hands.* She couldn't bring herself to stare into her laptop more than she did already, particularly on Sunday morning when she had read the paper for all the days she could remember. She paused, turning the page of smudged print: "Service Learning Provides High Schoolers With Responsibility." *Hummmm—The human interest section of the paper was full of articles on various aspects of volunteerism this morning.*

(continued)

(continued)

Madeline knew volunteerism. She had been the Director of Volunteer Programs for almost 20 years. She had seen all the trends, heard all the fads, attended workshops and conferences, experimented with new strategies, and helped others in the community set up their programs. There wasn't much she didn't know, but lately it seemed that there was a new movement afoot, something she couldn't quite describe. *It's as if volunteerism had been replaced by civic engagement; no one is defining it and everyone is probably thinking about it a bit differently,* she mused to herself.

She had watched intently during National Volunteer Week as President Obama had ceremoniously signed the Edward M. Kennedy Serve America Act (H.R. 1388) into law on April 21, 2009, an Act to reauthorize and reform the national service laws. The President's words had been strong and clear: "Programs like these are a force multiplier; they leverage small numbers of [Corps] members into thousands of volunteers. And we will focus their service toward solving tomorrow's most pressing challenges: clean energy, energy efficiency, health care, education, economic opportunity, veterans and military families." And even though the Act did not take effect until October as P.L. 111-13, the President urged "every American to make an enduring commitment to serving your community and your country in whatever way you can." Madeline had been inspired by his words and the sincerity in which they were delivered, and it was only later that she had wondered: *Exactly what does all this mean? Is it politically incorrect not to volunteer?* But those questions passed quickly as she got caught up in the wave of support and enthusiasm that made her job almost more relevant to the agency than it had ever been and in preparations for the Call to Service Campaign mandated to take place 180 days after the enactment of P.L. 111-13.

This reauthorization was hailed as a symbolic recognition of the importance of volunteerism by a wide variety of stakeholders, including the Child Welfare League of America and the Gerontological Society of America, literally spanning the generations. The League proclaimed national service as a way for young people to become part of their communities and applauded the provision to incorporate new projects as service-learning through all schools grades 6 to 12 and post-secondary institutions. The Gerontological Society lauded the Act as symbolic of continual involvement on the part of older citizens as a life-long commitment to service. The Act specifically recognized the coming wave of Boomers who were targeted as a skilled resource to be captured for community service roles. Web sites such as ENERGIZE carried articles on the role of volunteer managers in staying up to date and leading in the implementation of the Act, and foundations such as the Atlantic Philanthropies stepped up their initiatives to help local communities engage diverse population groups in multiple ways. Town hall meetings around the country focused on innovative civic engagement programs.

The first thing Madeline did was to read the Public Law—all 147 pages of it! She was overwhelmed by the complexity of it, but as she took her time, she could understand what the stated intent here was. What she was uncertain about was what might be useful to her agency, her city, and her state. Here is what she found.

It seemed as though the overall priority of the law was creating or generating volunteers through an emphasis on education and establishment of an ethic of civic responsibility for primary, secondary, and higher-education students, while also taking advantage of the skills and wisdom of people 55 and older (she smiled when she noted that in early legislation 60 was the cut point). In the Act there is support of higher education in creating options for community service and service learning. There is a focus on energy conservation and the health of economically disadvantaged, as well as on creating economic opportunities for the economically disadvantaged. She noted that there were even specific definitions of who would be considered "disadvantaged." There is attention to encouraging social entrepreneurs and nonprofit community organizations to become involved in responding to national and local challenges.

It seemed as though the whole purpose was to leverage federal moneys to increase state, local, business, and philanthropic resources to address national and local challenges. She even found attention paid to the involvement of veterans in national service programs. There was particular targeting of families of veterans and those on active duty. There were specific provisions for the medically underserved, Native Americans, Native Hawaiians, and predominantly black colleges.

(*continued*)

(continued)

She was surprised to see what activities were prohibited and also the detail to which the bill goes to in defining what constitutes scientific research, which appeared to be just traditional positivist and quantitative. And there was always that element of "sustainability" and the difficulty of being able to sustain a program when administrative costs seemed to be pretty low (6%). She was pleased that there were provisions for evaluation and accountability but surprised that the evaluation was to start 12 months after enactment. That seemed like a rather short timeline, especially since one of the most interesting research requirements was to create a civic health assessment related to volunteering. She thought that many of the elements that were going to be required by the civic health assessment resembled many of the measures of a healthy community and what many of her board members asked about when she made her reports on volunteer activities. This civic health assessment was added to a whole series of studies that were expected: a study of involvement of veterans, volunteer generation, increased service programs for displaced workers in services corps, evaluation of agency coordination, volunteer management corps study, and, of course, the 12-month program effectiveness study.

As she was trying to make sense of the public law, she finally realized that this law was really an update of the National and Community Service Act of 1990 and the Domestic Volunteer Service Act of 1973, so there were lots of updates and revisions to information that she was familiar with in those Acts. From her reading, she knew that the idea of VISTA (Volunteers in Service to America) arose in 1963 when President Kennedy wanted to create a domestic volunteer program modeled after the Peace Corps that was created in 1961. VISTA and Peace Corps were merged in 1973 under a new federal "ACTION" agency tasked with running all domestic volunteer programs as a result of the Domestic Volunteer Service Act. She knew that although the original ideas came to fruition through Democrats, John F. Kennedy and Lyndon B. Johnson, this Act was introduced by Senator Alan Cranston (D-California) and was supported by Republican President Richard Nixon.

Certainly there were changes along the way that encouraged fewer outside volunteers and more community self-help through retired senior volunteers and foster grandparents. For a long time, it seems that literacy and adult education were of primary interest, but then there was a swing back towards national volunteerism for all the needs of the poor. This culminated in the National and Community Service Act of 1990, which included President George H.W. Bush's "Thousand Points of Light" and the Commission on National and Community Service. When President Clinton was in office, The National and Community Service Trust Act of 1993 created the AmeriCorps program. This represented yet another Democratic approach to volunteer service.

Madeline even remembered some news coverage on the 35th anniversary of VISTA in October of 2000. Senator Jay Rockefeller of West Virginia entered into the Congressional Record a written statement by a prominent former VISTA volunteer, the CEO of Land-O-Lakes, who outlined the impact VISTA had on society. It was all about the importance of the volunteer experience for the volunteers themselves, including taking responsibility and creating opportunities, the role of teamwork, the importance of building alliances, the gifts of diversity, and the need to identify leaders and build leadership skills in America, all of which have been accomplished through VISTA. Madeline really did see a thread to all this, whether it was supported by Democratic or Republican ideology. This might even have a link to President George W. Bush's USA Freedom Corps, which he established in 2002.

Now it seemed the combination of all the former elements may have created a comprehensive Act that covered the activities of lots of federal agencies. She even noted that in order to get allotments under this Act, each state needed to prepare a three-year plan that also stipulated how to provide access to local allotments. There certainly were some cost-sharing responsibilities, since there was an expectation of federal, state, and local participation, with the cost sharing mostly at the 80/20 level, 80% coming from the feds.

Madeline was actually looking at which elements of the law would apply not just to her agency but to the city in which she lived and worked. There was great potential here for expanded services through volunteerism. She thought it would be good to understand all the sections of the Act before diving into the part that her director told her to carefully examine.

(*continued*)

(*continued*)

The first provision that caught her eye was Learn and Serve America. This section was focused on primary and secondary school studies to set up service learning and school-based learning programs. It also focused on capacity building for educators in aiding students to embrace civic responsibilities. Higher education was also targeted for service learning, but interestingly the cost sharing at the university level was just 50/50. She wondered why. There were federal work study provisions and the creation of 25 "Campuses of Service." She wondered if either the private or state college in her city might be interested in this.

She also found the National Service Trust Program, which seemed to house the National Service Corps. Within that was an Education Corps, a Healthy Futures Corps, a Clean Energy Service Corps, a Veterans Corps, an Opportunity Corps, and National Service Programs. It seemed that there was room to establish state priorities related to each of these programs that might be different from national priorities. But it also seemed that preparing people for a life of service or for a service profession, as well as creating a cadre of volunteers committed to clean energy was a big push. There was something called Community Corps that seemed to be an aspect of interest to her agency; however, it might just be for campuses and professionals. She would need to look a bit more closely. She was confused by the need to do tutoring and maybe citizenship training, as well as disaster service if you were going to develop a Community Corps. In all this, there seemed to be a real interest in emergency and disaster preparedness relief and recovery, as well as getting retirees involved in all this, including improving education. Somehow there also seemed to be an interest in engaging the services of alums of service programs. She thought this was good, since many of the young folks who volunteered for her were former VISTA volunteers, and now she was beginning to see some older Returned Peace Corps volunteers in her resource list.

When she looked at the National Service Education Awards, she wondered if there was anything there that might be of interest to her son, Ben. He seemed to be at loose ends and might get a bit more focus through some sort of volunteer adventure. What she found that might be of interest to him were the National Service Positions and the Summer Service Positions. She would have him look a bit closer at these. What was also of interest for her agency were the Silver Scholar Positions and the Encore Fellowships, both being for those 55 and over. The Encore Fellowships would only have 10 per state. Maybe they could get one of those for a technology position for the agency.

The next section was entitled: Corporation for National and Community Service. She knew this corporation well. Over the years it had provided much support for volunteerism. She looked closely at the National Civilian Community Corps Program and the summer National Service Program under the corporation, noting that this is residential or campus-like and combines the best practices in military and civilian services. That probably would not be for Ben, but she really wondered if this was the old Job Corps? There was also the National Service Reserve Corps with relationships to the National Senior Service Corps, and she wondered how this focus on former or veteran volunteers would really work and whether or not VISTA and Peace Corps Volunteers would be eligible for training as reservists mostly in emergency and disaster situations. There was a section for Social Innovation Funds, and these were directed toward social entrepreneurs and nonprofits, perhaps like their program efforts with women eligible for TANF who wanted to start their own day care businesses.

This section also spoke of clearinghouses, but it looked as though there would for sure be only one. Since the university in town had been doing service learning and even had a center for community engagement, she wondered what the chances were to have that clearinghouse locally. That would be a great help for everyone in the area. Finally, there was a section on nonprofit capacity building, aimed at what were called "intermediary" nonprofits, to provide technological support and other capacity-building efforts throughout the state. Because there would be only one per state, she wondered if NETWORK, the local on-line clearing house, might want to apply. *If that could be combined with a university-based clearinghouse, this area of the state could really have a major impact on volunteerism!*

One of the last major sections of the law seemed to be an update of the 1973 Act in that it spoke of Volunteers in Service to America, better known as VISTA, the special literacy volunteers, and the

(*continued*)

(*continued*)
National Senior Service Corps. It seemed as though everything
remained the same for the Retired Senior Volunteer program, the
Foster Grandparent Program, and the Senior Companion program,
except that the age requirement was lowered to 55 and eligibility
for Foster Grandparents seemed to have remained only for the
"disadvantaged." The final item under this section referred to a
"Volunteers for Prosperity Program." She didn't remember ever
hearing about this, but it seemed to be related to international
volunteer service for professionals through USAID (US Agency for
International Development). Surprisingly for her, there was
no mention of Peace Corps. Perhaps they had their own special
public law.

Madeline must have been getting tired as she was looking at the
last sections of the Act, as she noted the effort it would take to have
Global Youth Service Days, The Call to Service Campaign, and
the September 11 Day of Service noted as the major supports at the
federal level to implementation of this law. Of course, there were
all sorts of provisions for consultation, training, and technical
assistance throughout the document, but to enact all of this was
going to be a big job. And she wasn't even sure that what was in
the official document could ever hope to achieve the stated goals.
She wasn't sure that all this could be done through volunteerism.
At least this is what she thought was represented in the law.

To be certain, she began reading everything she could get her
hands on about the implications of PL111-13 for her as a local
volunteer program director. She read the highlights provided by
The Corporation for National and Community Service, and she
talked with her colleagues around the country to see what they
thought about it and how they were keeping up to date on funding
opportunities through the Corporation and other sources. She
found herself following the *Federal Register* for the first time to be
sure she didn't miss important potential funding possibilities.

So one Sunday morning, Madeline was not surprised to see the
Times featuring civic engagement and service learning, because it
followed closely on the heels of a Town Hall Meeting sponsored
by that same local newspaper. She had been one of the panel of
experts asked to provide a brief overview of their volunteer
programs and to talk about plans for expansion. A host of local
stakeholders had attended the event, and a number of people had

spoken about how they were engaged in their communities and how there were so many needs for volunteers to address. One man had talked about how he was giving a full day a week to helping adolescent boys who had gotten in trouble with the law and that in the process he had learned a great deal about how their families were barely making ends meet. Subsequently, he had worked with the local school system to form a group for single parents raising teens that met twice a week at the high school. He wondered where the city school system and the department of welfare were with problems like this.

A young woman talked about a youth group that was raising funds for the local Alzheimer's chapter in an attempt to educate young people about the increasing numbers of persons experiencing early onset of the disease. She expressed some frustration, because what they raised and what the chapter said was necessary to put together a campaign were really very far apart. She was here to find out other sources of funding so that the project could be done professionally.

Still others wanted to know how to become involved, citing stories of how they had applied to volunteer at a local organization only to have no one follow up with them. One woman had said, "You try to give your time and no one cares enough to follow up? What's that all about?" Madeline had responded to this concern by suggesting, "You need to go on-line through the NETWORK, the local online volunteer coordination service to which over 400 agencies subscribe. There you'll be able to find out what's available." She added, "We're all on this NETWORK because we sincerely want to recruit interested people to our causes."

NETWORK had been established by a local mover and shaker who had worked in the field of volunteer management for many years. It was a useful clearinghouse, but with this new public law, perhaps its span of responsibilities and services could grow to meet social needs as well as the needs of the human service agencies. To be sure, Madeline had received a number of really good applicants through the coordination service and had noticed that more and more applications were coming in lately. NETWORK was really helping her to support her agency's efforts.

To be on NETWORK, you had to have a paid volunteer coordinator (at least part time) and a fairly established volunteer program.

(*continued*)

(*continued*)

It was recommended that sample job descriptions be available as well as links to the organization's policies and procedures. Criticism from the community had come from local groups that wanted to recruit members but did not have the funds to hire a coordinator. (This new law with the 6% administrative cost probably would not help that.)

NETWORK was originally conceived as a city-based coordination effort, but more and more the city was moving into the counties and these small communities were beginning to face some of the same social problems as the city. On one hand, some formal nonprofits wanted "in" to NETWORK, but on the other hand, some civically engaged members from a number of small communities on the city's periphery felt that the neighborly acts they were already performing were being denigrated to the "God of Formal Volunteerism." Yes, Madeline had read those very words in a recent article—*The God of Formal Volunteerism indeed!* Yet when she really thought about it, she wondered: *What would happen if formal volunteerism was so privileged that the invisible acts that people did for one another would carry no currency and people would turn to those places that gave them recognition; communities could literally fall apart. No, I'm not going there,* she thought. It's a slippery slope! And then there was the other on the other hand. . . . *Why were all the formal systems so enthusiastic about civic responsibility and civic engagement? Did any of this have to do with taxes and government services?*

As she read the paper on this quiet Sunday morning, those thoughts kept coming back to her. An op-ed piece carried the headline "Elitism Trumps Natural Helping." This grabbed Madeline's attention. "Has anyone considered the implications of all this hoopla about the Call to Serve Campaign? It's Points of Light and every other administration's plan, Democrat or Republican doesn't matter, to move back to the days of private charity. It rewards those in power already who do not have to work two jobs, who have time on their hands, to serve the 'needy.' Instead of stimulating job development to pay a living wage, let's encourage volunteerism so that we don't have to pay social workers to take care of people in the streets. Let's make the homeless population into a corps of volunteers. They have plenty of time on their hands!"

The op-ed went on for two more paragraphs, but Madeline could read no more ranting. *Maybe there was a point there,* she thought, *but what the heck was it? Could anyone really be <u>against</u> volunteering? It was as American as apple pie.*

After another cup of coffee and one more swipe at the paper, Madeline turned to her laptop. Monday was a big day, because she was scheduled to lead a workshop on episodic volunteering for the state's Volunteer Managers Association (VMA), an organization she had helped form over a decade ago. *Maybe they might serve as the state's intermediary nonprofit.* She began composing her speech, thinking about what she would say. But the words of the op-ed kept ringing in her ears. *What if this movement was just a way to control what people did in their communities? What would I say if I was speaking to the Black Neighborhood Association or to the Advocates for Immigration Reform? Would I say the same thing? What if I was talking with a support group of elder caregivers or a group of disabled persons? Would I approach things the same way? STOP IT,* she said to herself. *I'm a professional volunteer manager. I know about episodic volunteers and how to capture them. Write the presentation!*

But it was as if her fingers were going in another direction from where her mind told them to go. VMA had had a number of conversations and programs about episodic volunteering over the last few years. It seemed like they needed to tackle some of the implications of this Act for how they would be doing business. She began writing. *The Act identifies target groups that we are encouraged to engage with in various ways, with the intent of increasing the diversity of volunteers in our local communities: boomers, court-involved youth or adults who are reentering the community, students, vets, individuals with disabilities, displaced workers, professionals who volunteer with specialized skills, even social entrepreneurs. In addition, the Act empowers the Corporation for National and Community Service to deploy Ameri-Corps members to leverage community volunteering. How will we work with Ameri-Corps and what will be their role? Will they have the training we have as volunteer coordinators or will they bring different skills to us? How will we work together to mobilize these new resources so that we're not stepping on one another's toes?* Madeline's fingers clicked along the keyboard at an accelerated rate as more and more questions arose, and as she realized she could not, at this point, totally imagine the potential impact (intended and otherwise) of the civic

(continued)

(*continued*)

engagement movement and the policies it was spawning on the work she had been doing all these many years.

She was actually quite surprised about her own professional trajectory. She herself had started out as a volunteer with this new upstart low-income housing organization almost 30 years ago. At that time, the agency was located in an ugly low-income neighborhood and had started by taking advantage of some of the federal money available in the late 1960s and early 1970s to focus on impoverished communities. By the time she had become a full-fledged employee, the agency was a well-established non-profit organization receiving funds from both federal grants and the United Way. What had started as an agency that with the use of VISTA volunteers had renovated lots of dilapidated houses in the catchment area had morphed into a full-service community agency.

She had started first with a hammer and found that she was quite organized and able to get others to become enthusiastic about the work, once the VISTA volunteers had completed their service. Little by little, with great support by the other volunteers and agency professionals, she sought further education and developed important skills that the agency seemed to need. Now she was a proud MSW who directs a volunteer recruitment and retention program that serves the agency needs around health care, literacy, legal assistance, and community-based family services. Based on some changes in the community, they were even looking to the startup of the first Head Start program in the area. This was quite an exciting time, even if the economic times were tough. She really wondered what would emerge from this iteration of policy in support of volunteer services—or did she now need to speak in terms of civic engagement?

CHAPTER 3

Rational Policy Analysis

I N CHAPTER 2, we introduced the positivist/postpositivist paradigm and the idea of classical, rational (linear) approaches to policy analysis. In this chapter, we deepen the original discussion by exploring the rational themes, assumptions, and major theories that undergird both this paradigm and rational models of policy analysis. Note that we are using the word "model" when it is paired with "rational" because these approaches are prescriptive, fitting the definition of "model" as a predetermined approach. The two preceding chapters have provided the general underpinnings of how to go from the identified purpose, through ideology or worldview, to focus on analysis. In this chapter and the one that follows, you will see the details of what is possible when a rational approach is applied to policy analysis.

We begin with the themes of rational thought and linear reasoning by providing a short history of logical positivism and logical empiricism, the basis of positivism and postpositivism. We will demonstrate how certain purposes of policy analysis lend themselves to rational approaches and detail what should be contained in a well-constructed rational policy analysis. Examples of rational policy analysis aimed at differing units of analysis built on a brief overview of theories that inform rational approaches will illustrate how these exemplars are both rational and compatible with the type of rigor expected in positivist or postpositivist systematic knowledge building. This chapter closes with ways to determine whether a policy analysis approach is, indeed, rational, followed by a thorough discussion of what is gained and what is lost in applying this model. In Chapter 4, we demonstrate how to apply selected models of policy analysis when the policy research or analysis goal is to sustain and strengthen existing social and policy structures.

In this and the following chapters, we will frequently refer back to the case presented at the end of Chapter 2: Service, Engagement, and Volunteerism: What's the Policy All About? We will use that case to illustrate major points, as well as to demonstrate that how one looks at the case will differ as different sets of assumptions are used. So when we refer to Madeline, remember that she is the Director of Volunteers in the previous case.

REASON AND RATIONALITY

To make the argument that policy analysis is research, it is necessary to provide a short discussion about science and systematic knowing. In this chapter, we focus on traditional ways of knowing based on positivist/postpositivist thought. In other chapters, we will examine alternative ways of knowing that developed in contradiction to or as a criticism of this traditional perspective and the way it has evolved over time. The appreciation of reason and rational, linear approaches to knowledge building is embedded in the history of how knowledge is developed. This also explains why, until recently, most approaches to policy analysis were rational models, embedded in the assumptions of positivism and postpositivism.

There are many ways of knowing that do not include the scientific method. Traditionally, knowing comes from customs, habits, and repetition. One type of knowing comes from personal experience. Tacit knowledge based on hunches (sometimes called practice wisdom) is also a type of knowing. There is also common sense, practical judgment based on experiences, wisdom, and prejudices. Early thinkers recognized that each of these ways of knowing had specific challenges arising from a confusion of knowledge with beliefs, values, or magical thinking. To counter these challenges, as early as the 1700s efforts were underway to develop science as the branch of knowledge concerned with systematizing facts, principles, and methods. These early rationalists and empiricists began to define science by distinguishing it from religious and moral beliefs. They asserted that scientific knowledge is based on empirical verification rather than personal experience.

European philosophers, particularly the Vienna Circle with such great thinkers as Schlick, Carnap, and Ayers, among others, furthered the development of logical empiricism and logical positivism into what has come to be known as the scientific method. The scientific method is empirical, based on direct observation and on operationalization when indirect measurement is undertaken. It is systematic in that the procedures are organized, methodical, open to the public, and replicable. The scientific method is deterministic. It assumes that order in the natural world can be discovered and is predictable, not due to chance alone. Knowledge derived from the scientific method is provisional. Tentative conclusions are subject to questions and refutation that are assumed to lead to a more accurate picture of the world. Finally, the scientific method is objective. It attempts to remove biases and values or at least make them more explicit. This rational way of viewing the world "turns policy decisions into something like an objective exercise, where values only need to be measured for the different contributing factors and the course of action that maximizes the total value chosen" (Lejano, 2006, p. 12).

Embedded in this definition of what constitutes science is the assumption of the role of reason, a certain kind of reason. Induction or making inferences of a generalized nature from particular instances became the preferred method of consolidating the observational link between reality and scientific knowing. This was accepted over deduction, where knowledge inductively generated is applied to situations not yet observed. Induction, going from the general to the specific, became preferred over deduction, going from the specific to the general. Inferences based on induction were seen as reason, while those based on deduction, where premises do not empirically or logically warrant conclusions, were seen as "unreasonable," or even "irrational."

The preferred type of reason, the reason that can reduce information to its most elegant or parsimonious form, fits nicely with the emerging definitions of the scientific method and positivism. Almost immediately, "real" reasoning became linear reasoning. Rational, linear thinking became scientific thinking and was accepted as reason. This is why rational, linear approaches to knowledge building are the only accepted ways in traditional, positivist science. Any other approach, no matter how useful to the individual, is seen to be not only nonrational but irrational, even when it is part of the creative processes of the researcher. In later chapters you will see some of the basic criticisms of this narrowed approach to reason that have led to more interpretive and critical approaches to science. These will become the philosophical underpinnings of the alternative perspectives for policy analysis in later chapters.

RATIONAL ASSUMPTIONS OF THE POSITIVIST/ POSTPOSITIVIST PARADIGM

The positivist/postpositivist paradigm is objectivist in its perspective. Recall that in Chapter 2 we provided a framework (Figure 2.1) containing a continuum between objectivism and subjectivism. The positivist paradigm is objectivist in its orientation. Being objective means seeing reality as outside the human mind (there is an external truth), assuming that this reality can be known and that one can approach reality in an inductive manner.

With a rational approach to policy analysis, there are a number of assumptions linked to positivism and postpositivism. First, there is an assumption that a single "best" policy truth is within the universe and it is the task of the policy maker to figure out what that is. This "one best way" perspective dominated the organizational and policy literature for years, creating a sense that there was a perfect policy solution to whatever social problem arose, if only it could be found. Today, there is recognition that perfection may not be achievable and that human decision makers have their limitations. Still, the rationalist will reach far beyond himself or herself in search of the best way, assuming that one can get there incrementally and that getting there is possible.

This objectivist approach is based on reason as the basic building block to policy analysis. Reasonable people are assumed to be those who very systematically establish measurable outcome-based objectives, study viable alternatives that will reach toward those outcomes, and then debate the consequences of each alternative. The selection of the alternative is based on the current market economy, in which the policy selected to be implemented is the one expected to be the least costly for the benefit achieved. Box 3.1 provides a list of these major assumptions.

Box 3.1 Rational Policy Analysis Assumptions

- There is a single "best" policy truth.
- Reason is the basic building block of policy analysis.
- "Best" is based on a market economy (getting the biggest bang for the buck).
- Expect the most benefit for the least cost in policy.
- The goal of policy analysis is predicting what is best based on objectives, alternatives, and consequences.

Take note that embedded in these assumptions is a belief in stability and control. Belief that this is possible is specifically related to the policy analysis goals of classical, rational models of analysis. See if you can directly link the strategies for rational policy analysis listed in Box 3.2 to the major assumptions of the positivist/postpositivist paradigm.

Box 3.2 Rational Policy Analysis Strategies

- Policy analysis is linear.
- Policy analysis is constructed through a series of well-defined steps.
- Analytical steps follow a fixed sequence.
- Decisions are made based on precision and linearity.
- Policy decisions are based on objectivity and determinant rules.
- Decisions are made by selecting from alternatives and minimizing objections.

Seeing this linkage will help in the decision making about both the quality and the appropriateness of a particular model for a policy analysis project.

RATIONAL MODELS OF POLICY ANALYSIS

In our journey to show how policy analysis can be most productive when considering it as research, we have laid out a multidimensional framework for ways of systematic knowing; we have also provided a framework derived from that approach to systematic knowing for understanding the various policy analysis tools. These can be found in Figures 2.1 and 2.2 in Chapter 2. In the two previous chapters, we briefly covered the role of theory in policy analysis and showed that policy analysis models differ in their approaches to analysis and their focus of analysis. Now it is time to focus directly on how classical rational models of analysis can provide a systematic way of understanding a policy when the goal of the policy analysis is sustaining and strengthening existing social and policy structures.

Just as in any systematic approach to knowledge, theories are central to a research design. In positivist or postpositivist research, a theory (or multiple theories) will be guiding the operationalization of variables, the hypotheses to be tested, and/or the research design to be used. Based on the themes and assumptions just identified, there are multiple theories about policy that drive its analysis. It has been our experience that some policy analysis models have been provided without the user of the model being able to explicitly see the theories that are behind the questions being asked. This is similar to what happens in the development of a policy. The substantive theories behind the social problem addressed in the policy are seldom articulated in the policy content; they are simply implied. Just as social problem analyses reveal important underlying theoretical perspectives that have led to a proposed policy solution, knowing what theories support one's policy analysis approach will provide clues as to why certain questions are being asked (and why other questions may not seem important to ask).

In Chapter 1, we discussed three types of theory: prescriptive, descriptive, and critical. Prescriptive theories are closely aligned with the positivist/postpositivist paradigm because their intent is to achieve the goal of prescribing a way to maintain or regain stability and control. Descriptive and critical theories will be highlighted in later chapters because of their connections to other aspects of the paradigmatic framework we are using. The theories we briefly highlight in this section are largely prescriptive and supportive of classical, rational models of policy analysis. Later, you will see their linkages to specific analysis models.

Understanding the worldview that undergirds a particular policy-analysis process is sometimes difficult because of two challenges. The first is that some policy analyst scholars do not lay out their approach in a succinct manner, preferring to lead the reader by narrative through their analytic process. This means that sometimes, even though there are precise steps to their approach, those steps can be lost in the discussion of the product of the analysis. The second challenge is that it is rare that the policy scholar explicitly states the paradigmatic assumptions upon which the approach is built or even acknowledges the theory that guides it. This is particularly true with those rational approaches that are built on positivist or post positivist assumptions about knowledge and how to come to know it. In this section we outline two well-known rational approaches to policy analysis with differing targets of analysis and representing different disciplines involved in policy analysis. We will demonstrate why they are both positivist (or at least postpositivist) and rational in their way of engaging in the policy analysis process.

Another note of caution is needed here. Depending on whom one reads, the terms *framework, theory,* and *model* may be used in different ways and sometimes interchangeably. Lack of specificity can be quite confusing, so we need to repeat how we have framed this. For us, frameworks (e.g., Guba's paradigmatic framework) serve as a way to gather theories that share the same sets of assumptions. In policy analysis, from those theories can be derived either models (within a positivist aspect of Guba's framework) or approaches (within an interpretive aspect of the same framework). Do not be confused if other authors use different language. Instead, always try to understand how the words are being used. What is important is that in rational policy analysis, theories provide direction and are easily translated into models that are by definition prescriptive. The following discussion is not a comprehensive exposition of the theories informing classical, rational models of analysis; however, it offers a briefer treatment that will most easily exemplify what we mean.

Rational Choice Theories

Ostrom (2007) lumps a number of theories under what has been called "institutional rational choice," focusing on "the institutional analysis and development (IAD) framework" (p. 21). Especially compatible with IAD are "economic theory, game theory, transaction cost theory, social choice theory, covenantal theory, and theories of public goods and common-pool resources" (p. 26). Ostrom explains the steps inherent in the IAD framework and reveals in the process a rational approach to prescribing a sequential process. The first step is to identify a unit called an action arena in which there are seven variables: (1) participants, (2) positions, (3) outcomes, (4) action-outcome linkages, (5) control exercised by participants, (6) information, (7) costs, and (8) benefits associated with the outcome. The interactions among these variables are seen as governed by rules participants use to order their relationships, external forces within the world that influence what happens, and the structure of the community in which they are operating. These factors come together in a complex structure, and multiple action arenas may be interlinked. Note the way in which this theory is rational in its assumptions. From the beginning there is an assumption that outcomes can be predetermined and that there are logical steps to use in assessing and analyzing the situation. Once an action unit is identified, there is a bounding of the analysis that may help to make it more manageable but could leave out variables that do not conform to what is expected.

Decisions are viewed as actions taken to choose the optimal choice among competing alternatives. To make a judgment, there is a need to make a choice that is informed. This means having the capacity to identify all the viable options and then to systematically compare each one with another. This develops what is known as a preference structure, in which one begins by comparing pairs of alternatives and then moves to rank-ordering the preferences. When there are too many alternatives to compare, a value (or utility) is assigned to each. Within this process Ostrom (2007) identifies three types of rules. Operational rules guide the day-to-day decision making among participants. Collective-choice rules influence operational rules by determining who is eligible to participate in the policy process and how participants go about changing operational rules. Constitutional-choice rules override both collective-choice and operational rules and lead to the crafting or recrafting of both (p. 44). Thus, there are multiple levels of analysis based on a hierarchy of rules at play.

One could look at health care reform efforts from a rational choice perspective; in fact, some of the challenges that have been experienced over the several decades of reform efforts related to arriving at a reform decision are at their base the result of a process of rank-ordering preferences related to solving the problems of accessibility and affordability in health care. The argument, when understood from a rational-choice theoretical perspective, is how to establish the priorities that create the most options for the least cost. The pivotal decision about "least cost" rests on what is valued. Collective choice about the best choices regarding health care seems not to have been possible for almost half a century.

Decision Theory   Decision theory is prescriptive in that it is concerned with identifying the best decision one could make, assuming that the ideal decision maker is fully informed, able to figure out all possible outcomes, and fully rational. To make an informed decision, one has to be able to list the best among a set of alternative possibilities and then compare each alternative with any others. When all alternatives have been compared with all others, then one is said to have a complete preference structure. Obviously, having many alternatives is problematic, because it takes far too much time to compare every possible combination and such a process requires an understanding of probability. The goal then may be to translate alternatives into numerical combinations. An argument against this utilitarian approach is that there are some things or situations to which numbers cannot have been assigned when it comes to social problems. Thus, translating alternatives into numbers can lead to assumptions with which one cannot ethically or philosophically agree (Lejano, 2006).

Two important concepts in decision theory are optimization and satisficing. Optimization is the idea that if one can identify what is best for society, subsequent decisions can move one toward that societal good. The difficulty, of course, lies in determining what is "best," on what basis that determination will be made, and by whom. Thus, the concept of bounded rationality is particularly important in decision theory. Herbert Simon (1957) argued that human beings are fallible and cannot be expected to become the prototype of the ideal utility-maximizing individual, nor is it possible to figure out all possible alternatives to an action and compute optimality. Simon introduced the concept of *satisficing*, a mode of decision making in which individuals simply score alternatives within the limits of what is known, knowing that all possibilities will not be fully assessed. If one waited until all information was available, one would never make a decision. Simon's view of the human decision maker is "that of a limited analyst seeking out alternatives until he or she comes upon some one alternative that is good enough. This is still rational behavior but in a bounded, limited sense" (Lejano, 2006, p. 46).

The decision-making process of identifying the issue or problem, ruling out unacceptable alternatives, making an informed decision based on potential outcomes, and then selecting the most logical alternative to obtain one's preferred outcome has been seen as universally applicable to all policy situations. Lejano describes the process as one of scoping (listing decision criteria), choosing alternatives (coming up with a range of possibilities), screening (testing among alternatives), and choice (choosing the best alternative). This process occurs so systematically in Western decision making that most people would not recognize that they are operating under the assumptions of a rational approach. "Rational choice arguments are used to analyze almost any and every social situation" (Lejano, 2007, p. 50), everything from group membership to religion and fertility.

Criticisms of rational decision theory is somewhat filtered by the acknowledgment of fallibility and the recognition that rationality is bounded. Other fundamental concerns are that decision theory has been used to describe what happens in collectivities (beyond individuals), personifying entire bodies such as city councils, states, and even nations. The idea of a unitary body that can make decisions that impact large numbers of people raises concerns of authoritarianism and representativeness. In addition, anyone involved in policy making (even on the periphery) is aware that multiple competing forces, constituencies, and motivations are present in any issue that arises. Thus the application of decision theory to collectivities is often used to manage what is so complex as to be overwhelming.

Determining the best policy to support transportation needs within a particular community with a burgeoning population and an existing set of roads provides an example of how decision theory impacts policy concerns. In this community the infrastructure is not able to support the amount of traffic that has resulted from economic development and population growth. When an ideological position requires that local taxes cannot be increased, decisions must be made that optimize the financial support options that might allow sufficient funds to add or repair roads and to quell citizen dissatisfaction, while not requiring added taxation. A policy instrument that would optimize the ability to support transportation needs while not increasing taxes would be increased user fees in the form of gasoline taxes and road tolls. These fees would provide some support to solve the most immediate challenges but would not totally solve the transportation challenge. This would be considered a satisficing policy decision under decision theory.

Game Theory   Game theory is about rational decision making and is based on the concepts of utility, games and information, trees, and matrixes. *Utility* is based on how much welfare a participant gains from an object or an event. A participant is typically referred to in game theory as an agent who has preferences. In a policy situation, agents interact, and each brings his or her own preferences to the mix with the motivation to increase their utility (what they gain from the situation). Game theory is focused on formal reasoning. The concept of *utility function* is a device for assessing the maximization of utility in mathematical terms. In other words, game theory is designed to determine what agents get out of a situation and how that can be rank-ordered or translated into a number. Situations in which one agent can act to maximize his or her utility by figuring out how others will maximize theirs is called a *game,* and the participants are called *players.*

In game theory, players are considered economically rational in that they can assess outcomes, figure out how to get to outcomes, and select actions that get them to their preferred outcomes despite the actions of other players. Each game player has two or more potential *strategies,* which are predetermined actions to take in response to whatever other players might use. Ideally, a game is played when players have information to inform their selection of strategies, but it is recognized that most situations are, in effect, games played with imperfect information. How strategies are played out can be viewed as trees or matrixes, depending on whether players move sequentially or simultaneously. Entire games may involve a mixture of both types of move (Ross, 2006).

"The theory of games is perhaps the most extreme form of the rational model . . . [and has] been so influential in policy discourse despite its extreme reductionism" (Lejano, 2006, pp. 59–60). From decision theory, game theory has inherited several assumptions: that social policy is best described as making choices among multiple alternatives, that decision makers are utility-maximizing agents, that utilities (values) can be assigned to what happens in the process, and that decision makers expect utility even when outcomes are uncertain. However, unlike decision theory, game theory does not assume that a collective group can stand in for individuals, because game theory is built around individuals as the units of analysis rather than groups or collectivities (Lejano, 2006, p. 60).

Game theory seems quite present in modern policy-setting processes at all levels. It is particularly notable at the national level, where Democrats and Republicans are operating as utility-maximizing agents in their actions and decisions regarding most bills introduced in Congress. In addition, game theory is at play when a Congressperson assesses how decisions might impact voter decision making during the next election cycle. Individual constituency perspectives (such as members of the "tea party") influence policy maker positioning when the outcome of the policy-making process remains in question.

The positivist/postpositivist paradigm and the theories that are based on rationality bring a number of strategies to the policy analysis process. Review again the content of Box 3.2. Since policy analysis is linear, the strategy is to construct an analysis through a series of well-defined steps that follow a fixed sequence. This same process can be applied to any policy situation anywhere, regardless of the content of that policy or the level at which the policy is being questioned—organization/community, county/state, regional/national or international. Thus, this strategy is universally applicable. Decisions are made based on precision and linearity as well as on objectivity and determinant rules. The strategy, then, is to make selections from alternatives, minimizing objections and working in a narrowing process to find the best solution to the policy problem.

CLASSICAL, RATIONAL MODELS

Chambers and Wedel (2009) have developed a well-known social work model for policy analysis that integrates both policy and programs. It is called a "value critical" appraisal (p. 41). We are including it here in Box 3.3, not just because it is well known and respected, but because its use of language might suggest that it does not totally fit within the assumptions of positivist and rational thought. When reviewing the dimensions of their model, try to see why this model is both positivist and closely, though not explicitly, linked to decision theory.

Box 3.3 Chambers and Wedel's Policy/Program Analytic Framework

Problem Analysis Component	Policy and Program Basic Element
Problem definition (terms)	What are the eligibility rules; goals to be achieved?
Subtypes	Who are the target populations?
Quantifications	What is the justification for one goal rather than another?
Causal analysis	What must be done to address the problem (benefits/ personnel to deliver services)?
Ideology and values	What type of eligibility rules, goals, and financing are chosen?
Gainer and loser analysis	What are the types of losses, methods of financing?

Policy Elements	Subtypes
Goals and objectives	What are the principles or purpose? How long term or short term is the proposed program/policy? What are the intermediate/ultimate objectives? What is manifest/latent in these goals/objectives?
Forms of benefits and services	Will personal social services (expert services) be provided? Will hard benefits (e.g., cash, goods, commodities) be offered? How will positive discrimination happen? Will credits/vouchers be used? Will subsidies be given? Will government loan guarantees be offered? What protective regulations will be developed? How will deviance be supervised?

Eligibility rules	Who will have decision-making power?
	Will there be means/assets tests?
	What will constitute administrative rules?
	Will there be private contract provisions?
	What about prior contributions?
	How will professional discretion be factored in?
	Are judicial decisions relevant here?
	What about attachment to the workforce?
Administration and service	Will the structure be centralized?
	Will there be a federated structure?
	Is case management needed?
	From what agencies will referrals be given?
	What about indigenous worker staffing?
	Will ethnic, racial, feminist, or faith-related auspices be used?
	Will administrative fair hearings be provided?
	How will due process protections for clients' procedural rights be put into place?
	Is citizen participation a priority?
Financing	Is there a prepayment and insurance principle?
	Is this a publicly regulated private contract?
	Will voluntary contributions be solicited?
	Will tax revenues be appropriated?
	Will fees for service be charged?
	Will private endowments be solicited?
Interactions	How will various constituencies relate to one another?

Source: Adapted from *Social Policy and Social Programs: A Method for the Practical Public Policy Analyst* (5th edition), by D. E. Chambers and K. R. Weidel, 2009, Boston, MA: Pearson.

This model looks at the way the problem is defined; the cause(s) to which the problem is attributed and its more serious consequences; the ideology and the values that make the events of concern come to be defined as a problem; and major gainers and losers with respect to the problem. It approaches the understanding and assessment in a logical, linear way. The analysis begins with a definition of the problem. From that definition it is necessary to understand or identify the cause or causes of the problem. There is an assumption that if you know the cause, you will be able to rationally determine what is necessary to eliminate the problem. Based on an assumption of decision rules that require the best benefit for the least cost, the next step in the analysis is to look at what choices have been made to create the policy response, including who is eligible for services to eliminate the problem and what resources are being allocated to eliminate or ameliorate the problem. The identification of gainers and losers allows some closer interrogation of the power and politics that are at play. This helps to clarify what caused the current programmatic choices. These, then, are more closely interrogated in the second part of the analysis, which looks at the programmatic aspects derived from the policy. Note that this model recognizes complexity in that it guides the analyst to look at the interactions between the various elements of the program so as to promote understanding of the causal dimensions of the findings.

This model is based on the assumption that knowledge rests in evidence-based verification. It aims towards clarification of the basic concepts that go into the creation and implementation of policy. There is a linear logic as to how to proceed with the analysis, along with a specific methodology and validation procedures. This model uses induction and deduction, but induction is the primary reasoning tool. In sum, this model creates an analytic process whereby variables must be carefully defined along with the sample frames and the data collection mechanisms. In fact, there is an unspoken assumption that generalization by way of universal programming, in the right instances, is actually possible. This analytic method aims to provide rational explanations of the social policy.

If we were to use this approach to policy analysis with the case example on Service, Engagement, and Volunteerism, we might assume that Madeline wants to focus on her agency by first looking at the current federal policy and determining what goals are expected to be achieved at that level, based on the specific decisions that have been made to address the problem as it has been defined. It would be important for her to understand the choices that have been made regarding who is eligible, what the goals are, and how financing will occur at the various levels of the policy. Once Madeline understands this, she would step back to identify gainers and losers at all levels prior to moving toward the programmatic issues at her agency. What are the goals and objectives and how do those relate to the long-term and short-term elements of the federal policy? Are the services in keeping with the information garnered about what should be done to address the problem? Are eligibility rules congruent with the problem definition? In other words, do the target populations match? Who delivers the service, and how is that related to the problem analysis?

What about financing? Is it sufficient to overcome the problem as defined? Finally, in the process of analysis, were any interactions, either positive or negative, identified?

Another different, but wholly positivist and rational approach can be seen in Hofferbert's model (1974) which is well known and well cited in the fields of public policy and political science. We include it in Box 3.4 because it presents an interesting, linear view of the policy making "process as a 'funneling' of influences toward a formal decision-making event . . . [portraying] an external environment (historic-geographic circumstances plus socioeconomic conditions) processes through a political system (the public, governmental institutions, and elite policymakers) that yields policy outputs" (Blomquist, 2007, p. 267).

Box 3.4   Hofferbert's Model for Comparative Study of Policy Formation

What were the politically relevant incidents?

- Historic-geographic conditions?
- Socioeconomic composition?
- Mass political behavior?
- Governmental institutions?
- Elite behavior?

What became the formal policy conversion?
What is the policy output?

Source: Adapted from *The Study of Public Policy* (p. 228), by R. Hofferbert, 1974, Indianapolis, IN: Bobbs-Merrill.

Hofferbert assumes that socioeconomic conditions and mass political behavior mediated by government institutions and elite behavior drive policy decisions. This model allows for understanding both the direct effects and the developmental sequences of the politically relevant incidents in the formation of a particular policy and assumes that this will help in the understanding of the "whys" of a particular policy output. Think about how this model could be influenced by game theory.

In the case of the Edward M. Kennedy Serve America Act, using Hofferbert, we would want to understand why this policy, constructed in this way, would be seen to be acceptable in April of 2009. We would also want to understand geographic conditions that might have been politically relevant. For example, were there particular areas of the country in need of volunteer services for some reason? We would wish to investigate the socioeconomic composition of the Act and what might be the basis of the various cost-sharing elements contained in it. We would want to investigate the public positioning both in favor of and against all the elements in the Act, along with the general position of government institutions that might be impacted either positively or negatively by the Act. We would also look at elite behavior by those in government and business related to this Act, such as the CEO of Land-o-Lakes, in order to understand in great detail why all the parts of the policy were placed together as they were to create PL111-13.

In many ways, a determination of the degree to which an approach is both positivist and rational is where a sophisticated process of selection of which model of analysis to apply ends. Rarely, does even the most critically thinking analyst take the next step in method selection. It is at this level that the real opportunities for precision and for understanding policy analysis as research are found.

In Chapter 2, we talked about four foci to enact policy analysis as research: (1) formulation (policy intent or goal), (2) product (policy choice), (3) implementation (policy action), and (4) performance (impact). Note that the Chambers and Wedel (2009) model in Box 3.3 focuses on product or policy choice, identifying all the elements needed to analyze what is included in a particular policy product, whereas the Hofferbert (1974) model in Box 3.4 targets formulation. It is noteworthy that Hofferbert's model is flexible, leaving it up to the analyst to determine whether the particular location in which formulation occurs is a city council, a state legislature, or any other formal public decision-making body (Schlager, 2007, p. 314). Note that as the location changes, so does the unit of analysis for the research.

EXAMPLES FOCUSING ON DIFFERENT UNITS OF ANALYSIS

All of the following policy-analysis models are built on positivist or postpositivist assumptions and incorporate an objectivist perspective that embraces realism and places reality above and beyond individual knowledge. They assume that knowledge about social reality is hard and concrete and exists beyond the individual and that reality shapes action and perceptions deterministically. Natural science methods, with quantitative data collection being preferred over qualitative approaches, should be applied in the analysis in order to conform to or create law-governed or nomothetic stances. Generalizability of the results of the policy analysis would be the goal in order to strengthen or maintain existing social and policy structures. Each of the following models differs in its focus of analysis, principally looking at different units of analysis. See if you can determine which rational theory relates to each model. Accomplishing this, in view of this section's discussion, your capacity should be extended to make informed decisions about which model to apply, depending on the purpose and focus of your analysis. This is the final step (other than doing the actual analysis!) in engaging in policy analysis as research within a positivist or postpositivist frame.

Formulation Example In Box 3.5 is Jansson's six-step policy analysis model (2008). As you can see, its focus is on policy formulation or policy-in-intention (Guba, 1984). Beginning with gaining familiarity with the social problem to be addressed, Jansson moves through a rational process in which alternatives are brainstormed, options are compared and contrasted, an approach is selected, and that proposal is put forward by its advocates. Look back at Box 3.2, in which policy analysis is constructed through a series of well-defined steps following a fixed sequence. Jansson's model proposes a series of steps that could be applied to whatever problem or issue is being considered, and it is firmly grounded in the positivist/postpositivist paradigm.

Box 3.5 Jansson's Six-Step Policy Analysis Framework

1. What is the specific social problem or issue—or interrelated problems or issues?
2. What relevant policy, programmatic, and resource options could, singly and together, define a strategy for addressing the social problem or issue?
3. What are the relevant merits of competing options?
4. What specific policy proposal flows from the preceding three stages of policy analysis?
5. How are supporters for the proposal solicited?
6. What key factors need to be communicated about the substance of the proposal?

Source: Adapted from *Becoming an Effective Policy Advocate* (pp. 216–220), by B. S. Jansson, 2008, Belmont, CA: Thomson Brooks/Cole.

If Madeline from the Service, Engagement, and Volunteerism case example had a particular question that looked at how the agenda for the policy was derived with an emphasis on logical decision making, she would use Jansson's approach to understand the problem that volunteerism or civic engagement is intended to address. She would look at the minutes of hearings and other reports to understand what options were considered and why this particular policy option with all its aspects was selected by understanding who supported this particular policy approach and who did not.

In our previous theory discussion, the example regarding health care and transportation would be considered at the policy-formulation stage. Each could be understood and analyzed with Jansson's approach, either while the decision-making was in process or after the policy decisions had been made. Either way, Jansson would help to clarify why particular policy options gained favor.

Product Example In Box 3.6 is Huttman's policy analysis model (1981). Whereas some models are succinct and involve just a few steps, Huttman provides a very comprehensive approach to examining a policy product. Note how it focuses on questions that are directed to the content of the policy, attempting to get to the underlying needs addressed or the intent of the policy. The unit of analysis is based on the policy instrument itself.

Box 3.6 Huttman's Policy Analysis Model

What are the unmet needs?

- What particular needs or social problems will this policy address?
- What are the dimensions of this problem, including the size and characteristics of the group affected?
- What changes in American society and what gaps in institutional performance of basic societal functions will this policy cover?

What are the goals and outcomes of this policy?

- What will be the goals and outcomes in terms of
  - Greater social equality—that is, income or resource redistribution?
  - Greater opportunities for disadvantaged groups?
  - Changing the power position of the poor in comparison to other groups?

- To what degree will this policy improve the quality of life of those affected and the community in general?
- To what degree will this policy improve societal functioning?
- To what extent will this policy improve intrasocial relations and decrease individual and group tensions and conflicts?
- What will be the indirect or side effects of this policy, and will it generate other social problems?

What are the policy implementation strategies in terms of eligibility requirements, type of assistance given, and type of organization and staff utilized?

- What part of the target group will be eligible for benefits, as determined by such policy decisions as means testing? In other words, to whom will these benefits be allocated?
- What types of benefits are provided—case, material goods, or services?
- What types of organization and staff is used in providing services, and to what degree does the organizational arrangement fulfill the need of consumer accessibility and coordination of services?
- Will the rules and regulations of this policy be workable at the user level?

What is the scientific basis for policy?

- Is this policy in accord with research findings?
- Does this policy follow social work principles and practice?

What are the values embodied in this policy?

- What types of basic value premises are embedded in this policy?
- Will influential groups with different values provide opposition to implementation of this policy?
- Are there value compromises in the policy?
- To what extent is the policy influenced by historical precedent and present and past institutional arrangements?

What are the power bases for support for this policy?

- What interest groups and power bases will support or oppose this policy, and what is their respective strength and size?
- How much interest do these respective groups have in the policy?
- Is political decision making on this policy likely to be of the elitist or of the pluralistic type?
- In general, will the policy be politically acceptable?

What is the level of resource scarcity in relation to the policy?

- What is the resource situation of the funding body (usually, a national government), and what proportion can be used for this policy, under strictly traditional budgetary allocations or under special conditions caused by the economic and political climate?

(*continued*)

(continued)
- What demand will this policy put on changing the priorities in resource allocation, say between defense and social welfare spending?
- Is the policy economically feasible?

What are the costs and benefits related to this policy?
- What is the cost-effectiveness of this program versus the present program or other alternatives in terms of the degree to which it will reduce the problem, help a large number of people, or give high levels of help?
- What are the funding mechanisms, and are these cost-effective?

Source: Introduction to Social Policy (pp. 17–18), by E. Huttman, 1981, New York: McGraw-Hill. Used by permission.

Look at how rational assumptions are embedded in this model. It is expected that there will be goals and predetermined outcomes, based on scientific findings. Questions about policy implementation strategies are designed to interrogate the policy for inclusion of content relating to the elements specified to provide direction for the policy action. Again, these questions presume predetermined approaches to making content come alive. Of particular note are the questions about values and power, which could be seen as more interpretive. Still, embedded in the questions are issues of cause, so that no matter where the Huttman model is placed between the objectivist and subjectivist continuum, when it comes to these sets of questions the model remains rational and positivist. Rationality is also demonstrated in the questions about resource scarcity and costs and benefits. Cost-effectiveness questions are based on rational choices. Could that offer a clue about the theoretical basis of the model?

In the Service, Engagement, and Volunteerism case example, if Madeline had a question about the policy itself, she would try to identify how the policy, as constructed with all the different volunteer programs, meets the needs of the disadvantaged, as defined in the policy, at the national and local levels. She would search for goals and outcomes that would provide clues to what predetermined end states the policy is designed to pursue.

Again, in our theory discussion, we suggested that a particular policy instrument might be selected to respond to transportation challenges in an imaginary community. The policy option selected was user fees in the form of gasoline taxes and tolls. Huttman's model would allow a clear understanding of the cost/benefit considerations that were present in the choices involved within a context of resource scarcity.

Implementation Example   Holcomb and Nightingale's Implementation Analysis Model (2003, p. 50) is located in Box 3.7. When implementation is the focus of analysis, policy action and performance are examined. Note how they begin with a policy-intent question, asking about the major goals and assumptions of the policy, but quickly focus on the context in which the policy is being operationalized. Since implementation of a policy often results in a program being developed, this is another model that is programmatic in its orientation. Questions concern organizational context, staff roles, structure, management information, clients, and the task environment in which implementation will occur. A rational approach is embedded in the questions asked, which conform to the acceptable expectations one would consider important in developing a well-conceived program, one that tracks and monitors clients and responds to the labor, fiscal, and political context in which it is developed. Client outcomes are specifically mentioned, reinforcing the accountability of effectiveness-based programming and alluding to predetermined measures of success. Consider how game theory might be an influence on this model.

Box 3.7   Holcomb and Nightingale's Implementation Analysis Model

What are the major goals and assumptions underlying the policy that was adopted?

- What are the policy's underlying premises and assumptions?
- What is the policy intended to accomplish?

What is the organizational and service delivery structure and context in which the policy is operationalized?

- How is the organization structured?
- What are staff roles and responsibilities?
- What organizational arrangements and linkages are in place to deliver services?
- What types of interagency and interprogram interactions and collaborations are involved?

(*continued*)

How are key management functions carried out, and what role do they play in the program?

- How is program planning structured?
- Who is involved?
- What types of management information are used and for what purposes (e.g., planning, monitoring, performance analysis, performance improvement, evaluation)?

What is the sequence and timing of client activities?

- How do clients learn about and access services?
- How do clients move through a program (e.g., intake, eligibility determination, work orientation, activities)? How is a client's progress tracked and monitored?

What role do contextual factors play in shaping program operations and client outcomes?

- Labor market conditions?
- Fiscal/budgetary conditions?
- Political environment?
- Historic program experience?

Source: Adapted from *Conceptual Underpinnings of Implementation Analysis*, by P.A. Holcomb and D. S. Nightingdale, 2003. In M.C. Lennon and T. Corbett (Eds.), *Policy in Action: Implementation Research and Welfare Reform* (pp. 39–55). Washington, DC: The Urban Institute Press, p. 50. Used by permission.

If Madeline were interested in the programmatic implementation that her program had to achieve in the case example, this policy model would be helpful. She would focus on the organizational and service delivery aspects of the program and would use this approach to track how the agency structured its service delivery in response to the policy, including management and direct practice activities as well as who the client is and how the client is served. Using this model, some contextual issues such as the current socioeconomic and political climate would be interrogated.

Returning to the examples in our theory discussion, Holcomb and Nightingale provide a useful tool to track the implementation of the user fees in the form of gasoline taxes and road tolls. The level of local, county, and state jurisdictional cooperation or confusion related to the collection and distribution of those fees, the costs related to implementation of new fees, shifts in customer usage, and other elements of the socioeconomic and political context would become clear.

Impact Example Segal and Bruzuzy's Questions for Social Welfare Policy Analysis (1998, p. 66) model is contained in Box 3.8. As you can see, they move forward in a rational manner, beginning with questions about the social problem being addressed and the goal of the policy. They spend some time on the politics surrounding the policy, asking about hidden agendas, supporters, and opponents. Think about how game theory may be evident here. Are any other theories influencing the structure of the model? The focus of their model is on implementation and impact. Questions about the affected populations and both intended and actual impact are explored, focusing on consumers' experience of the policy. Note how they reinforce costs and benefits as part of their actual impact statement.

Box 3.8 Segal and Bruzuzy's Questions for Social Welfare Policy Analysis

What is the social problem?

- What is the problem?
- Definitions?
- Extent of problem?
- Who defines this as a problem?
- Who disagrees?
- Related social values?
- Competing social values?
- Underlying causes or factors?

What is the policy goal?

- What is the general goal?
- Are there subgoals?
- Do the subgoals conflict?

What is the relevant policy/legislation?

- What is/are the relevant public policies?
- If there are no public policies, why?
- What are the objectives of the policies?
- Are there hidden agendas?

(continued)

(continued)
- Who supports the policies?
- Who opposes the policies?

How was Implementation?
- What is/are the social programs implemented as a result of the policies?
- Are the programs effective?
- Strengths?
- Weaknesses?

Who are the affected populations?
- Who is touched by the policy and programs?
- Are there positive effects?
- Are there negative effects?

What is the intended impact?
- What is supposed to be the result?
- Who was supposed to have been affected?
- How has the social problem supposed to have been changed?

What is the actual impact?
- Costs and benefits?
- Is the social problem changed?
- If so, how?
- Are there unintended results?

Source: Social Welfare Policy, Programs, and Practices (p. 66), by E. Segal and S. Bruzuzy, 1998, Itasca, IL: F. E. Peacock. Used by permission.

In the Service, Engagement, and Volunteerism case, if Madeline were interested in another way to follow the social problem through to the policy response and actual impact—especially if she was interested in seeing what caused what at each stage of development—she would identify the social problem, the goals of the Serve America Act, and what was included in the policy as well as how implementation progressed, at least during that first year. In looking at implementation, who was actually affected and whether or not what happened was intended or unintended would be considered.

Imagine that health care reform, as discussed in the theory section, resulted in a mandated insurance purchase for all citizens. Once that part of the health reform policy was totally implemented, using Segal and Bruzuzy's model would be appropriate to determine whether accessibility and affordability in health care had indeed increased as a result of the reform efforts. Other intended and unintended consequences of the health policy changes would also be made clear.

HOW TO ASSESS THE DEGREE TO WHICH AN ANALYSIS APPROACH IS RATIONAL

If the policy analyst is engaging in rational policy analysis in which stability and control are intended, the purpose of the policy work might be to answer such questions as: What are the dimensions of the social problem? What is the cause of the problem? Why does the problem exist, or why is it being recognized now? How can the problem be eliminated? How was the policy agenda established? What are the outcomes of the policy? These questions follow from the modern positivist and postpositivist concern for providing explanations for the status quo, social order, consensus, social integration, solidarity, and satisfaction of needs. These questions imply no priority to searching for meaning or to spending time questioning values. They are aimed at provoking answers that will provide a sense of the acceptable social structure and control of what works by incrementally changing what does not. These questions are focused on current or potential outcomes rather than process. Objective sources of information obtained by traditional means support the thrust of these questions. They can be best answered by a positivist/postpositivist approach to policy analysis, which implies that if one carefully and systematically analyzes the policy situation, powerful generalizations about policies can be made. To achieve this, the positivist assumption is that the rational, pragmatic methods of the natural sciences are appropriate for studying human affairs.

QUESTIONS RELEVANT TO ASSESSING THE RATIONALITY OF AN APPROACH

From this discussion, it should be clear that there are numerous viable guides for engaging in rational policy analysis. Once the analyst knows that the policy questions guiding the analysis are situated within the positivist/postpositivist approach to knowledge building, it is important to be certain that the available model can actually provide meaningful answers to the questions at hand. Rather than reverting to questions of ontology and epistemology, a simpler way to make that determination is to decide whether the model is rational in its methods. The following are useful screening questions for that decision making:

- Is it based on the assumption of a single best policy truth?
- Is it based on a belief that the best policy (or best analysis) is made through a series of well-defined steps, following a precise linear sequence?
- Are variables carefully defined (can the unit(s) of analysis be determined)?
- Are there specifically stated questions to guide the analysis?
- Are there mechanisms for empirically based data collection?
- Is the theory guiding the architecture of the model identifiable and based on positivist or postpositivist assumptions?

Once the analyst is certain that the policy analysis approach is indeed a classical, rational model, there is one more area of consideration prior to final selection.

GAINS AND LOSSES WHEN RATIONAL MODELS ARE USED TO ANALYZE POLICY

It is important to remember that there is no perfect model of policy analysis, just as there is no perfect paradigmatic perspective or theory to capture the complexity of lived experience. There is no perfect science, so findings from the positivist/postpositivist approach to systematic knowing must be held tentatively until better, more accurate or generalized knowledge is possible. At this stage in knowledge development, one must use a critical lens to understand the choices that are being made when a rational model of analysis is selected to interrogate a particular policy. The following issues should be thoroughly considered when making a selection.

Gains and Benefits   A classical, rational model brings assumptions about objectivity and the preservation of the status quo. The goal of rationality is to control and structure in order to reduce complexity for easier management. In rational approaches, the analyst aims to provide an answer based on an identified problem-solving process that is predictable and deterministic. This often provides a welcome relief to overwhelmed decision makers who are sorting through hundreds of pages of written documents, trying to figure out how to address a social problem.

A rational approach provides an assessment of the most benefit for the least cost in environments that are often mired in budgetary deficits or in agencies that are strapped for funding. Some would call this satisficing decision making—the best possible within identified constraints. Decisions are empirically and logically based on conformity to objective and determinant rules used to forecast costs and benefits. With those decisions usually comes a glimmer of hope that something can be resolved by finding the best solution to a problem. Linear reasoning helps to make appropriate selections among alternatives so as to minimize objections while maximizing benefits, thereby giving decision makers a sense of being in control of final outcomes, even if that is nearly impossible in the twenty-first century.

Costs and Losses   On the other hand, reduced complexity may lead to simplistic assessment or policy decisions that are somewhat naïve. One universal answer cannot respond to or account for the uniqueness of personal experiences or for cultural differences in a pluralistic society. This reductionism cannot take the social problem into account with the particulars of a unique context for the identified social problem.

The simplifying nature of a rational approach may create a false sense among policy makers that they have solved a problem, when in fact their solution may simply be a temporary Band-Aid for a population at-risk. This type of incremental policy response tends to preserve the status quo or create a narrowed response which generates another social problem as a result. Thus, reductionism is necessary to enact this approach, but any answer must be held tentatively until a better one appears; therefore, this analytic style will never really achieve a perfect response. This means that policy action is never static, never resolved, and always subject to incremental change strategies.

All of these gains and costs should be considered when selecting a classical, rational model for policy analysis. A summary of gains and costs appears in Box 3.9.

**Box 3.9   Gains and Benefits, Costs and Losses
in Rational Approaches**

Gains and Benefits

A rational approach reduces complexity for easier management.
A rational approach gives an answer based on an identified problem-solving
   process.

(continued)

(continued)

A rational approach provides an assessment of the most benefit for the least cost.

Decisions are empirically and logically based on conformity to objective and determinant rules used to forecast costs and benefits.

Linear reason helps to make appropriate selections among alternatives so as to minimize objections while maximizing benefits.

Losses and Costs

Reduced complexity may lead to simplistic assessment and policy decisions.

One universal answer cannot respond to or account for the uniqueness of personal experiences connected with the social problem or for the particulars of a unique context for the social problem.

Reduction may be necessary to enact this approach, but it is all but impossible, so that any answer must be held tentatively until a better one appears.

CONCLUSION

This chapter introduced the rational approach to policy analysis. There was a short history of the philosophy of science to show both our society's historic appreciation of reason and the sources of Western notions of reason that led to preferences for positivism and linear rational thought for matters scientific. A brief overview of sample theories was introduced, along with an exploration of the dimensions of rational approaches to policy analysis, providing examples of models that are clearly situated in a positivist/postpositivist paradigmatic perspective. The understanding of the possibilities and the challenges of rational models of policy analysis were further explored by looking at examples of models that target differing units of policy analysis.

The following chapter is based on the assumptions and approaches introduced here, but it has a much more applied focus. You will see how to actually use rational approaches to achieve policy analysis goals that fit within a positivist/postpositivist perspective. After reading through this section (Chapters 3 and 4), you should be able to assess the paradigmatic perspective of a particular policy analysis model to determine whether it fits within a positivist worldview and whether it is rational in its approach to policy analysis; identify the unit(s) of analysis that are the focus of the particular model; and know what is necessary to determine how to enact analysis using a particular model based on a positivist/postpositivist rational approach.

DISCUSSION QUESTIONS

1. Early in this chapter, we argued that linear thought is much more congruent with positivist and postpositivist thought. First, define and give an example of linear thought. Then, identify at least three ways in which linear thinking is congruent with a positivist ontology or frame of reference.
2. Review the theories that were discussed in Chapter 3. Why would you consider them to be prescriptive theories? What are the benefits of prescriptions guiding work? What are the costs of the prescriptions these theories provide?
3. Look at rational choice, decision, and game theories to identify how they are similar and how they differ. Now, using the media (radio, TV, the Internet, or any other news source), see if you can identify policies at the formulation, product, implementation, or impact levels that can be better understood using one or all of these theories as a guide.
4. Rational choice, decision, and game theories are relevant at many levels of practice. Select a policy issue within an organizational setting. How do these theories inform your thinking about this issue? Select a policy issue within a community with which you are familiar. How do these theories inform your thinking about this issue?
5. What do you see as the strengths and challenges of using rational approaches to policy analysis, especially with issues impacting nondominant groups?

CHAPTER 4

Applications of Rational Policy Analysis

IN CHAPTER 3, we provided a background for understanding the underlying assumptions of rationality, and we introduced a number of frameworks that fit with those assumptions. All the approaches presented in Chapter 3 fit within a positivist/postpositivist perspective. They all represent a policy ideology in which it is assumed that there is a best way to formulate a policy solution to a social problem and that well-articulated policies can provide stability and control. The Service, Engagement, and Volunteerism case was discussed in Chapter 3 and will be used extensively in this chapter to demonstrate how rational policy questions can be used in the analytic process. How these rational approaches can be applied in a systematic manner is the primary focus of this chapter.

This chapter's principal subject is the "doing" of rational policy analysis as a type of research. Starting with identifying the purpose of the policy analysis, which also determines the paradigmatic perspective for the research aspect of the process, this chapter will take you through a decision-making process that results in the determination of an appropriate rational approach for use in analysis. Based on this chapter, you should be able to identify or construct a policy research question that fits within the positivist/postpositivist perspective. Anchored in the identification of the purpose of the research, you will be able to identify rational policy analysis strategies and defend the use of those strategies to answer the policy research question. With your knowledge of how to determine the form, level (and scope), and focus of the social policy, you should be able to select and defend the selection of a particular rational approach to policy analysis. In this chapter, you will learn how to engage in various types of rational policy analysis through the application of several models. The chapter ends with a discussion of what rational approaches can and cannot offer when policy analysis is undertaken. Finally, you will understand what is gained and what is given up when one engages in positivist/ postpositivist policy analysis research.

Recall that rational approaches to policy analysis are prescriptive and are typically called *models*. Rational approaches assume that there is a single best policy truth that can be identified through a series of well-defined steps in a linear manner. Variables are carefully defined, questions are specifically asked, and there is an attempt to narrow the process so that the analyst achieves manageability. The policy analysis approach itself will generally have a specific focus in the policy process. That focus can be on formulation, the product, implementation of the policy, or the quality of the policy performance to eliminate the social problem it was designed to address. The focus of the approach must match the reason for engaging in policy analysis in order to produce useful findings. Awareness of all these aspects of a policy analytic process, in addition to the appropriate and thorough application of a particular approach in the analysis, makes policy analysis a type of research.

Now let's see how all this works by looking more deeply at the policy analytic interests and the selected approaches that were introduced in Chapter 3. We will continue our interrogation of P.L. 111-13 using most of the models already introduced. So how does one begin this sort of interrogation and how does one know that a particular approach will be appropriate? In the sections that follow, we will demonstrate the essential elements that require critical decision making and lead to the selection of a particular model to use for policy analysis. We will then provide some guidance about applying the selected approach. It is beyond the scope of this effort to engage in a series of full-blown policy-analysis processes with well-articulated products. Instead, based on the kinds of questions contained in the selected approaches, we will suggest where one might find answers needed to complete an analysis of P.L. 111-13, as discussed in our case example and guided by a particular rational approach. This should give you the required level of familiarity to discover what can and cannot be accomplished by a particular rational approach to policy analysis. Since it is as important to know how to select an appropriate resource for analysis as it is to know how to apply it, each section will detail the decision making that suggests why the approach is appropriate for the desired analysis before demonstrating the potential data sources for the type of inter-rogation that would be useful when applying the approach to a particular policy question.

USING THE CHAMBERS AND WEDEL POLICY/ PROGRAM ANALYTICAL FRAMEWORK

In Chapter 3, we introduced the work of Chambers and Wedel (2009) as an example of a rational approach to policy/program analysis that includes a number of problem analysis components and policy ele-ments. To refresh your memory, Chambers and Wedel's approach is presented again in Box 4.1.

Box 4.1 Chambers and Wedel's Policy/Program Analytic Framework

Problem Analysis Component	Policy and Program Basic Element
Problem definition (terms)	What are the eligibility rules; goals to be achieved?
Subtypes	Who are the target populations?
Quantifications	What is the justification for one goal rather than another?
Causal analysis	What must be done to address the problem (benefits/personnel to deliver services)?
Ideology and values	What type of eligibility rules, goals, and financing are chosen?
Gainer and loser analysis	What are the types of losses, methods of financing?
Policy Elements	**Subtypes**
Goals and objectives	What are the principles or purpose?
	How long term or short term is the proposed program/policy?
	What are the intermediate/ultimate objectives?
	What is manifest/latent in these goals/objectives?
Forms of benefits and services	Will personal social services (expert services) be provided?
	Will hard benefits (e.g., cash, goods, commodities) be offered?
	How will positive discrimination happen?
	Will credits/vouchers be used?

Eligibility rules	Will subsidies be given?
	Will government loan guarantees be offered?
	What protective regulations will be developed?
	How will deviance be supervised?
	Who will have decision-making power?
	Will there be means/asset tests?
	What will constitute administrative rules?
	Will there be private contract provisions?
	What about prior contributions?
	How will professional discretion be factored in?
	Are judicial decisions relevant here?
	What about attachment to the workforce?
Administration and service	Will the structure be centralized?
	Will there be a federated structure?
	Is case management needed?
	From what agencies will referrals be given?
	What about indigenous worker staffing?
	Will ethnic, racial, feminist, or faith-related auspices be used?
	Will administrative fair hearings be provided?
	How will due process protections for clients' procedural rights be put into place?
	Is citizen participation a priority?
Financing	Is there a prepayment and insurance principle?
	Is this a publicly regulated private contract?
	Will voluntary contributions be solicited?
	Will tax revenues be appropriated?
	Will fees for service be charged?
	Will private endowment be solicited?
Interactions	How will various constituencies relate to one another?

Source: Adapted from *Social Policy and Social Programs: A Method for the Practical Policy Analyst* (5th edition), by D. E. Chambers and K. R. Wedel, 2009, Boston, MA: Pearson.

First, let us look at how one might begin to apply this framework in analyzing P.L. 111-13. In Chapter 3 we suggested,

Madeline wants to focus on her agency by first looking at the current federal policy and determining what goals are expected to be achieved at that level, based on the specific decisions that have been made to address the problem as it has been defined. It would be important for her to understand the choices that have been made regarding who is eligible, what the goals are, and how financing will occur at the various levels of the policy. Once Madeline understands this, she would step back to identify gainers and losers at all levels prior to moving toward the programmatic issues at her agency. What are the goals and objectives and how do those relate to the long-term and short-term elements of the federal policy? Are the services in keeping with the information garnered about what should be done to address the problem? Are eligibility rules congruent with the problem definition? In other words, do the target populations match? Who delivers the service, and how is that related to the problem analysis? What about financing? Is it sufficient to overcome the problem as defined? Finally, in the process of analysis, were any interactions, either positive or negative, identified?

To accomplish this, let us first test the idea that the Chambers and Wedel approach is appropriate in this case. Then let us look at how one might proceed to conduct the analysis.

TARGETING THE RESEARCH

Based on the Service, Engagement, and Volunteerism case, Madeline could ask the following *policy research question*: What are the goals and important elements of this policy? Note that this is a rational question asking for the facts about this policy. If Madeline wants a description of relevant facts, rational policy models provide her with the tools she needs to move forward in a step-by-step manner.

Before moving forward, however, Madeline needs to systematically think about the policy *form*, the *level* at which the policy is being studied, and the *focus* of the policy analysis. Form-wise, Madeline's question seeks to know more about the enacted statute; in this case, the form is statutory law. And since the Act was signed into law by the president, it is at the national level. The focus of the analysis, given the research question, is the policy product. At this point, Madeline is asking what is the policy's content. She does not ask how this came about or what forces supported or disapproved it; she simply wants to know the facts about the policy product.

Use of the Chambers and Wedel framework can be *justified* because it provides a comprehensive overview of the components and elements that one would expect to identify in a policy. It does not ask why these components and elements are in place; it assumes that they are logically a part of a well-articulated policy and are taken into consideration if the policy is complete. Madeline will find the questions straightforward, providing her with details that will be informative and helpful as she thinks about how policy content will drive implementation in her agency.

APPLYING THE APPROACH

While the questions that one might ask under the guidance of a particular approach to policy analysis are important, the feasibility of the enactment of a particular approach is actually most related to whether or not the analyst knows and has access to the needed information or data at each stage of the analytic process. So rather than engage in a completely developed policy analysis in this section, we present ways to locate the needed information to answer the questions present in the approach. Sometimes minor adjustments to the questions may also be necessary to target the particulars of the analysis, given a policy research question. This allows a look at each aspect of the approach while also offering some suggestions about what might be useful data sources for the process.

Problem Analysis Components Chambers and Wedel begin with four problem analysis components. Problem definition may or may not be stated in the policy itself. Often policy products are intended to solve a problem and speak to that resolution, simply implying what the problem is. So the first thing Madeline may want to do is see whether there is a problem statement in the policy itself. She will want to look for other information as well: How are important concepts defined? What entities are expected to implement the policy? Who is the target population? What are the eligibility guidelines? She will want to refer to the *Federal Register* to identify proposed rules for implementation along with any published comments related to those rules. Notice that those rules will represent a different form of policy and could be subject to the same type of analysis using Chambers and Wedel later. For a full idea of the history behind what went into the final version of the law, she will also want to look at the hearing minutes from the particular committees in both chambers of Congress to trace how the social problem came to be defined as it was.

   To determine why one goal was chosen over another, she will return to the same committee minutes as well as minutes of both the House and the Senate. She may want to look at the various versions of the law that failed to be adopted. In addition, various Web sites such as that of the Corporation for National and Community Service would be interrogated to find information on what must be done to address the problem; what types of eligibility rules, goals, and financing are favored; and who is seen as gaining and losing in the method of financing or in any other aspects of the legislation. Advocacy Web sites could be investigated to identify various other views. These alternative perspectives could serve as an interesting background in the process of sorting out what finally became the official record.

Policy Elements   P.L. 111-13 serves as the source for the identification of goals and objectives, forms of benefits and services, eligibility rules, administration and service, financing, and interactions. Madeline will be looking for specific information on the principles and purpose, the outcome objectives, the services to be provided, and a host of details designed to make her fully knowledgeable about the reach of this legislation. The Internet will be a good source of summaries of the law, key findings, and frequently asked questions geared to interested parties such as directors of volunteer services such as herself.

Because the Edward M. Kennedy Serve America Act reauthorizes and reforms the National and Community Service Act of 1990 (NCSA) and the Domestic Volunteer Service Act of 1973 (DVSA), Madeline will need to read these acts to determine how they have been changed as a result of the new legislation. National volunteer organizations will be a resource for commentary and for summaries of changes and how those will affect their members. In addition, Web sites such as those of the Points of Light Foundation and Energize will provide summative information. Most likely, much of what she will learn in this policy analysis will require her to make minor adjustments to her program but not to engage in a major program redesign.

CRITIQUE OF THE APPROACH

This approach provides a straightforward, detailed set of questions to guide an analysis aimed at knowing the contents of a policy. The process is particularly useful for policies involving incremental changes of existing policies. The systematic approach allows the analyst to know what has changed and what remains the same. Chambers and Wedel's approach does not assess why changes were made or identify the underlying reasons for change. This rational approach assumes by the questions posed that the analysis should address the specifics of the law and the way in which it will alter practice. It asks who, what, when, and how questions that will make the analyst knowledgeable about the content and how it came to be, rather than assuming the role of a critic of the content or language of the policy. It does not challenge the status quo or seek deeper insight as to why the law was reformed.

Since this is a rational approach that is attuned to cause and effect, this process provides precise predictive information for implementation. It specifically provides those interested in implementing the policy with the exact steps needed to successfully implement the policy to assure the detailed results. In short, this approach simplifies the policy process at every level. It does not expose complexity or look beyond historical context, thus narrowing the analytic focus so that interested parties can move toward incremental changes in the status quo. It does, however, allow for the assessment of off-targeting once a program has been implemented, by allowing a look at the original problem and desired policy response in light of who was and was not served.

USING JANSSON'S SIX-STEP POLICY ANALYSIS FRAMEWORK

Another approach that can be used in response to the information recounted in Chapter 3 is based on Jansson's (2008) framework. Again, to refresh your memory, Box 4.2 provides the six steps that Jansson includes in his policy analysis approach.

**Box 4.2   Jansson's Six-Step Policy
Analysis Framework**

1. What is the specific social problem or issue—or interrelated problems or issues?
2. What relevant policy, programmatic, and resource options could, singly and together, define a strategy for addressing the social problem or issue?
3. What are the relevant merits of competing options?
4. What specific policy proposal flows from the preceding three stages of policy analysis?
5. How are supporters for the proposal solicited?
6. What key factors need to be communicated about the substance of the proposal?

Source: Adapted from *Becoming an Effective Policy Advocate* (5th edition, pp. 216–220), by B. S. Jansson, 2008, Belmont, CA: Thomson Brooks/Cole.

In Chapter 3 we stated,

> *[I]f Madeline had a particular question that looked at how the agenda for the policy was derived with an emphasis on logical decision making, she would use Jansson's approach to understand the problem that volunteerism or civic engagement is intended to address. She would look at the minutes of hearings and other reports to understand what options were considered and why this particular policy option with all its aspects was selected by understanding who supported this particular policy approach and who did not.*

Here, Madeline is interested in knowing what options were considered and the rationale behind the options that were selected in P.L. 111-13.

TARGETING THE RESEARCH

Given the foregoing, Madeline could develop another *policy research question* that would take her in another specific analytic direction. Her question might be: What happened in the policy-making process? By asking this question, she would gain descriptive background information about how P.L.111-13 came about, including reforms and reauthorizations of other bills. This is a rational question asking for the facts of what happened. Madeline is not asking why these changes happened or asking in depth about the politics of the process. She wants to know what occurred so that she will be informed.

Before using Jansson's six steps, it is important to target the research by identifying the form, level, and focus. As in the case of the application of Chambers and Wedel's framework, the *form* is the policy instrument, the statute. Again, the *level* remains the same. Madeline continues a *focus* on the national level policy, though she may encounter active stakeholders at other governmental and community levels. Those data sources will be important to this analysis only in terms of the degree to which they participated at the national level.

Jansson's six steps are well suited for examining the agenda-setting process. Its focus is on formulation. Madeline's policy research question is about what happened to bring this policy into being. She is interested in a description of the basic facts and wants a reasonable summary of the formulation aspect of the policy process. *Justification of the analytic approach* is clear in that Madeline needs to be an informed director of volunteers who can explain in a understandable, logical manner to others how this policy was formulated. Jansson's model can enable her to do this.

In the following subsections, we provide a look at each aspect of Jansson's model while also giving some suggestions about useful data sources for the process.

Specifying the Problem   Madeline will need to talk with a number of her colleagues at the national level who were involved in the development of P.L. 111-13 about what constituted the problem from their perspectives. She will want to be familiar with the host of programs combined under P.L. 111-13 and mobilized under the rubric of civic engagement. She can access a number of Web sites that have summaries of how the law developed. To determine what the problem was that this statute was supposed to address, she can locate government documents of public hearings as well as summaries prepared by a number of national organizations focused on volunteerism. In her analysis, she needs to determine why national service is being promoted and why the use of volunteers and quasi-volunteers is so central. She needs to understand the relationship between the identified problem and social entrepreneurs, the increased use of public and private investments in nonprofits, the leveraging of federal investments, the expansion of service learning, the coordination of citizen services in emergencies or disasters, the increased opportunities for retired professionals along with numerous other activities that were folded into this reform effort. In addition, she will need to look at empirical evidence about government and the promotion of national service. In a rational way, then, Madeline may find Jansson's first step helpful because it suggests that there may be interrelated problems or issues that set the stage for policy development.

Defining a Strategy   To consider the strategy that led to the legislation, Madeline should read the original House and Senate bills that were combined to become P.L. 111-13 along with the public hearing minutes that led to those original bills. The print media at the time along with records of talk shows and other media will provide a picture of what was going on before the bills were proposed and how the ideas were managed in the media. Much of what was happening among the major players before the bill's introduction will not be part of the public record, but informal conversations with her friends at the Points of Light Foundation and at AmeriCorps might give her some ideas about the important players. These conversations will also allow her to gather information on the facts they presented to influence the legislation. In short, she should be able to recognize and document the strategies that came together to address the opportunity for enhanced national service.

Determining Merits of Competing Options   To determine the merits of competing options, the first step could be an analysis of the original House and Senate bills. In addition, looking at hearing minutes and talking with her contacts at the national level will indicate what may have been proposed that never got into either bill in order to identify alternative or competing options. The idea is to become knowledgeable about how different groups assessed the merits of various proposals and what was finally voted into law.

Identifying the Policy Proposal   Linguistic analysis of competing bills as well as attention to differing emphases throughout those bills will help to highlight compromises that occurred to create the final policy product. This, in addition to what she learned in her previous steps, will help her see why P.L. 111-13 is so packed with details about all government programs that relate to volunteerism and national service.

Identifying Supporters   Beginning ideas about supporters should be available as a result of Madeline's noting position statements in hearings, in the media, and on the various Web sites that she has accessed. Written material from various national membership organizations will also help in the identification of supporters. To understand how supporters were solicited, informal conversations with national contacts could help her understand the network of associations. Colleagues who lobbied for the bill may be able to identify individuals and organizations that were original supporters and how others had to be persuaded about its merits. If possible, it would be well to determine what the cost of that persuasion was. In some ways, looking at "strange bedfellows" regarding who sponsored the bill and spoke on its behalf in each house of Congress will also provide data that might be useful in understanding why other strange associations happen in other bills introduced later. Those who opposed the bill would be important to identify as well.

Communicating Key Factors   Jansson's last step is one that summarizes and narrows the analysis into the key factors that need to be communicated about the substance of the proposal. Madeline should summarize what she learns in the first five steps to create a set of talking points about the Act itself. This sort of communication is useful for stakeholders after the fact of a policy's enactment, but it can also be used as a way of informing advocates about positions to be taken during the policy-making process.

CRITIQUE OF THE APPROACH

Jansson's six-step model is straightforward and logical. It is designed to provide a descriptive overview of what is happening or how it came to happen. This analysis produces a focused summation that can convey a good deal of information in a concise manner. Whereas Chambers and Wedel ask much more detailed questions that delve into the programmatic aspects of the policy, Jansson focuses on the overview of the originating proposal. It provides the "front-end" fine points of policy setting. This approach allows the analyst to gather detailed information and narrow it down into a manageable and knowledgeable format.

Note that this is a very rational, linear process in which one step leads logically to the next. The step analogy portrays the manner in which the process of policy making is assumed to proceed. If the analyst wants precise predictive information, this approach will serve well. Jansson's model provides guidance for the exact steps needed to successfully analyze a proposal to assure the desired results. However, its prescriptive, reductionist focus will not encourage the analyst to understand the complexity surrounding why the particular results were the ones chosen over various other options.

USING HUTTMAN'S POLICY ANALYSIS MODEL

Huttman's (1981) policy analysis model was introduced in Chapter 3 as an example of a framework that could be used to examine in detail policy content (product). This rational approach can take Madeline in yet another direction in policy analysis. As a refresher, Huttman's model is reproduced in Box 4.3.

Box 4.3 Huttman's Policy Analysis Model

What are the unmet needs?
- What particular needs or social problems will this policy address?
- What are the dimensions of this problem, including the size and characteristics of the group affected?

(continued)

(continued)

- What changes in American society and what gaps in institutional performance of basic societal functions will this policy cover?

What are the goals and outcomes of this policy?

- What will be the goals and outcomes in terms of
  ○ Greater social equality—that is, income or resource redistribution?
  ○ Greater opportunities for disadvantaged groups?
  ○ Changing the power position of the poor in comparison to other groups?
- To what degree will this policy improve the quality of life of those affected and the community in general?
- To what degree will this policy improve societal functioning?
- To what extent will this policy improve intra social relations and decrease individual and group tensions and conflicts?
- What will be the indirect or side effects of this policy, and will it generate other social problems?

What are the policy implementation strategies in terms of eligibility requirements, type of assistance given, and type of organization and staff utilized?

- What part of the target group will be eligible for benefits, as determined by such policy decisions as means testing? In other words, to whom will these benefits be allocated?
- What types of benefits are provided—case, material goods, or services?
- What types of organization and staff is used in providing services, and to what degree does the organizational arrangement fulfill the need of consumer accessibility and coordination of services?
- Will the rules and regulations of this policy be workable at the user level?

What is the scientific basis for this policy?

- Is this policy in accord with research findings?
- Does this policy follow social work principles and practice?

What are the values embodied in this policy?

- What types of basic value premises are embedded in this policy?
- Will influential groups with different values provide opposition to implementation of this policy?
- Are there value compromises in the policy?
- To what extent is the policy influenced by historical precedent and present and past institutional arrangements?

What are the power bases for support for this policy?

- What interest groups and power bases will support or oppose this policy, and what is their respective strength and size?

- How much interest do these respective groups have in the policy?
- Is political decision making on this policy likely to be of the elitist or of the pluralistic type?
- In general, will the policy be politically acceptable?

What is the level of resource scarcity and policy?

- What is the resource situation of the funding body (usually, a national government), and what proportion can be used for this policy, under strictly traditional budgetary allocations or under special conditions caused by the economic and political climate?
- What demand will this policy put on changing the priorities in resource allocation, say between defense and social welfare spending?
- Is the policy economically feasible?

What are the costs and benefits related to this policy?

- What is the cost-effectiveness of this program versus the present program or other alternatives in terms of the degree to which it will reduce the problem, help a large number of people, or give high levels of help?
- What are the funding mechanisms, and are these cost-effective?

Source: Introduction to Social Policy (pp. 17–18), by E. Huttman, 1981, New York: McGraw-Hill. Used by permission.

In Chapter 3 we stated,

[I]f Madeline had a question about the policy itself she would try to identify how the policy, as constructed with all the different volunteer programs, meets the needs of the disadvantaged as defined in the policy at the national and local levels. She would search for goals and outcomes that would provide clues to what predetermined end states the policy is designed to pursue.

Here, Madeline is interested in identifying which part of the statute in its final form will be important to her practice as a director of volunteers. She is probably thinking about writing her grant application and wants to make sure that her program's measurable objectives can be designed to achieve the outcomes expected by the policy.

TARGETING THE RESEARCH

Madeline may be responsible for the oversight of a number of volunteer programs, some covered by P.L. 111-13 and others that do not have a federal mandate. One of the programs that she oversees is the Foster Grandparent Program originally under the Domestic Services Act and part of ACTION (the federal agency that used to administer domestic service programs, including VISTA and Peace Corps), and which has since been subsumed under the Corporation for National and Community Service. Given this, Madeline might want to ask this question for her policy research: What changes have been made in the current policy regarding the Foster Grandparent Program? This research question allows her to focus on a particular program within the larger grouping of volunteer initiatives within the Act.

Before applying the Huttman model, Madeline will target her research by identifying its form, level, and focus. As in her previous analyses, Madeline's *form* is the policy instrument, the statute, but only that content that pertains to the Foster Grandparent Program. Depending on the timing of her analysis, she may have only the statute available to her, but as administrative rules and regulations are developed by the agencies that have been tasked with the implementation of the policy, she will want to see what those provisions contain as well. Rules and regulations will flesh out details that are not fully articulated in the policy itself. They become just as important to the analyst interested in carrying out the policy at the programmatic level. The *level* remains the national level policy, although Madeline is aware that her analysis will be relevant to all Foster Grandparent Programs including the one in her agency.

Justification of the analytic approach can be made on the basis that Huttman's approach allows the analyst to systematically examine policy content from needs assessment to costs and benefits. By using Huttman's detailed questions to guide her analysis, she will have a good grasp of current expectations of the Foster Grandparent Program and, therefore, what has changed.

Assessing Unmet Needs   As a director of a Foster Grandparent Program, Madeline knows of some of the needs of low-income elders and the children they help, but a look at the history of the program would help her to understand what was originally seen as the need in the 1970s when the program was initiated. She will need to trace the modifications made to the legislation over time by looking at the policies themselves as well as at the content of the hearings at the times of reauthorization. This will give her a background for assessing the unmet needs as articulated in P.L. 111-13.

Madeline must also look at impact data over time from her own agency and from others funded through the policy as it has changed.

The goal here is to determine why the policy continues, after all these years, to target elders with low incomes and to provide them a stipend for the time they spend with their assigned children. What needs remain unmet after all this time? A look at census data will help her trace the dimensions of the size and characteristics of the group targeted by the law. Some investigation of the literature on both elder and children's needs could also help add another empirical dimension to the needs picture, especially related to the changes in the aging population and the changing needs of disabled children.

Identifying Goals and Outcomes of This Policy   The goals and outcomes of the Foster Grandparent Program will become apparent to Madeline as she uses Huttman's questions to interrogate the amendments to the Domestic Services Act under Title II, Subtitle B. She will need to attend to its language and the changes that might have occurred in the program over time. Name changes and changes in what programs are now associated might give information about differing goals and expected outcomes.

Aside from the language of the particular section of the bill itself, commentaries on mandates from such national entities as the National Senior Service Corps will help in articulating goals and outcomes. Contacts at the program office could serve as a sort of triangulation between what she is reading and what the program office interpretation of it is. She will want to hear from her contacts about how drug abuse rehabilitation and treatment, mentoring for low-income youth, energy conservation and environmental protection, and crime prevention activities directed toward low-income or formerly incarcerated youth fit for foster grandparent and other senior programs.

Determining Policy Implementation Strategies   The section of the policy of interest to Madeline should be interrogated to identify eligibility requirements, types of assistance given, and type of organization and staff to illuminate the changes she reads in the policy. In addition, the *Federal Register* will provide information about new proposed rules that will have a direct impact on her program. Fact sheets from national offices related to services for elders and volunteerism will also help. Newsletters and Web sites of volunteer associations may have information on how program changes influence their stakeholders. Guided by Huttman's question "Will the rules and regulations of this policy be workable at the user level?", she will wish to fully study the soon-to-be released rules and regulations. She knows that to be workable in her local area, the rules and regulation will have to be flexible enough to allow her to integrate what seem to be broadened boundaries into her program. Contacts in the state office who oversee the foster grandparent programs will be helpful for local interpretations.

Finding the Scientific Basis of the Policy   To determine the scientific basis of the policy (and to be in line with the latest thinking in empirically based programming), Madeline will want to access the latest research on older volunteers to see how the amended policy conforms with the available evidence and to ascertain what research might guide implementation. Professional organizations such as the American Society on Aging and the National Council on Aging should have material available regarding "best practices" for her to see how these correspond to what she is reading in P.L. 111-13. She needs to look at the research sponsored by such associations as the American Association of Retired Persons (AARP, 2004), well-known foundations such as The Pew Charitable Trust (Pew Research Center, 2005), or Atlantic Philanthropies' support of the American Society on Aging's Civic Engagement project (ASA, 2009). Madeline will want to access gerontological or nonprofit journals that are publishing conceptual and empirical pieces on the subject of civic engagement and aging (e.g., Kaskie, Imhof, Cavanaugh, & Culp, 2008; Morrow-Howell, Hinterlong, Rozario, & Tang, 2003; Tang & Morrow-Howell, 2008; Wollebaek & Selle, 2002) in order to get the facts and compare those with what she sees in the policy.

Since Huttman is a social work professional, her model asks whether this policy follows the principles and practices of the profession. The intent is to require consideration of how professional standards and codes may interface with the policy changes that are occurring. Depending on the professional background that Madeline brings to the situation, she will want to determine whether the principles and practices explicated in the policy fit with her code of ethics.

Identifying the Values Embedded in the Policy   Huttman raises a number of helpful questions that Madeline will want to consider that will make her aware of potential controversies and conflicts as well as compromises and consequences, both intended and unintended, reflected in the final bill. In a way these questions will assist Madeline in being politically savvy rather than simply taking each change at face value. Note that from a rational perspective, the reason one would want to know about the value premises, the groups that have opposed the policy, the compromises made, and the historical precedents, is not for Madeline to oppose the new policy or even question whether it should be implemented. From this approach, she needs to be knowledgeable about the potential conflicts and issues that could precipitate a reaction during implementation. She should be able to determine some of this by looking at the way the media covered the creation of the policy. She should also look at alternative ideological Web sites in addition to those that have been supportive to the process in order to identify potential areas of future conflicts as the policy is implemented.

Locating the Power Bases That Support the Policy   Madeline is in a good position to think about power and special interests, as well as the political decision making that surrounds the making of this policy, particularly in P.L. 111-13, at the national level because she was actually involved as a local advocate for the changes that were being proposed and was very supportive of the final bill that made its way through the Congress. In that process, she recognized that not everyone embraced the changes in the various programs, and she was quite aware of a cadre of foster grandparent directors who worried that broadening the program would dilute their focus.

In order to be a bit more systematic in identifying the power bases that supported the policy, she may want to examine it at both the Congressional and the professional levels. Through membership lists of professional associations, she can identify many of her colleagues who direct other programs. She can develop a grid based on informal conversations to list both concerns and positive positions. Based on hearing testimony, she can do the same at the Congressional level, looking closely at who appeared to provide testimony and categorize that by type. She should also see which legislators were associated with various aspects of the bills as they moved through Congress to actually understand both political and professional power on which the final bill was based. She has some personal and professional experience here, but she must engage in systematic inquiry, which will require her to interrogate both the media and formal hearing records in addition to what she "knows" personally.

Identifying Resources   Review of the final bill will provide information about how resources are intended to be allocated, both geographically and programmatically. She will want to look at any hearing minutes and at rules and procedures to identify the thinking related to resources. She will also want to look closely at the language of the bill to determine what sorts of program resources are acceptable under it. The reports from the Office of Management and Budget should also be investigated to determine whether what is expected based on both state and federal allocations will be feasible. Her main interest is in identifying any additional resources for the expanded vision of the bill. She will also need to use her contacts at the state level to determine what the thinking is related to state and local planning and the resources that might be available there. Of interest as well is knowing whether there is commitment at the state and local levels for long-standing programs or instead there is more enthusiasm for greater competition through allowing new applicants to develop programs in strict compliance with the new rules, while established programs struggle with being forced to change. Her major concern now is the change that allows programs to accept donations. This releases program staff to solicit other sources of funds to support what they do, but it adds different responsibilities to her program.

Identifying Costs and Benefits   Through a thorough analysis of the bill, Madeline is beginning to see that small changes may have big costs. The freedom to solicit funds means less dependence on a particular, predictable grant funding source. Madeline realizes that the directors of many of these programs, including herself, do not have a fundraising or development background. The push toward a diversified funding base may require the development of a new set of skills that many program directors do not have.

There will be many other costs and benefits as program implementation evolves. At the onset, it is clear that the cost-effectiveness mandates of P.L. 111-13, while important for survival in a rational, outcomes-based environment, will require much more program evaluation competence particularly related to statistics and management of quantitative data. Over the years, Madeline has relied on narrative comments that she has collected from her foster grandparent volunteers, to tell the stories of how working with children makes their lives new again. Madeline needs to return to the initial hearings in both houses of Congress to understand what exactly is expected, so that she can make recommendations to her director and the board about ways to assure measurement of program effectiveness according to policy expectations. She notices that the cost-benefit analysis in the policy is an economic one, based on decisions about effectiveness or biggest "bang for the buck" rather than on an assessment of who "wins" and who "loses" as a result of this program. Although being able to show numbers and assess per unit costs are important to hard-pressed decision makers who have multiple policies to monitor and evaluate, she worries that the stories of her foster grandparents will be lost.

CRITIQUE OF THE APPROACH

The Huttman model is comprehensive in that it seeks to look at every aspect of the policy product. It is rational, using words such as *outcomes, strategies,* and *cost-benefits.* The section on the scientific basis of the policy is tied to a traditional, evidence-based practice approach that honors numbers and measurable objectives. Yet the Huttman model contains elements that touch on the subjective elements inherent in any policy, such as values and power. These questions are posed so that the analyst can be politically savvy, understanding the causal elements involved in politics, power, and ideology. The model is not designed to move the analyst to challenge the policy or to advocate for something different. In subsequent chapters on nonrational or critical policy analysis, values and ideology will be central aspects of the analytic process, leading to different analytic results.

USING HOLCOMB AND NIGHTINGALE'S IMPLEMENTATION ANALYSIS MODEL

In Chapter 3, we introduced yet another rational policy analysis approach that is particularly helpful in studying implementation. Holcolmb and Nightingale's (2003) implementation analysis model is reproduced in Box 4.4, and can be added to Madeline's toolbox.

Box 4.4 Holcomb and Nightingale's Implementation Analysis Model

What are the major goals and assumptions underlying the policy that was adopted?

- What are the policy's underlying premises and assumptions?
- What is the policy intended to accomplish?

What is the organizational and service delivery structure and context in which the policy is operationalized?

- How is the organization structured?
- What are staff roles and responsibilities?

(continued)

(continued)
- What organizational arrangements and linkages are in place to deliver services?
- What types of interagency and inter-program interactions and collaborations are involved?

How are key management functions carried out and what role do they play in the program?
- How is program planning structured?
- Who is involved?
- What types of management information are used and for what purposes (e.g., planning, monitoring, performance analysis, performance improvement, evaluation)?

What is the sequence and timing of client activities?
- How do clients learn about and access services?
- How do clients move through a program (e.g., intake, eligibility determination, work orientation, activities)? How is a client's progress tracked and monitored?

What role do contextual factors play in shaping program operations and client outcomes?
- Labor market conditions?
- Fiscal/budgetary conditions?
- Political environment?
- Historic program experience?

Source: Conceptual Underpinnings of Implementation Analysis, by P. A. Holcomb and D. S. Nightingale, 2007. In M. C. Lennon and T. Corbett (Eds.), *Policy in Action: Implementation Research and Welfare Reform* (pp. 39–55). Washington, DC: The Urban Institute Press, p. 50. Used by permission.

In Chapter 3 we suggested,

[I]f Madeline were interested in the programmatic implementation that her program had to achieve in the case example, this policy model would be helpful. She would focus on the organizational and service delivery aspects of the program and would use this approach to track how the agency structured its service delivery in response to the policy, including management and direct practice activities as well as who the client is and how the client is served.

Using this model, some contextual issues such as the current socio-economic and political climate could be interrogated.

TARGETING THE RESEARCH

From the foregoing statement, it seems that Madeline is ready to think about how the new amendments will be implemented in her program. Madeline has a specific policy research question in mind, one that is particularly close to her daily work: What needs to be done in order to accurately implement this policy in compliance with the legislative mandate? Although the *form* of the policy remains P.L. 111-13, she now chooses to examine the policy at a different *level*—the program level. The *focus* of the analysis is now on implementation, and that process occurs in local communities.

Madeline's *justification* of her selection of Holcomb and Nightingale's implementation analysis model is that it primarily focuses on the organizational, managerial, and client concerns in the policy. Her interest is in implementation planning, so this will be a useful model.

Major Goals and Assumptions Using the Holcomb and Nightingale model, Madeline will return to identifying the major underlying premises and assumptions of P.L. 111-13 through a detailed reading of the policy instrument itself. She will need to interrogate the policy for explicit statements about goals and attempt to uncover assumptions that are either explicitly or implicitly stated. She will need to review meeting and hearing records, especially those in the *Congressional Record*, to identify the range of assumptions that were present and to identify those that remained in the final document. She will also need to look for both explicit and implicit goals in the language of the policy. This becomes a baseline from which she can move to implementation.

Operationalization and Service Delivery Once the basic goals and assumptions have been identified, Holcomb and Nightingale move the analysis to implementation. Madeline will be considering her organizational context. She is quite familiar with her agency's structure and her role within it as director of volunteers. She has a copy of the organizational chart that depicts staff roles and copies of job descriptions readily available. She also knows that in carrying out the Foster Grandparent Program, numerous linkages within the organization and across organizations must be nurtured and sustained in order to carry out the programmatic mission. She can articulate these linkages in writing. She will also need to identify the linkages that are in place to deliver services, including the more informal interagency and interprogram collaborations that are involved. She should compare the existing service delivery structure with the stated policy expectations.

Because she is not starting from scratch in implementation, she must look at her current program design to understand what changes must occur for it to remain compliant with the national legislation. At some point, she will need to communicate these changes to the volunteer stations where grandparents connect with children, but more analysis will be necessary before determining the changes that may be needed in operation or service delivery.

Before enacting changes, she knows that she needs to put an information system in place to monitor and evaluate her program's effectiveness, given that P.L. 111-13 is riddled with references to evidence. The Corporation for National and Community Service Web site provides information to illustrate what is now required in order to fully evaluate effectiveness.

Holcomb and Nightingale's questions about interactions and collaborations bring up a host of important issues that must be identified and considered for compliance with policy expectations. In her case, Madeline recognizes that the increased push for accountability implicates teachers in classrooms, day care providers, and a host of other stations in which staff are overextended already. She will need to determine the degree to which she will need to mandate data collection and to have systems in place that assure that appropriate informed consent is obtained for release of these data. Once everything has been determined, she realizes the changes put pressure on her to communicate these mandates to everyone involved in the agency's foster parent operation.

Key Management Functions   Based on her reading of P.L. 111-13, Madeline should be able to respond to the questions raised by Holcomb and Nightingale regarding program planning, who is to be involved, and information management expectations. At her level, she will need to articulate who is involved in program planning under P.L. 111-13 and how the program planning is structured. She will also need to identify who is involved at all levels of the program. Finally, she needs to identify from the law itself and the rules and procedures that have come from either the federal or the state level what data will be necessary for program planning and the monitoring of all aspects of the program, including performance analysis and improvement, as well as program evaluation. She is interested in determining what is expected and what will be possible among the various organizations involved in her program. She will need to know how data are collected in order to push for a plan that leads to the most uniformity possible. In order to carry out the required management functions, she must find a rational way to combine the requirements of the various organizations with which she works into a reasonable, quantifiable management information system for her program.

Client Activities   Questions about clients and how they move through the program allow Madeline to define exactly who her clients are. As a director of volunteers, Madeline sees the volunteers as her clients, yet they are being recruited to serve others (and these are her secondary clients). She needs to determine the profile of the volunteers including their skills and interests as a beginning point for effective interventions with the populations they serve. If she does not have information in her existing information system, she will need to identify in a systematic way how volunteers learn about her program. She also needs to be clear about the various activities in which they can be involved in the current program and how it may need to change. If she were to develop a traditional management information system in which recruitment, retention, and recognition form the basis of her practice, she would have forms in place to document every step, including criminal background check and health assessment forms to aid in responding to and assessing this aspect of the policy analysis.

Contextual Factors   After having focused internally on policy and program implementation, Holcomb and Nightingale raise questions about the role of contextual factors in shaping program operations and client outcomes. Madeline, using media and other financial sources, should investigate how labor market conditions and the current downturn in the economy may be impacting volunteerism. Aside from financial and traditional media sources, Web sites on the subject and fugitive data available through agency and advocacy groups will be of help. She will want to study the trends in civic engagement that are being tracked by national think tanks such as Independent Sector. These trends will relate to fiscal and budgetary conditions in a political environment in which there is a great deal of uncertainty. She may also wish to check YouTube and talk radio to capture the general political environment beyond her own personal ideology in order to assess objections or other problems with this particular policy at the state and local levels. These have the potential to influence her own program design and implementation. It is also useful to look at past program experiences with other policy changes. What do historical annual reports, grant funding reports, and board minutes suggest about challenges and opportunities for which she might be prepared?

CRITIQUE OF THE APPROACH

This approach provides a process analysis of implementation based on a rational view of the world. It is based on an effectiveness-based program perspective that seeks predetermined, measurable client outcomes. Beginning with identifying policy assumptions, the analyst using this model moves through a set of traditional questions about organizational and service delivery issues. Built into the model are additional assumptions that there will be a traditional set of managerial functions structured in an identifiable way and focused on the linear process of planning, monitoring, performance analysis, performance improvement, and evaluation. Unlike some rational models, this one pays attention to context in order to determine what may enhance or impede policy or program implementation.

The strength of this approach is that its linearity aligns well with the expectations of a law such as the one Madeline is implementing. The amendments are aligned with an evidence-based, traditional approach to accountability and documentation. On the other hand, the questions asked script the analyst into a traditional managerial and program-matic process and do not open the possibility of using a nonrational or nontraditional approach to planning and implementation.

USING SEGAL AND BRUZUZY'S QUESTIONS FOR SOCIAL WELFARE POLICY ANALYSIS

The final important aspect of policy practice and policy research is at the "so what" level. What did the policy produce related to the social problem that the policy was intended to address? In Chapter 3, we introduced some possible questions to ask about impact and we reintroduce those in Box 4.5.

Box 4.5 Segal and Bruzuzy's Questions for Social Welfare Policy Analysis

What is the social problem?
- What is the problem?
- definitions?

- Extent of problem?
- Who defines this as a problem?
- Who disagrees?
- Related social values?
- Competing social values?
- Underlying causes or factors?

What is the policy goal?

- What is the general goal?
- Are there subgoals?
- Do the subgoals conflict?

What is relevant policy/legislation?

- What is/are relevant public policies?
- If there are no public policies, why?
- What are the objectives of the policies?
- Are there hidden agendas?
- Who supports the policies?
- Who opposes the policies?

How was implementation?

- What is/are the social programs implemented as a result of the policies?
- Are the programs effective?
- strengths?
- weaknesses?

Who are the affected populations?

- Who is touched by the policy and programs?
- Are there positive effects?
- Are there negative effects?

What is the intended impact?

- What is supposed to be the result?
- Who was supposed to have been affected?
- How has the social problem supposed to have been changed?

What is the actual impact?

- Costs and benefits?
- Is the social problem changed?
- If so, how?
- Are there unintended results?

Source: Social Welfare Policy, Programs, and Practice (p. 66), by E. Segal and S. Bruzuzy, 1998, Itasca, IL: F. E. Peacock. Used by permission.

In Chapter 3 we stated,

> [I]f Madeline were interested in another way to follow the social problem through to the policy response and actual impact—especially if she was interested in seeing what caused what at each stage of development—she would identify the social problem, the goals of the Serve America Act, and what was included in the policy as well as how implementation progressed, at least during that first year. In looking at implementation, who was actually affected and whether or not what happened was intended or unintended would be considered.

Segal and Bruzuzy's model allows Madeline to investigate causal notions related to policy action.

TARGETING THE RESEARCH

Because Madeline will have a great deal of interest in what happens as a result of this policy, she might frame a *research question* as follows: Was the agency's foster grandparent program effective? Madeline is wondering whether her program implemented under P.L. 111-13 worked. The policy *form* then is programmatic, and it is at the organizational *level*. The focus of Madeline's policy research is on policy impact or performance. *Justification of the analytic approach* rests on her interest in accountability and the expectation in the Act that accountable programs with well documented, predetermined outcomes will be produced. Segal and Bruzuzy's model will help her to do so.

To demonstrate the application of this model, it will be necessary to imagine that Madeline is engaging in her policy analysis research one year after the Act's implementation. Imagine that P.L. 111-13 has now been in force for over a year and Madeline has carefully followed the steps for developing an evidence-based program. She begins her analysis with an examination of the social problem.

Social Problem   Madeline, based on her thorough analysis of P.L. 111-13, is aware of the social problems that the public law was intended to address. For this analysis to make sense, she must compare the understanding of the social problem at the national level with the way it has been defined locally—and more specifically in her program. She will want to compare the national information with what was developed in the state plan that was the source of her funding to see whether there are major discrepancies there, before moving to an analysis at her agency and programmatic levels. As she tries to identify the local problems with foster grandparents and the children they serve, she looks to the information system used by the agency. To determine how her program has performed in relation to the problems that the program is expected to address, the agency management information system must be able to manage performance-based programming, including all the elements required at the state and national levels for accountability.

A year ago and for many years before that, her agency was reporting inputs. Because the change in the law called for outputs and outcomes rather than inputs, much work was done to change the agency's accountability system. Soon after the signing of the legislation, Madeline and other volunteer manager colleagues joined together to develop information systems to collect relevant data on their program's performance. This took a great deal of time and required returning to some college texts on standardization and performance-based measurement, but as she prepares an annual report she is confident that she will have the needed data.

Goal Based on her reading of the law and her assessment of much of the commentary on relevant Web sites and printed material from organizations and associations interested in the content of the Act, she is able to articulate the goal of the overall bill and the specific goals of the Foster Grandparent Program. In preparation for implementation, Madeline located best practices for meeting these goals by searching Web sites of programs in other parts of the country and used this information in shaping the changes in her own program.

Policy and Legislation Obviously, these changes were driven by public policy. Madeline, a year into the process of implementation, is well aware of the content of P.L. 111-13, especially as it relates to the Foster Grandparent Program, but she continues to watch the public dialogue on traditional media sources as well as Web sites to see whether the original supporters and opposers are still present. Because many conversations have occurred over the year with colleagues and state-level decision makers, she has a sense of the political will regarding the current state of the policy in general and her program in particular.

Implementation So many programs were affected by P.L. 111-13 that Madeline has lost count. She is focusing on the Foster Grandparent Program, but that is one of a triad of programs that comprise the

National Senior Service Corps. The policy had amended the National and Community Service Act of 1990 as well, and there were four sets of programs affected: (1) the School-Based and Community-Based Service-Learning programs and Higher Education Innovative Programs for Community Service, also known as Learn and Serve programs; (2) National Service Trust programs, also known as AmeriCorps; (3) the Civilian Community Corps Demonstration program; and (4) the Investment for Quality and Improvement program.

Madeline realized that each set of programs should be examined for effectiveness, but she really is focused only on her own program's effectiveness as she prepares for another round of requests for proposals and grant proposal writing. She has the effectiveness data for her own program, but she is interested in seeing how her data compare with other similar programs and, in fact, all the programs implemented under P.L. 111-13. She thinks this comparative data might be instructive for her agency, and if her data hold up in the comparison, it might be helpful as the agency applies for further funding. She searches the Internet to locate programs that have reported data. She could also ask program officers at the National and Community Service Corporation for model effectiveness-based programs that have outcome measurements built into their systems. Her idea is to compare what her logic model has produced with other program evaluations that use performance-based programming.

Affected Populations   To determine populations affected by her programs, Madeline could list all the stations (various sites) in which she placed grandparents by types and by numbers and types of children served. As the program shifted due to P.L. 111-13, different locations were added serving slightly different kinds of youth. She would need to look at the differences between the "old" stations and the newer ones as she measured positive and negative effects related to such dimensions as increased social skills, increased acceptable behaviors, and increased flexibility in social interactions and settings. She would measure the degree to which volunteers were able to provide advice, emotional support, companionship, and opportunities for socialization (Newman, 2002). The Center for Evidence Based Social Sciences gave her ideas about what older adult mentors could provide, but she could also look at what they gained or gave up as a result of their efforts.

Intended Impact   Rather than totally relying on herself to develop impact measures, Madeline was able to access a number of tools and examples for evaluating volunteer and service programs available through the National Resource Center Web site. These are the preferred measurement tools, because they are rather standard and the data they produce will be what reviewers will expect when they review her continuation grant application. When she and other directors met to develop information systems, they were quite aware of the National Resource Center's impact measures, and she, for one, folded them into the changes in the agency's management system. She is aware that the language of reporting changed as well, not only because of what was present in P.L. 111-13, but also based on what she has seen in "exemplary reports" that were shared with her by the state program officers. In her proposal she avoided narratives whenever possible and proposed numbers to document impact according to categories of service in relation to community need with service activities, inputs, outputs, and outcomes to declare her intended program impact.

Actual Impact   Madeline has restructured her program evaluation to assess costs and benefits, so for the first time she has the capacity to respond to questions that go beyond service activities and inputs. Because she may not have the statistical ability, she may want to locate a faculty member at a local university to assist in designing an impact study for her.

One problem she encountered, however, was in determining immediate, intermediate, and ultimate (final) outcomes. Impacting the social problem is an ultimate outcome, and no matter what she was able to collect, her outcomes seemed modest. For example, she had data that indicated youth who had foster grandparents expressed increased self-esteem, but she did not have comparative data for youth who did not have a grandparent volunteer. In addition, she hypothesized that increased self-esteem would serve youth well in terms of continuing in school, graduating, and eventually becoming self-sufficient. These would be ultimate outcomes, but they would have to be tracked longitudinally, and a year was simply too short a time to know whether the program has been effective in addressing the social problem identified in P.L. 111-13.

CRITIQUE OF THE APPROACH

Segal and Bruzuzy's approach begins with background information on the social problem, goal, and policy/legislation and then moves to areas that are more aligned with impact. The underlying assumption is that there is a causal relationship between the problem, the goals, and the impact. The impact is intended to reduce the problem and hopefully eliminate it. Traditional ways of thinking about impact from a rational perspective are reflected in the questions asked. There is an inherent assumption of linearity in this approach, which fits well with the contemporary evidence-based movement. This approach does not seek great complexity. In fact, it is reductionist, moving from stating a social problem to resolving it. This is a clear causally linked process that does allow for the identification of off-targeting if the intent is different from the actual impact. However, there is little attention given to the socio-political context or to any opportunity to assess the more affective or ideological dimensions of the policy process and its implications.

DISCUSSION

Rational approaches to policy analysis are linear and reductionist, requiring a focused stance and a somewhat narrowing analytic space. Though our discussion of approaches throughout this chapter appeared to have similar starting points in the application of the approaches, this is because most models, even if they are focused later in the policy process, are built on the "if/then" aspect of linear causal modeling, which requires clarity about the problem definition and the goals of the policy in order to make any assessment of the subsequent steps. The rational process takes a step-by-step, fairly prescribed approach that is intended to lead the analyst toward a tidy ending. One begins at the beginning in a rational approach as opposed to the interpretive, nonrational approaches presented in the following chapters; in these, one starts where one can.

The types of policy questions that are usefully answered by application of rational approaches typically seek manageability and reduce complexity. Description and causation are of interest. Questions that focus on causation do not seek deep meanings or multiple understandings; rather, they push the analyst to focus on what can be measured and well documented to link cause with consequence. Questions that assist the analyst in coming to a parsimonious conclusion about what is right or wrong or true or untrue are congruent with this perspective, because the production of a succinct report of findings is desired in rational models. Probably the major reason for this is that decision makers are overstretched and interested in "bottom line" information for decision making. Rational models are not focused on how everyone "feels" about the policy, but politics and influence are important aspects of the analysis in that it is important to know the arguments the opposition is making to be able to counter them throughout the entire policy process. Evidence is assumed to be more powerful than values and ideology. Policy questions asking for cause, prediction, objective costs, and efficiencies are appropriate here.

From this chapter's discussion, most of the skills necessary to effectively and productively engage in rational policy analysis should be clear. The policy analyst using a rational approach will principally need quantitative skills. Managing numbers and statistics will be a primary undertaking. Qualitative or word data will be only descriptively useful, and the terms used should be defined or operationalized. The rational analyst should be a skilled library researcher as well as a focused person capable of conveying a well-articulated message in a logical and cogent manner.

CONCLUDING REMARKS ABOUT RATIONAL POLICY ANALYSIS

Typically, the best defense of a rational approach to policy analysis is the ability to demonstrate that a particular policy research and analysis question can be appropriately answered through the application of the chosen approach. Being able to articulate why the approach is well targeted to the form, level, and focus of the question will also be helpful. Further defense of what is done in the analytic process can be made on the basis of the rigor of the analyst. The well-positioned analyst will knowingly assert that the underlying assumptions of the policy question establish a paradigmatic location for the analysis. This is done by evaluating the aims and goals of the analysis for fit. In doing so, the analyst must be certain that there are no assumptions present that suggest an incorrect understanding about what can be accomplished by a rational policy analysis approach. Then the analyst applies the standards for the analysis design with the quality or rigor that is consistent with a rational paradigm.

The models presented in this chapter are objectivist. Generalization could be possible if they are used within the rules of rigor needed for generalizability. This sort of analysis recognizes the importance of finding the best way, the best practices, and a consistent measurement of success in implementation. Although context and issues surrounding the policy must be recognized, this information is required to avoid being surprised or taken off guard, rather than to delve into the complexity. There is efficiency built into the rational approach, in hopes that there will be no time wasted in processing ideas and different perspectives without coming to the right conclusion and to move things forward to the desired conclusion.

DISCUSSION QUESTIONS

1. Many people are challenged by the demands of rational modes of thinking, especially if their first language is not English. Those who think nonrationally sometimes feel that they are incompetent thinkers because of their holistic approach to information processing. Where is your comfort zone for rationality? What is necessary for you to skillfully engage in this approach to policy analysis research?
2. Look at all the approaches to policy analysis discussed in both Chapters 3 and 4. Identify the theories (rational choice, decision, and/or game theory) that are guiding each. Can you identify any dimensions of those theories present that were not discussed? Are there also other theories influencing the structures of the rational models of policy analysis?
3. Your research question will determine the approach needed. Based on a policy with which you are familiar, write a research question that would require a rational approach. Show why this question fits with a rational approach.
4. The approaches highlighted in this chapter are not standardized tools. Thus, there may be other questions that one might ask that are equally helpful to the analytical process. If you were constructing a rational policy analysis framework to examine a policy approved by a local human service agency's board of directors, are there particular questions that you would want to include? Provide a rationale for your choices.
5. Rational policy analysis approaches typically narrow rather than broaden the complexity of a situation. When do you think it is important to be more focused and to narrow the analysis process? If you were working in a nonrational environment, in which getting to generalizable information was not highly valued, how might you persuade your colleagues to use a rational approach?
6. Pose a question about a policy with which you are familiar. Practice targeting your research by identifying the form, level (and scope), and focus of your analysis. Then select an appropriate framework and analyze the policy. Upon completion, talk about what you learned in the process, what you would do differently in the future, and the benefits and challenges you encountered.

CHAPTER 5

Nonrational Policy Analysis

I N CHAPTER 2, we introduced the interpretive/constructivist paradigm and the idea of interpretive, nonrational approaches to policy
analysis. In this chapter, we provide more detail by exploring
nonrational themes and assumptions, along with the major theories
that inform nonrational approaches and nontraditional strategies for
understanding policy. The research aspect of nontraditional approaches
to policy analysis also begins with determination of the reason or goals
for the analysis. In this chapter, we continue the discussion of the history
of the development of science, with a focus on the basis of the
criticism of positivism and postpositivism and the limits of rational
thought and linear reasoning. We will demonstrate how certain
purposes of policy analysis lend themselves to particular analytical
approaches; this time we focus on nonrational analysis. We will detail
what is contained in a well-constructed nonrational approach to
policy analysis and end with various examples of nonrational
approaches aimed at differing units of analysis, demonstrating
how these exemplars are compatible with more interpretive goals of
developing policy through diverse participation based on recognition
and management of power and politics. We close this chapter by
presenting ways to determine whether an approach is indeed nonrational and a discussion of what is gained and what is given up by
applying this alternative. In Chapter 6, we demonstrate how to apply
selected nonrational approaches to policy analysis.

REASON AND NONRATIONALITY

Although there were diverse strands of thought that have questioned
rationality, Lejano (2006) credits Wittgenstein's (1922) challenge of the

notion of logic as the "most profoundly" influential in opening doors for alternative ways of thinking about policy (2006, p. 89). Wittgenstein argued that all knowledge was a "form of language game . . . [thus] if everything was a language game, then all alternative constructs were equally valid." This challenged the core concepts of the Enlightenment, "namely the primacy of the ratio (the cognitive subject) and sense (the empiricist route to knowledge). Later, writers "would argue how science itself was a social construct, subject to tradition, consensus, and prejudice" (Lejano, 2006, p. 89).

Recognition of nonrationality, along with more heuristic or circular ways of knowing, came to the forefront of philosophical thought with the development of mid-twentieth-century postmodern philosophy of science. With the postmodern critique of positivism also came recognition (with the help of continental rationalism) that nonlinear thought could be a valid and systematic way of knowing. Thus, the "many ways of knowing" literature included a variety of ways of being rational (see Dean, 1989; Fraser, Taylor, Jackson, & O'Jack, 1991; Gottschalk & Witkin, 1991; Hartman, 1990; Imre, 1984). Nonrationality, for the most part, ceased being lumped with irrationality and magical thinking and took its rightful place as a legitimate and respectable aspect of scientific and paradigmatic thought.

Given the authority granted to nonrationality, the idea of what constitutes legitimate science expanded. Not only was science as a product (that which has been arrived at through reductionist means) important, but science as a process was recognized (Heron, 1981). Practical knowledge coming from both skill and creativity as well as experiential knowledge coming from intuition and experience were seen to be important in context-embedded reciprocal, open inquiry. No longer was induction preferred over deduction; both were appreciated. No longer were space and time irrelevant or controlled for. It was not as though "anything goes"; in fact, new and rigorous ways to avoid reductionism were developed.

To get to the complexity of the modern world, it was recognized that reductionism must be replaced by holism. The assumption was that complexity was not static but was an emergent social process created by those engaged in the process. Knowledge building began to be considered as a mix of rationality, serendipity, and intuition (Dilthey, 1976; Polanyi, 1962)—an essentially nonlinear, iterative, emergent way of enacting the business of science. The preferred type of reason in this way of thinking about systematic knowing became nonrational because of its ability to hold paradoxical positions when confronted with complexity. A more fluid notion of thought, using induction and deduction, analogy and metaphor, along with information coming from measurement, was recognized as a means to allow more holistic findings to emerge. The reductionism of rational, linear thought was rejected based on the recognition that in complexity (where cause cannot actually be identified, only networks of associations), anything may be important and should be considered in order to make the best sense out of what is being interrogated. The amorphous, comprehensive, circular thought pattern of nonrationality fit well with the alternative, more interpretive approach to knowing seen in the interpretive/constructivist paradigm.

NONRATIONAL ASSUMPTIONS OF THE INTERPRETIVIST/ CONSTRUCTIVIST PARADIGM

It is likely that the interpretivist/constructivist paradigm and nonrationality as a systematic way of knowing have probably always been present, but because of the strength of the promise of positivism, they all but disappeared in any explicit discussion of science and the scientific method. The subjective, interactive nature of the creativity at the base of nonrational thought probably continues to be present in positivist scientific "breakthroughs." It is probably part of the decision-making process as research designs emerged in traditional research projects. Until the critique of positivism and postpositivism was in full swing, we suspect some degree of subjectivity was recognized by scientists, but it was not much talked about—or worse, it was feared to be an indication of less than rigorous science.

In many ways, interpretivism/constructivism is a reaction to the limits of positivism and postpositivism. In other ways, it is a wholly new way of enacting science. To fully understand the need for the creation of alternative paradigms including interpretivism and the critical paradigm that we will explore later, it is important to understand some of the major criticisms of positivism. Lincoln and Guba (1985) provide a succinct characterization of these criticisms:

- Positivism leads to an inadequate conceptualization of what science is.
- Positivism is unable to deal adequately with the problem of induction and the theory-ladenness of facts.
- Positivism is overly dependent on operationalism.

- Positivism has at least two consequences that are both repugnant and unfounded—determinism and reductionism.
- Positivism has produced research with human respondents that ignores their humanness, a fact that has not only ethical but also validity implications.
- Positivism falls short of being able to deal with emergent conceptual/empirical formulations from a variety of fields.
- Positivism rests upon at least five assumptions that are increasingly difficult to maintain:
  ○ The assumption of a single, tangible reality "out there" that can be broken apart and studied independently.
  ○ The assumption about the possibility of separation of the observer from the observed.
  ○ The assumption of the temporal and contextual independence of observations, so that what is true in one time and place is also true at another time and place.
  ○ The assumption of linear causality—that there are no effects without causes and no causes without effects.
  ○ The assumption of value freedom guaranteed by methodological control (Lincoln & Guba, 1985, pp. 25–28).

Interpretivism/constructivism attempts to counter these and other criticisms through the creation of an alternative paradigmatic perspective. Recall the framework from Figure 2.1 in Chapter 2. Interpretivism/constructivism seeks meaning or understanding, rather than order, control, or generalizability (Imre, 1985; Tyson, 1995). It does this through a decidedly relativist stance, allowing for a multiplicity of meanings to form the complexity necessary to arrive at a deep and rich understanding of a situation. There is recognition that individual consciousness and subjectivity are basic to complex understanding (Dilthey, 1976; Polanyi, 1966). Finally, this perspective is nonrational.

A nonrational approach to policy analysis links to interpretivist/constructivist assumptions. First, the nonrational policy analyst is a relativist, believing that there are multiple, competing truths. Depending on the context, one truth might be pragmatically better than another for now, but maybe not forever. Second, the analyst is subjectivist in orientation in that personal needs satisfaction (read power and politics) are assumed to play an important part in the policy process.

This subjectivist position suggests that the meaning of all aspects of the policy process becomes important in understanding any other aspect of the policy. It is assumed that influence in all its various forms, rather than objective facts, plays an important part in decisions at all levels, so that determining what is "good" or "bad" in policy represents managing truths that are multiple and competing. The process will be fraught with conflict, if not dialectical discussions and power politics. The selection of the policy alternative, then, is based on the position(s) having the most influence. Box 5.1 contains a list of the major assumptions about policy analysis that characterize this approach.

Box 5.1 Nonrational Policy Analysis Assumptions

- There are multiple, competing truths.
- Reasoning is by metaphor and analogy.
- Decisions are based on power and politics.
- Context will have everything to do with the selection and success of a policy.
- The goal of policy analysis is to include diversity and recognition of power to lead to better understanding in selecting the "best fit" within context.

Recognized multiplicity and the existence and types of influence in policy suggest a belief in the power of connection and collaboration in successful policy making and analysis. There is a belief that diversity and recognition of power will allow better understandings of policy and policy contexts. This is, in fact, the goal of nonrational analysis. Nonrational approaches to analysis are assumed to be better suited for this type of multilayered analysis. Primary strategies that assure that the approach is multiperspectival, pragmatic, and pluralistic are listed in Box 5.2. These strategies are intended to capture the diversity of perspectives for a full and rich understanding of the policy.

Box 5.2 Nonrational Policy Analysis Strategies

- Policy analysis is nonlinear; one starts where one can.
- Policy analysis must include multiple understandings or perspectives.
- There are no fixed sequences of analytic steps; one goes where sense can be made.
- Decisions are made with clarity and reason, but of a more fluid and circular type.
- Decisions are made based on influence.
- Policy decisions result from making sense of paradox and politics.

Review again the interpretive/constructivist perspective in Guba's (1999) framework (Figure 2.1 in Chapter 2) to assess the degree to which these assumptions and strategies are paradigmatically linked. Here, as with rational models of policy analysis, understanding the paradigmatic linkage will aid in assessing the quality and the appropriateness of an interpretive, nonrational approach for an analytic project. Failure to assure that both the policy question and the analytic approach are situated in the same paradigmatic perspective will create havoc in the process and product.

NONRATIONAL APPROACHES TO POLICY ANALYSIS

Classical, rational policy analysis assumed that a social problem was like a disease—that conditions cause problems and needs are real. In Chapter 3, we saw models that generally followed some aspect of the following four steps: (1) description of problem and cause, (2) discussion of competing solutions, (3) general implementation problems, and (4) evaluation of policy implementation for improvement. In a rational approach, the idea is that the prescriptive analytic process can produce recommendations that allow a focus on the democratic ideal of improving the social order. While what we consider here is also focused on improving the social order; there are no prescribed steps when an interpretive/constructivist perspective guides the nonrational policy analysis. Rather, more philosophical ideals are present. Nonrational approaches are much more fluid and much less linear ways to establish the context-embedded nature of the multiple truths that are nonrationally interrogated. Here, you will see that there are no steps that must precede subsequent steps. Rather, one starts where one can to construct the information necessary to complete the analysis, and the analysis is complete when all aspects of the approach have been attended to.

A nonrational approach creates quite a challenge for those who are willing to see policy analysis as research, as long as it fits within the traditional positivist/postpositivist expectations for rigor and good science, because the approach is so different. Hopefully, in this section, aside from expanding your horizons about tools and resources for policy analysis, we can also expand your vision of what can constitute rigor in an alternative but still systematic research process. In an interpretive/constructivist perspective about knowledge building, there are differing expectations about what constitutes good science and what degree of rigor is appropriate to support the epistemological assumptions of the paradigm.

The interpretive/constructivist paradigm is concerned with understanding the world as it is: the fundamental nature of the world at the level of subjective experience. This embraces an "emic" or insider's view rather than an "etic" or outsider's view of reality. Rather than establishing expectations of rigor consonant with the traditional scientific method, in this view, rigor becomes a matter of making the values and biases of all stakeholders explicitly part of an evolving inquiry process. Rigor requires clarifying the contextual influences in the meaning-making results. The inquiry process emerges through iterative stages. Language is personal and informal and based on definitions that emerge during the inquiry. The real test of the quality of the results rests with the participants and whether or not they see relevance and meaning in the product. Because no generalizability is expected or desired, all findings are held tentatively; the usefulness of the inquiry product must be determined not only by those engaged in the process, but also by those who are interrogating the results who will determine the degree to which the result in one context can be transferred to another context.

It may come as little surprise that this approach to rigor and the general assumptions of the context-embedded nature of knowledge plays havoc with the usefulness of traditional classical theories. Most theories or theoretical frameworks have been developed with the assumption of objectivity for generalizability. In short, most theories are prescriptive. Such theories will be of little help in expanding the context-embedded assumptions of an interpretivist/constructivist paradigm. Here, in most cases, the useful theory is the one that grows from an inquiry process and is used to capture knowledge grounded in a particular time and place. Generally speaking, these are descriptive (nonprescriptive) theories. We highlight three such theories here: multiple streams theory, social construction theory, and advocacy coalition theory.

MULTIPLE STREAMS THEORY

Kingdon (1995) uses the phrase "an idea whose time has come" to capture the basic premise underlying multiple streams theory (MS). The intent of MS is to recognize that it is often hard to fully understand just how one issue rises to the surface and becomes the emergent concern at a particular time, when other issues do not even get to the agenda-setting stage. Why do individuals and decision-making entities attend to certain subjects and not even seem to notice (and certainly do not pursue) others? MS is particularly concerned with the predecision process in which something bubbles up, and in understanding how things happen, what makes them take a spotlight in the political arena, and why some endure whereas others do not capture the public's attention.

Multiple streams theory was developed with national government public policies in mind, yet it applies to a variety of policy types. Its focus is on the ambiguity (having many different ways of thinking about the same situation) that accompanies policy making as a process, with a special applicability to agenda setting and decision making (formulation). Three separate but parallel streams (problems, policies, and politics) are seen as converging into the policy process. Each stream has its own rules and dynamics, and the streams flow together at critical junctures when policy entrepreneurs see windows of opportunity opening (Zahariadis, 2007). Policy windows are often fleeting, and they may open at unexpected times. But when they do open, policy entrepreneurs defined as "individuals or corporate actors who attempt to couple the three streams" and who "are power brokers and manipulators of problematic preferences and unclear technology" must "immediately seize the opportunity to initiate action" (Zahariadis, 2007, p. 74).

Kingdon (1995) has a specific definition of agenda as the list of subjects or problems to which policy makers pay attention. The agenda-setting process is one in which that list is narrowed and it is not easy to predict what will make the short list. A decision agenda is one in which the items that remain on the list are actively pursued and a set of possible alternatives form the potential actions that can be taken. Kingdon is clear that agendas and alternatives are different, one being the list of problems and the other being the list of potential solutions. Since there is ambiguity and unpredictability in the process, Kingdon carries on the tradition of Cohen, March, and Olsen's (1972) garbage can approach to decision making in organizations in which choice is more than the aggregation of what a number of individuals think about the problem. It is a contextually driven process in which cognitive and affective thinking intertwines. Since the systems in which policies are developed are constantly changing, there is more than one way in which change can occur. Choice is seen as a garbage can into which various perspectives about the situation are dumped, without any one person controlling the dynamic process. "The problem under conditions of ambiguity is that we don't know what the problem is; its definition is vague and shifting" (Zahariadis, 2007, p. 67).

When there is ambiguity, participants in the process will attempt to make sense out of what is happening, to search for some form of order, and to reduce the contradictions and paradoxes. This sense-making process (Weick, 1979) holds three basic assumptions: (1) "individual attention or processing is serial, systemic attention or processing is parallel; (2) policy makers operate under significant time constraints; and (3) the streams flowing through the system are independent" (Zahariadis, pp. 68–69). Serendipity plays a role in the policy process, making this theory fit within the interpretive/constructivist paradigm in which it is simply not possible to predetermine an outcome. Depending on what happens in the process, policies will emerge in somewhat unpredictable and unique ways.

In an example illustrating multiple streams theory, one state legislature is attempting to deal with the public school challenges involving aging structures, incomplete responses to the Americans with Disabilities Act (ADA), technological needs, low test scores, and a growing dropout rate during a time of shrinking resources. These problems are being identified at many levels just as a great push is being made for both charter schools and a voucher system to bring private schools into the state funding process. This is all occurring at a time of great pushing and pulling between the conservative and liberal wings of both the Democratic and Republican parties in the state. Movement towards charter schools began informally when the newly elected governor appointed as the Secretary of Education someone who has a national reputation regarding charter schools, but the legislative session ends before any specific decisions can be made other than significantly cutting state support to local school systems. In this case, depending on what happens as a result of the serious budget cuts, the policy-making process may well include not only charter schools but vouchers.

SOCIAL CONSTRUCTION THEORY

Building on the original work of Berger and Luckmann (1976) regarding the social construction of reality and the evolution of constructivism and constructionism (see Gergen & Davis, 1985; Keeney, 1983; Maturana, 1988; Varela, 1989; Watzlawick, 1984) in the 1980s, policy theorists introduced the idea that policy makers socially constructed target populations and rated their worthiness or unworthiness as well as the potential benefits or burdens that should be provided to address these populations' problems. Given these social constructions, it becomes more understandable why policies reflect the prejudices held by dominant societal groups about citizens who do not conform to the worthiness criterion. This theory assists in understanding how inequities and privileges get built into policies. Social construction can be defined as "a world-shaping exercise or, at least, encompassing varying ways in which the 'realities' of the world are defined" that includes "images, stereotypes, and assignment of values to objects, people, and events" (Ingram, Schneider, & deLeon, 2007, p. 95). To complicate the situation, there are typically competing social constructions based on different beliefs, experiences, and projected consequences, making politics a continual struggle for one social construction to be accepted over another.

Social construction theory is largely contextually driven, recognizing that past and current policy designs convey messages about target populations that become part of institutions and culture. Even target groups internalize their experiences with how they are treated, incorporating their participation (or not) into the policy process into their view of themselves. Policy-making dynamics, based on what has come before and which social constructions have been privileged, lead to future policy designs, and the cycle reinforces itself. "These policy designs usually reproduce the prevailing institutional culture, power relationships, and social constructions, but at times depart from this pattern and introduce change" (Ingram, Schneider, & deLeon, 2007, p. 97).

"Like belief systems, social constructions influence individual choices and actions. Thus, the decision-making model within social construction theory requires people who respond to and manipulate symbols, whose beliefs filter information, and who act on their biases; otherwise, social constructions would have little staying power, and consequently, little explanatory power" (Schlager, 2007, p. 302). Regardless of whether one is examining a material resource that is distributed as a result of an enacted policy or of the lack thereof, social construction theory posits that each action (or inaction) has an accompanying symbolic interpretation that carries a message about what is valued and what is not valued.

Central to the theory are two dimensions that characterize the construction of target populations. The first dimension is the strength of the target group in terms of its political resources as well as how mobilized or united it is. In other words, is this group isolated from political power or is it an active player within the political domain, and how much power does the group already have to influence change?

The second dimension is the social construction of the group along a positive to negative perception. Ingram, Schneider, and deLeon (2007) identify four groups that reflect variance in these two dimensions. *Advantaged* groups have more resources and enjoy a more favorable social construction, whereas groups of *contenders* have political clout but are negatively seen as selfish or suspect. *Dependent* groups are those that are favorably constructed as deserving (e.g., widows and orphans) but lack political power, whereas *deviants* lack both positive social construction and political power. Deviants then receive disproportionate shares of punishments and burdens.

Based on the social constructions and power of target groups, there are various elements of policy design (e.g., rationales, rules, tools, and delivery structures) that can be used to move toward action. These built-in design elements become critical variables in analyzing the implementation of policy because the perceptions of the targeted group literally get folded into the policies and programs that carry out the policy directives. "Considerable evidence supports the contention that there are distinctive differences in policy designs for disadvantaged, contender, dependent, and deviant target groups, with advantaged being treated far better than the others" (Ingram, Schneider, & deLeon, 2007, p. 106). Differences may be found in how treatment is provided, what benefits are distributed, how people are perceived by service providers, what rules apply, what punishments are meted out, and in connection with many other intervention activities.

An example of social construction theory in a policy arena occurred within one state in which a bill had been introduced into the state legislature to add "sexual orientation and gender identity" to the State's Bill of Rights. The bill made its way through one chamber, to be tabled in a subcommittee of the other and left for dead since it was close to the end of session. The state's attorney general, seeing an opportunity to reinforce the fact that this status characteristic was not part of state law, sent a long memorandum to the public universities within the state indicating that their inclusion of sexual orientation and gender identity was out of compliance with state nondiscrimination policy. This set in motion a wave of rallies, forums, protests, and letter writing campaigns about the importance of sexual orientation and gender identity. Note the power of socially constructed terms packed with deep emotional meanings on the parts of protesters as well as on the part of conservative political figures who advocated against this language being incorporated into university or state policies.

Advocacy Coalition Theory

Recognizing the growing dissatisfaction with a highly rational approach to policy analysis in which one step leads to another in a linear way, Jenkins-Smith and Sabatier (1994) elaborated on their advocacy coalition theory (ACT). Designed to understand policy change over a long period of time (decades), ACT considers the relevancy of policy-driven learning that occurs during and over the long haul. Much like the concept of the learning organization, ACT recognizes the changing preferences and beliefs of the critical actors who participate in the process. As new information is filtered through actors' experience, beliefs may change in process. The emphasis of ACT is multiunit in that its focus is multidimensional problem definition, policy formulation, adoption, and evaluation (Schlager & Blomquist, 1996).

What makes ACT patently interpretivist is the locus of individual decision making, in which "the theory of advocacy coalitions empirically identifies the inner world of individuals and uses it to explain individual action. The parts of the inner world that are empirically verified are belief systems . . . a set of basic values, causal assumptions, and problem perceptions" (Schlager, 2007, p. 301). Belief systems become information filters through which information is processed and may be used to superimpose one's own thinking over the situation in question or to join with others who have solidarity among members of a coalition through a shared belief system. Originally, theorists focused almost exclusively on individuals' belief systems, but as the theory has been developed over the years, a number of assumptions about collective action and participating in coalitions have been developed to "capture the emergence and continuation of collective action" (Schlager, 2007, p. 303).

An example of ACT can be seen in the well-established long-term care ombudsman program, originally created under public mandate through an amendment to the Older Americans Act. The policy called for the selection of a state ombudsman who would be responsible for overseeing intrastate or regional ombudsmen, both paid and volunteer. This cadre of paid and volunteer ombudsmen formed an advocacy coalition that monitored state and local policies impacting nursing homes and responded to residents' complaints. Over the years, this group of advocates changed how they conceptualized long-term care, as it evolved to include a full continuum of services from home and community-based to assisted living and skilled nursing facilities. Their reconceptualization of long-term care changed their focus and spread their skills across more and different types of facilities, altering their target focus on skilled nursing facilities and "nursing home reform."

All three of these theories focus on policy change as a result of collective action, and each is based on understanding individuals and how they come together to organize themselves. They differ, however, in how they understand collective action. Schlager (2007) sees the multiple streams theory as paying the least attention to why people gather in an organized way to effect policy change and focuses instead on the critical roles played by policy entrepreneurs who attempt to anticipate events so that they can influence what happens in the emergent process. This coupling of policy entrepreneurs with events brings together coalitions that lead to policy action. Social construction theory focuses on how major players within the policy arena view target populations in context, and ACT works on understandings of the process over time. All three theories are nonrational approaches that recognize the serendipitous nature of policy process and development as well as the ambiguity posed by competing sets of assumptions that cannot always be reconciled but must be corralled in some way for action to happen. These theories recognize that talking about final outcomes (a rational approach) does not fit in highly diverse contexts in which policies emerge, as opposed to being predetermined.

INTERPRETIVE, NONRATIONAL APPROACHES

In interpretive, nonrational approaches to policy analysis, there are different strategies for defining problems and targeted groups from those used in rational models. At this point, it might be helpful to review the content of Box 5.2, which outlines nonrational strategies. Not only do nonrational approaches provide different ways to view policies and policy alternatives, there are also different presumptions about the function of policy studies or policy analysis. Interpretive nonrational approaches are designed for in-depth description and to push for deeper understanding. Once one unmasks the inequities within a policy, one's eyes may be opened to the need for change. These approaches begin by raising consciousness, which could lead to a questioning of the social order itself and to the more critical approaches, on which we will focus in Chapter 7.

In addition, rather than assuming that policies are constructed through a rational interplay between problems, solutions, and studies regarding both, nonrational approaches lead to being attentive to the sociohistorical context that informs what is seen as a problem. They do this by studying what is socially legitimized as a policy solution and what is acceptable policy analysis. Fortunately, there are some powerful tools for nonrational analysis. We will describe two strong approaches that are interpretive along with several that are useful for various units of analysis.

Widely cited and innovative, Deborah Stone's *Policy Paradox: The Art of Political Decision Making* (2002) offers a highly interpretive approach to policy analysis. We have used Stone's work quite extensively to help students make sense of policies that do not make rational sense. Stone's approach contextualizes a policy within the sociopolitical horizon and allows the understanding of politics, perspectives, and influence within the polity to underscore the paradoxical aspects of multiple positioning "for" and "against" any aspect of a social problem and its policy response. Stone's approach captures not the rationality of policy but the politics of the political reasoning that is at play to strategically and persuasively achieve a particular policy formation. This approach assumes that participants operate in an essentially political society where ideas are the medium of exchange and shared meanings motivate people to action. Stone's policy paradox approach is listed in Box 5.3. Note that unlike more rational models where specific answers are elicited, Box 5.3 contains areas to consider as well as questions that are so expansive that the analytic process would likely elicit even more questions to deepen the process.

Box 5.3   Stone's Policy Paradox Approach

GOALS

Equity

How are services distributed, and who are the members and recipients?
How is power used to rank or distribute resources?
Is power used to oppress or discriminate?
What is provided (items of service linked to need)?
What is the process of receiving service (how)—competition, lotteries, elections, boundaries, values, and so forth?
Is there distributive justice?

Efficiency

What is the objective measure to judge efficiency?
What are the costs of obtaining services?
Who is the constituency? For whom is it efficient?
What are the important inputs or outputs?

Is there duplication, and when is duplication seen or judged to be important?
Is there allocative efficiency?

Security

What has primacy—economic, physical, or psychological considerations, or
   military security?
What are the minimums necessary to meet security needs? Those that are
   directly visible? For the future? For those at risk? For the community?
What is the status of the political validation of need and goal claims?
Where is power/hierarchy located within this policy and its oversight?
Which is preferred—security or efficiencies?

Liberty

What is the degree of lack of interference?
What is the degree of individual choice/action?
Which overriding value combination is preferred—liberty/security; liberty/
   equity?

PROBLEMS

Symbols

What words or symbolic devices are used to portray the policy problem?
What language is used to shape the drama of the stories?
What political strategy is used to construct and reveal the hidden stories?

Numbers

What symbolic devices are used in the numerical language?
How are counting and measuring used to create the problem story?

Causes

What symbols and numbers are used to portray cause?
What does the causal theory reveal about control?
What cause is linked to a result?

Interests

How is language used to portray the problem as a contest between compet-
   ing interests?
Who are the villains and who are the heroes?
Where is the strength in the story of the problem?

Decisions

How are the preferred decisions being portrayed as rational choices?
How are numbers used to count up the costs and benefits of alternative
   pathways?
How are complexity and confusion being reduced to a single choice?

(continued)

(continued)

SOLUTIONS

Inducements

What rewards, punishments, incentives, or sanctions are being used to change behavior?

Rules

What commands are in place to act or not act?
Who are the people and what are the situations that determine permissions and entitlements?
What sanctions (inducements) back up the rule?

Facts

What strategies are used to persuade?
What cognitive strategies (rather than rewards and punishments) are used to provide information so that minds are made up in the desired direction?

Rights

What strategies are used to invoke government power?
Where is citizen enforcement to assure the desired solution?

Powers

What strategies are used to alter the decisions to change the size of the decision-making body, to shift authority from one part of government to another, and so forth?
Who else is being included among the decision makers?
How has the political power been restructured?

Source: Adapted from *Policy Paradox: The Art of Political Decision Making,* by D. Stone, 2002, New York, NY: Norton.

Stone (2002) is very clear in stating how her approach varies from rational models that use the metaphor of the market as their beginning point. The market is competitive and built on the concept of people pursuing what they need for their own welfare. Instead, Stone offers the concept of "polis" as an alternative metaphor, in which the Greek word for city-state "conjures up an entity small enough to have very simple forms of organization yet large enough to embody the elements of politics" (p. 17). Polis requires the formation of community (or multiple communities) and has a public interest and common problems to resolve. Cooperation and loyalty are essential among groups and organizations within its boundaries. Information is interpretive and always incomplete, and the polis is governed by "laws of passion as well as the laws of matter" (p. 32). Building on the polis metaphor, Stone's approach allows understanding how the will of the polis can become a collective will, how public interest can overcome individual interests, and how influence by way of collective education and persuasion can create the recognition of common problems.

Influence and cooperation are interrogated so that the coalitions and alliances are understood along with the loyalty that is required to reason politically and paradoxically. Stone's approach recognizes how the power of the social order and structures such as courts, legislatures, and agencies with political sanction shape information. Here paradox becomes the context of policies and political decision making. The participant that wields power interprets policies. Stone's approach allows the analyst to identify and interrogate multiple and competing meanings of what appears to be a single concept or "truth." The analytic process allows the analyst to uncover how understandings about social problems, preferences, and solutions are created and how they are manipulated as part of a political strategy. Note how the theories reviewed earlier may have relevancy here.

Returning to our case that looks at Service, Engagement, and Volunteerism, if Madeline were confused about what problem was being served by the volunteerism solution, or if she were to wonder exactly which goals were being attended to by this public law, Stone's political approach, which allows a look at the paradoxes that seem to be present in the law, would be more than helpful. Madeline could interrogate the law to determine whether equity, efficiency, security, or liberty was the priority, and she could begin to understand why all of them might be in play. Stone would help her to look at the other paradoxes contained in the problem definitions and the selected solutions as well.

Another interpretive nonrational approach, developed by Scheurich (1994) and heavily dependent on Foucault (1972), focuses on identifying how problems become socially visible and how the range of solutions are established. This approach allows the study of the social construction of the social problem and interrogates the social construction of the range of acceptable and unacceptable policy solutions. In rejecting policy analysis as a neutral activity, it joins the Stone approach in questioning the role of power and influence including the broader social functions of policy studies themselves. Box 5.4 summarizes the dimensions of policy analysis following a policy archaeology approach.

> ## Box 5.4   Scheurich's Dimensions of Policy Analysis Following a Policy Archaeology Approach
>
> *Arena I—social problem:* How did the social problem come to be constructed as it is?
> *Arena II—social regularities:* What are the dimensions of the network that constitute the social regularities of the social problem as constructed?
> *Arena III—policy solutions:* How did the range of acceptable policy solutions become constructed?
> *Arena IV—policy studies:* How does the policy analysis itself influence how the problem is addressed?
>
> *Source:* Adapted from "Policy Archaeology: A New Policy Studies Methodology," by J. J. Scheurich, 1994, *Journal of Education Policy, 9*(4), pp. 297–316.

In Box 5.4, the analysis process is iterative and recursive as the work in one dimension passes through all four arenas, each one reframing and altering the information and its meaning. The order of the arenas is not necessarily the order in which the analysis will occur. The analyst starts where it makes sense for the sociopolitical context of the analysis or where information is present. This analysis ends when the analytic effort no longer produces material that significantly refashions or alters any of the four arenas.

Arena I looks at how a problem is named, defined, and discussed as a social problem. It interrogates the social visibility of some problems as social problems and the invisibility of other problems as social problems to clarify the process of social construction. Here, a social problem is not necessarily a natural occurrence; it has a construction process that can be identified. Understanding the construction process is essential in problem understanding. Note that social construction theory is applicable here.

Arena II recognizes that social regularities constitute what is socially visible or credible, but regularities do not literally create material reality. Instead they constitute what is socially selected and verified as real. Policy responses result from a grid of social regularities that constitute what becomes visible as a social problem and what is seen as the range of credible policy solutions. These social orders are historically shifting, complex, dispersed systems with much influence at the margins that help to create unities and differences, continuities and discontinuities, while still producing and reproducing the dominant order. However, what constitutes that order is not necessarily within the awareness of social agents (including the analyst).

Arena III's assumptions are inextricably linked to the assumptions of the two preceding arenas. Here, it is assumed that there exists a range of possible policy choices that have been shaped by the grid of social regularities. The shaping of those choices is not necessarily intentional or conscious. Regardless, in the range some choices are seen as relevant and others are invisible. Some choices have privilege over others. The difficult aspect to grasp is that social regularities do not identify objects; they constitute them, and in the practice of doing so, conceal their own invention. The trick is to uncover how the social regularities (created by a grid containing gender, race, family values, class, morality, etc.) generate the range of possible and impossible solutions.

It is in Arena IV that the policy analyst should pause and question the social function of the policy analysis itself. Policy studies, like social problems and policy solutions, are constituted by social regularities. Policy analysis legitimizes constructions, constrains the range of choices, and refrains from questioning the social order. Without inter-rogation, traditional models of analysis serve a social order function. Thus, the analyst guided by this approach questions the function of the very policy analysis process she or he is conducting.

Scheurich's approach is clearly nonrational. Along with Foucault's, Scheurich's approach is built on assumptions that policies are symbolic and interpretive solutions to social ills and that the policy process is a struggle over symbols related to public concerns. For Scheurich solu-tions are symbolic, not real, and related to latent public concerns. As with Stone, policy and politics are central to the focus on the democratic ideal of improving the social order. Differing from Stone, Scheurich presents a way to understand a problem definition range, a goal range, and an acceptable solution range for consciousness raising and educa-tion. Here, there is still a concern for incremental improvement of the social order but without any interest in revolutionary change resulting from the consciousness raising and education that result from the policy analysis.

Using policy archaeology to assess P.L. 111-13, Madeline would be aided in her understanding of the particulars of the social problem as it is currently constructed. Is it so locally constituted that national need, combined with insufficient human resources, would make it difficult to adequately respond at her agency level? Does it represent what the society wants to do with "wounded warriors" and aging "boomers"? Once the "real" construction of the specific social problem has been identified in all its complexities, the social structures (such as govern-ment and nongovernmental institutions) and their relationships in response to this social problem (and other related social problems) will need to be articulated. These steps will allow an understanding of the range of solutions that were considered and why the policy brings together these particular programs for volunteers with the various stated goals. Finally, use of this approach would force Madeline to consider her role as an analyst within the context of the problem and policy solution.

As you read, keep in mind that by its nature this material is complex and sometimes ambiguous. Since nonrational approaches require complex critical thought, not reductionist approaches, moving through the material may be confusing and contradictory or even paradoxical. It is up to you to determine whether the possibilities of nonrational approaches outweigh the challenges they represent.

Examples Focusing on Different Units of Analysis

A note of caution is needed at this point. Although we have identified various foci of analyses, it is important from an interpretive perspective to recognize that there are limitations to identifying any categories that imply a step or stage progression. Whereas rationalists find a stages heuristic helpful in providing a logical set of steps in which the process of policy making occurs (agenda setting leads to formulation, which then leads to a policy, which is followed by evaluation and impact), the nonrationalist does not assume that things are so ordered. For the rationalist "the stages model has provided a useful conceptual dis-aggregation of the complex and varied policy process into manageable segments, particularly regarding agenda setting . . . and implementation" (Jenkins-Smith & Sabatier, 1994, p. 177). Such a linear approach is viewed by the interpretivist as "descriptively inaccurate," because things simply do not always work in a nice, stepwise fashion with a "legalistic top-down focus." Thus, before we point out ways to focus on units of analysis, it is important say that there may be "multiple, interacting cycles" in the analytic process much like what was already mentioned in relation to advocacy coalition theory (Jenkins-Smith & Sabatier, 1994, p. 177).

What is important in a nonrational approach to policy analysis is to recognize that just because one is focusing on a particular unit at the moment does not mean that one's focus will not shift to another unit or even back to a former unit of analysis. For example, if one is focusing on the implementation of a policy, one might simultaneously need to look at formulation of an amendment to that same policy that will alter its very nature. Similarly, if one is looking at policy content, one may want to focus simultaneously on implementation. In other words, the inter-relatedness of units of analysis must be considered and never assumed to remain static.

The following policy analysis approaches build on interpretive or constructivist assumptions based on a subjectivist perspective that embraces relativity and a socially constructed reality. Knowledge is not hard or concrete but interactively constructed and contextually based, with individuals constantly shaping that reality, their actions, and their perceptions in a creatively emergent process. Word data and emergent methods where the "right" question and the "right" inquiry design are determined in context with the stakeholders to the inquiry process are preferred over traditional means of knowledge building. Generalizability is considered not only impossible but also irrelevant for meaning making. Each of the following approaches is multiper-spectival, pragmatic, and pluralistic. Each recognizes the contest of competing perspectives in a back-and-forth narrative. Each uses a recursive, circular reasoning for the discursive practices and contests that are contained in the analytic processes.

Each differs in its focus of analysis, attending primarily to different units of analysis. Again, see if you can determine which theory relates to each approach and in what way. Being able to identify the focus as well as the theoretical guidance will aid in your decision making about which analytic frame to choose. It will also help to articulate the basis of your choices to those who might doubt the relevance, efficiency, or effectiveness of your analytic process.

Formulation Example Kingdon's (1995) policy as primeval soup or garbage can approach to policy analysis is in Box 5.5. As you can see, it is primarily focused on policy formulation or policy-in-intention (Guba, 1984). Beginning with agenda setting, Kingdon's approach is based on multiple streams theory, in which three streams of prob-lems, politics, and participants run parallel and then converge into the policy process. As a list of possible alternatives emerges, Kingdon asks how the choices are narrowed and how the coupling processes interrelate, forming a decision agenda. The approach recognizes the importance of windows of opportunity and allows a chronicling of how policy entrepreneurs seize these opportunities. This approach is a circular process in which policy entrepreneurs may identify other agenda items to be funneled into the process over and over again.

Box 5.5   Kingdon's Policy Primeval Soup Approach

AGENDA SETTING

Problems

1. Why has this problem come to occupy the attention of governmental officials (or other decision makers) more than other problems?
2. Is or was there a focusing event (e.g., a disaster, crisis, personal experience, etc.)?
3. How did the condition become linked to a problem that gained public attention?

Politics

4. What factors in the political stream facilitated addressing this problem?
5. How were decision makers and others persuaded to recognize this problem or settle on certain proposals?
6. Which interest groups are involved in this process?

Participants

7. Who are the visible participants and what roles do they play?
8. Who are the invisible participants and what roles do they play?

Alternative Specification

9. How is the list of potential alternatives for policy choices narrowed to the ones that actually receive serious consideration?

Coupling and Windows

10. How have streams of problems, policies, and politics become interrelated within a decision agenda?
11. Are problem windows or political windows open?

Entrepreneurs

12. Who are the entrepreneurs?
13. How are entrepreneurs softening up the system?
14. What are they doing to push proposals forward?

Source: Adapted from *Agenda, Alternatives, and Public Policies* (2nd edition, pp. 197–205), by J. W. Kingdon, 1995, New York, NY: Longman.

Returning to the Service, Engagement, and Volunteerism case, if Madeline had questions about alternative standpoints, context issues at the outset, or politics in action at the agenda-setting stage with P.L.111-13, she would investigate the stated problem and ask why it has come to the attention of decision makers at all stakeholding levels. She would identify the factors that have facilitated this effort to address the problem. This might include both financial and sociological issues. It would be important to identify all the players in favor and against the construction of the problem. Both overt and covert influences should be identified to understand what the alternatives were and what led to setting the agenda. Madeline, as a Director of Volunteers, would probably be aligned with certain stakeholders who advocate for the professionalization of volunteerism, raising a host of issues about where volunteerism and professional roles overlap.

In our preceding theory discussion, the examples of state education and of nondiscrimination (sexual orientation and gender identity) would be considered at the policy formulation stage. Each could be understood and analyzed with Kingdon's approach, either while the decision making was in process or after the policy decisions have been made. Either way, Kingdon would help to clarify why particular policy options gained favor and others did not.

Product Example Prigmore and Atherton's (1986) policy analysis approach can be found in Box 5.6. We have characterized this approach as a nonrational example of a policy product, because Prigmore and Atherton begin with a consideration of values. Coming from a social work perspective, they ask whether the policy is compatible with social work's professional values and ethical system. If one wanted to consider another profession's perspective, the question would still hold, as their intent is to see how congruent (or not) the policy is with the values of one's profession. As with other interpretive exemplars, this approach is iterative and recursive. However, it is important to note there could be some paradigm jumping in the questions posed under knowledge consideration, unless "testing" is interpreted to mean using methods such as member checking for congruence with multiple perspectives rather than testing for generalizability. Similarly, depending on one's definition of effectiveness and efficiency under elements of costs and benefits, these questions would be handled differently with differing paradigmatic assumptions guiding the work.

Box 5.6   Prigmore and Atherton's Policy Analysis

Consideration Related to Values

1. Is the policy compatible with contemporary "style"?
2. Is the policy compatible with important and enduring cultural values, particularly equity, fairness, and justice?
3. Is the policy compatible with social work's professional value and ethical system?

Dimensions of Influence

4. Is the policy acceptable to those in formal decision-making positions?
5. Does the policy satisfy relevant interest groups?

Knowledge Considerations

6. Is the policy based on knowledge that has been tested to some degree?
7. Is the policy workable? That is, can the programs that flow from the policy be carried out in the real world?
8. Does the policy create few problems for both the public and the intended beneficiaries?

Elements Related to Costs and Benefits

9. Is the policy reasonably effective?
10. Is the policy efficient?

Source: Social Welfare Policy: Analysis and Formulation (2nd edition, p. 46), by C. S. Prigmore and C. R. Atherton, 1986. Used by permission.

In the Service, Engagement, and Volunteerism case, if Madeline had questions about the multiple values and meanings that had the most influence in the shaping of the policy content, Prigmore and Atherton's policy analysis approach would be helpful. It would be important to examine the expectations regarding the reauthorization of the bill supporting volunteerism. She would need to identify the predominant cultural values that served as a context for this particular reauthorization. As a social worker, she would be interested in determining the value congruence of the reauthorized policy content with the profession, along with determining who had influence in shaping the final policy product. Of particular interest would be the degree to which the selected solutions had been assessed and whether or not all aspects of the policy are feasible and with the potential to be effective in overcoming the social problem as defined in P.L.111-13.

The Older Americans Act, in which the ombudsman program is mandated, was discussed in our theory section. This federal policy is an example of a product that could be analyzed using Prigmore and Atherton's policy analysis approach. Since this Act begins with the ultimate objectives of what the nation wants for its elders, the exploration of values in the Prigmore and Atherton approach would be especially relevant, particularly in light of economic downturns in which these ideals are not likely to be realized.

Implementation Example The next example treats policy as behaviors or activities that are displayed in the process of implementing policy. This approach allows assessment at various distances from the point of action. It also allows various assessment points for what Guba (1984) calls "policy determiners" (p. 65), which include program implementers, supervisors as well as other actors at the street level (Lipsky, 1980). Note this is only one aspect of Guba's rather circular approach to policy analysis.

Guba's policy-in-action is outlined in Box 5.7. When implementation is being analyzed, policy action and performance are the focus. Guba begins with behavior, then moves to norms of conduct, and then to action. The interpretive focus on behavior, norms, and expectations shapes an interpretive approach in which implementation analysis is focused on how the socially constructed policy comes together. This differs from a more rational focus on targeted outcomes. Throughout this approach is a concern for relationships in the implementation process and how people act in those relationships. Recall the theories discussed earlier and how the emphasis of advocacy coalition theory was on multidimensional problem definition, policy formulation, adoption, and evaluation. Guba's approach is closely aligned with this theory as well as with elements of social construction theory.

Box 5.7 Guba's Policy-in-Action Aspect of Policy Types Taxonomy

- What constitutes the sanctioned behavior?
  - Is it formal?
  - Was it established (or "sanctified") over time?

(*continued*)

(*continued*)
- What are the norms of conduct?
  - Are they related to the goals or intents of the policy?
  - Are they related to the policy decisions? Rules?
  - Are they related to any guides to discretionary action? Guidelines?
  - Are they related to a problem-solving strategy? Sets of tactics?
- What are the impacts of the policy-making system on the action?
  - What actions at other levels impact the expectations, norms, and effects of the policy?
  - What decisions at other levels impact expectations, norms, and effects?
  - What behaviors in bureaucracies at all levels impact the point of policy action being investigated?

Source: Adapted from "The Effect of Definitions of Policy on the Nature and Outcomes of Policy Analysis," by E. G. Guba, 1984, *Educational Leadership, 42*, pp. 63–70.

In the Service, Engagement, and Volunteerism case, if Madeline had questions about the meaning of mounting the policy response or the politics that narrowed or expanded the shape and direction of the program at its enactment stage, particularly in her agency, she would first wait until the program supported by P.L.111-13 was fully mounted (even though there is a one-year timeline for evaluation). To use the policy-in-action, she would identify the practices being supported both formally and implicitly. This would include the norms of conduct within the agency between employees, volunteers, and the clients they serve and how those are related to the intent and rules of P.L.111-13. It would also be important to interrogate how the federal, state, and local processes are being impacted and are impacting the work.

Three examples were presented earlier in this chapter when we discussed theory. First, an example of how charter schools emerged as a particular focus amid multiple possibilities in educational reform revealed the potential for a complicated implementation process in carrying out the intent of public law. Second, the implementation of nondiscrimination policy would require finding out who had actually filed complaints and how they were handled in light of the policy. And third, the long-established ombudsman program and what is revealed in its reporting system could be analyzed using Guba's policy-in-action framework. In each example behavior, norms and expectations would need to be investigated in order to understand how each of these socially constructed policies came together.

Impact Example Generally speaking, questions of impact are difficult ones for an interpretivist/constructivist perspective. Imbedded in impact questions are stated or unstated assumptions about cause; the policy "caused" something. However, the assumptions of this worldview suggest that causes may be consequences and consequences causes, depending on the time and circumstance of the investigation. If you are interested in a deeper understanding of the complexity of this position, you may want to read about quantum physics; at this stage, it is important just to realize that from the interpretivist/constructivist paradigm the most that can be garnered in research is the identification of networks of association and how they are related or associated. Cause or impact are impossible to identify. This means that the most a policy analyst can discover would be the description of or the meaning of the experience of the policy. From this perspective, that experience is heavily mediated by the context of the local culture, the reactions of those administering the policy, expectations of those around them, the expectations and experiences of those implementing the policy, and the resources available to do so.

Guba (1984) can be useful in understanding the perceived impact that policy has on the *consumer's* actual experience (not the practitioner's experience, but the experience of the persons whose original needs were targeted in the first place). Recall that we introduced Guba's policy-in-experience concept in Chapter 1. We use it now to illustrate how impact can be understood and analyzed in a nonrational way. Rather than focusing on rational outcomes as defined by professionals and policy makers as "success" or "effectiveness," the interpretive policy analysis redefines what it means to have an impact. Impact becomes the quality of the processes and changes that consumers experienced as a result of being beneficiaries of the policy's intent. It focuses on the meaning of the experience. These impacts could be similar to what policy entrepreneurs anticipated or expected, but they could be entirely different based on individual recipient needs and perceptions. For example, an older consumer of services might be rejoicing at the manner in which their views were heard by professionals, when there were no measurable outcome data generated. The consumers in this situation would see the policy's impact as positive for their quality of life because of feeling that they had been heard. The rationalist would be saying that this does not indicate anything about whether or not the policy really "works." The consumer may be focused on personal impact in tune with the interpretive, nonrational interests, whereas the rationalist's (positivist/postpositivist) focus is on generalizable impact that transcends one individual's experience.

Since the prevailing evidence-based interests push for outcome-based measurements to reveal impact, we encourage anyone choosing an interpretive approach to carefully identify the dimensions that should be considered for policy analysis that looks at meaning as impact. Determining an acceptable circumstance for this type of analysis would also be important. Box 5.8 lists elements to consider for the analysis of meaning in policy-in-experience.

Box 5.8   Possible Questions to Ask About Interpretive Impact

- Who would be the stakeholders who experience the policy in addition to those who were "carriers" of the social problem that the policy sought to address?
- Who might be beneficiaries? Victims? Where is there evidence of coercion and control or of consciousness raising and empowerment?
- What might be related to the experience that has something to do with how the policy became enacted at the street level? How is that enactment different from the original policy intent?
- What values are at play in the experience of the policy? How do those correspond to the values undergirding the original intent?
- Given the various constructions, what are the similarities and differences among the stakeholders on the answers to the preceding question? Where is consensus about the meaning of the experience of the policy?
- Where are there mismatches about the conditions that gave rise to the policy and the policy itself?
- What are the stakeholders' reactions to your results?

In our case example on Service, Engagement, and Volunteerism, if Madeline were interested in understanding the meaning of the experience of those with a stake in the policy, she would assess all those impacted by the policy beyond those who are "disadvantaged," noting both beneficiaries and victims at the individual and institutional levels. Based on this, efforts would be made to identify the values at play in the implementation of the policy and their congruence with policy intent. The idea is to identify and understand all the standpoints that are present. Consensus and the lack of it should be articulated, along with the needs that remain as a result of the mismatch between the original need and the policy itself. It would also be instructive for analysis in the future to capture stakeholders' reactions to this type of analysis.

The example used earlier in this chapter, in which the state's attorney general questioned the universities' right to include sexual orientation and gender identity in their statements of nondistribution, illustrates a conflict about policy impact. This is an example of how what is not covered in a social policy can negatively impact a group because the group's members do not perceive any protection coming from this policy if they experience discrimination. On the other hand, groups that are protected under the state's rights act may feel that they have the capacity to contest discriminatory action. Guba's policy-in-action could be used to analyze what this silence about sexual orientation and identity means as well as how those groups that are named experience the policy's impact on their lives.

HOW TO ASSESS THE DEGREE TO WHICH AN ANALYSIS APPROACH IS NONRATIONAL

If one is engaging in nonrational policy analysis where collaboration and connection for consensus are intended, then the purpose of the analytic process might be to answer such questions as: Who were the major players in establishing the shape and language of the current understanding of the social problem? What perspectives were not present in the construction of the social problem, and would that change how the social problem could be understood? What is the meaning of the social problem to all the stakeholders to the problem, including those who are "carriers" of the problem, those who are sanctioned to solve the problem, and those who must pay for the effort? What is the meaning to all involved of what it takes to mount the implementation action aimed at problem elimination? These questions are built upon the interpretivist/constructivist notions related to the status quo, social order, consensus, social integration, solidarity, and needs satisfaction. Differing from the positivist/postpositivist world-view, they are context and values imbedded rather than attending to causes and consequences. The idea is that multiple meanings from multiple perspectives, when gathered together in consensus, can provide acceptable, feasible direction for incrementally improving the social structures for a diverse society. Here, the assumption is that through diverse participation, consensus and political will develop to improve the lived experiences of all who have a stake in the social problem.

QUESTIONS RELEVANT FOR ASSESSING NONRATIONALITY OF APPROACH

Once it is clear that the questions guiding the policy analysis are situated within an interpretivist/constructivist worldview, it is important to determine whether the approach is congruent with that worldview. Lack of congruence will prove problematic not only for the process but for the product of policy analysis. For example, if the analyst is interested in the meaning of the social problem and uses an approach to produce the causes of the social problem, the results would be interesting, though not useful for the purpose at hand. Therefore, it is important to assess the degree to which the policy analysis approach being considered is interpretive and nonrational, if the question(s) guiding the analysis is interpretive. The following questions might help guide the analyst's decision-making process in selecting an approach:

- Is it based on the assumption that there are multiple ways to achieve a feasible policy?
- Does it recognize the management of power and politics in the policy process?
- Does it allow the analyst to engage in an iterative, emergent process in which one starts where one can and finishes when no new information develops?
- Are the important concepts developed in an "emic" or context-based, insider's way?
- Do the precise questions for the analysis emerge from the analytic process, such that what is important to be known is related to the context of the analysis and those participants who have a stake in the particular analysis?
- Are there mechanisms for rigorous data collection with a major focus on word data, with triangulation and other means to manage the power and politics of stakeholder agendas that might sway the process or the product of the analysis?
- What is the role of theory? Does it aid or thwart an emergent process? Is the theory explicitly or implicitly congruent with interpretivist or constructivist assumptions?

Once the approach is seen to be an interpretive, nonrational one, the gains and losses associated with nonrational approaches deserve thoughtful consideration. Because of the political and emergent nature of nonrational approaches, the policy analyst would be well advised to seriously consider the appropriateness and feasibility of this sort of policy analysis.

GAINS AND LOSSES WHEN NONRATIONAL APPROACHES ARE USED TO ANALYZE POLICY

Positivist/postpositivist policy analytic work cannot provide deep, individualized meaning; but it can be the basis for appropriately targeted incremental policy development or provide evidence to support causal hypotheses about what "works" or not. On the other hand, interpretivist/constructivist policy analysis is not generalizable. It can, however, provide complex, context-based deep understandings about the social problem and the policy response. Keep in mind that neither of these approaches can be held to a change standard that will be so central to the critical approaches that are discussed in the final section of this text. For now it is important to look seriously at what the nonrational approaches represent. The following issues must be understood and considered before selecting a nonrational way to engage in policy analysis.

Gains and Benefits An interpretive nonrational approach brings assumptions about subjectivity and the preservation of a consensual status quo. The goal is to develop policy through diverse participation based on recognition and management of power and politics. In nonrational approaches the analyst aims to recognize unique responses to diverse needs in a nonprescriptive, emergent way. This approach is respectful of difference, which is appreciated when diverse constituencies realize that their voices are being heard.

A nonrational approach is concerned with understanding, sense making, and meaning making. The interest is in lifting up complexity in the process rather than focusing on parsimonious or reductionist solutions to challenging problems or needs. Alternative ways of considering policy and policy contexts make this type of analysis expansive and inclusive. In this analytic process, educational and consciousness-raising methods are used so that a new consensus can emerge as participants gain more sophistication about the complexity of the issues related to the policy under analysis.

Costs and Losses The major complaint heard from rationalists is that interpretive approaches are so process oriented that nothing is ever accomplished. Since nonrational approaches require a great deal of

critical thinking, there are no formulaic steps, solutions, or predetermined outcomes to guide persons who are anxious to know where
things are going. Given a sense-making process attentive to behaviors
and norms, there is a time intensity that can create frustration for
persons who want to deal with problems in an efficient, timely
manner. There is little efficiency in a nonrational process, because
process takes time.

Another difficulty that arises in nonrational approaches is that they
are overtly political and attentive to ideologies. When dealing with
ideology, there may be strong reactions from participants who do not
agree. Thus, gaining consensus may be challenging. In this process,
persons who do not tolerate ambiguity may become uncomfortable
with the paradoxes they encounter. There will be no sense of certitude.
Discomfort may occur both with uncertainty and lack of trust in an
emergent process. A major criticism is that the analysis process will
never be complete because consciousness-raising and learning continue to reverberate uncontrollably.

CONCLUSION

In this chapter, we introduced nonrational approaches to policy analysis. There was a short history of the philosophy of science to document
how reason and logic can be understood more broadly than in the
classical, traditional approaches to rationality in Western thought. A
brief overview of interpretive theories was introduced, along with an
exploration of the dimensions of nonrational approaches to policy
analysis, providing examples of approaches that are situated in an
interpretivist/constructivist paradigmatic perspective. The understanding of the possibilities and the challenges of nonrational
approaches of policy analysis were further explored by looking at
examples that target differing units of policy analysis.

The following chapter is built on the assumptions and approaches
introduced here, but with an applied focus. You will see how to actually
use nonrational approaches to achieve policy analysis goals that fit
within an interpretivist/constructivist perspective. At the conclusion of
this section (Chapters 5 and 6) you should be able to assess the
paradigmatic perspective of a particular policy analysis approach to
determine whether it fits within an interpretive worldview and
whether it is nonrational in its approach to policy analysis. You will
identify the unit(s) of analysis that are the focus of the particular
approach and know what is necessary to determine how to enact

analysis using a particular approach based on an interpretivist/constructivist nonrational approach.

DISCUSSION QUESTIONS

1. Early in this chapter, we argued that circular or nonrational thought is much more congruent with interpretivist or constructivist thought. First, define and give an example of circular thought. Then, identify at least three ways that circular thinking is congruent with interpretivist/constructivist ontology or frame of reference.
2. Review the theories that were discussed in this chapter. Why would you consider them to be descriptive theories? What are the benefits of descriptions guiding work? What are the costs of the descriptions these theories provide?
3. Look at multiple streams, social construction, and advocacy coalition theories to identify how they are similar and different. Now, using the media (radio, TV, the Internet, or other news source), see whether you can identify policies at the formulation, product, implementation, or impact levels that can be better understood using one or all of these theories as a guide.
4. Multiple streams, social construction, and advocacy coalition theories are relevant at many levels of practice. Select a policy issue within an organizational setting. How do these theories inform your thinking about this issue? Select a policy issue within a community with which you are familiar. How do these theories inform your thinking about this issue?
5. What do you see as the strengths and challenges of using nonrational approaches to policy analysis, especially with issues impacting nondominant groups?

CHAPTER 6

Applications in Nonrational Policy Analysis

I N CHAPTER 5, we provided background for understanding the underlying assumptions of nonrationality, and we introduced a number of frameworks that fit with those assumptions. All the approaches presented in Chapter 5 fit within an interpretive/constructivist perspective as well as within a policy ideology in which it is assumed that through diverse participation and management of power and politics, consensual policies can be constructed, implemented, and understood. The Service, Engagement, and Volunteerism case that was discussed in Chapter 5 will be used extensively in this chapter to demonstrate how nonrational policy questions alter the analytic process. How these various approaches can be applied differentially is the primary focus of this chapter.

This chapter's intent is on the "doing" of nonrational policy analysis as a type of research. Starting with identifying the purpose of the policy analysis, which also determines the paradigmatic perspective for the research aspect of the process, this chapter will take you through an analytic process that results in the determination of an appropriate nonrational approach to select. Note that we are carefully choosing our words here, because a nonrational process is emergent and there is no one way to approach the analysis—in fact, there are multiple ways. Based on this chapter, you should be able to identify or construct a policy research question that fits within the interpretive/constructivist perspective. Anchored in the identification of the purpose of the research, you will be able to identify nonrational policy analysis strategies and defend the use of those strategies to answer a policy research question. Based on determining the form, level (and scope), and focus of the social policy, you should be able to select and defend the selection of a particular nonrational approach to policy analysis. In this chapter, you will learn how to engage in various types of non-rational policy analysis through the application of several nonrational approaches. The chapter ends with a discussion of what nonrational approaches can and cannot offer in undertaking policy analysis. Finally, you will understand what is gained and what is given up when one engages in interpretive/constructivist policy analysis research.

Recall that interpretive nonrational approaches to policy analysis are multiperspectival, taking into account the positions of multiple stakeholders with and without power. These approaches are pragmatic, accepting whatever works for now in a pluralistic society. Nonrational approaches recognize that along with competing perspectives come alternatives, as policies are interrogated and evaluated in a back-and-forth dialectical, discursive process that produces a particular policy product at an identifiable level with a specific form. The policy-analysis approach itself will generally have a specific focus in the policy process: formulation, the product, implementation of the policy, or the quality of the policy performance to eliminate the social problem it was designed to address. The focus of the approach must match the reason for engaging in policy analysis in order to produce useful findings. Awareness of all these aspects of a policy analytic process, in addition to the appropriate and thorough application of a particular approach in the analysis, makes policy analysis a type of research.

Now let us see how all this works by looking more deeply at the policy-analytic interests and the selected approaches that were introduced in Chapter 5. We will continue our interrogation of P.L. 111-13 using most of the approaches introduced in Chapter 5. So how does one begin this sort of interrogation, and how does one know that a particular approach will be appropriate? In the sections that follow, we will demonstrate the essential elements requiring critical decision making that lead to the selection of a particular approach to policy analysis. We will then provide some guidance about how one might go about applying the selected approach. It is beyond the scope of this effort to engage in a series of full-blown policy analysis processes with well-articulated products. Instead, based on the kinds of questions contained in the selected approaches, we will suggest where one might go to find answers in order to complete an analysis of P.L. 111-13 as discussed in our case example and guided by a particular nonrational approach. This should give you the level of familiarity needed to know what can and cannot be accomplished by a particular interpretive, nonrational approach to policy analysis. Since it is as important to know how to select an appropriate resource for analysis as it is to know how to apply it, each section will detail the decision making that suggests why the approach is appropriate for the desired analysis before demonstrating the potential data sources for the type of interrogation that would be useful in applying the approach to a particular policy question.

USING STONE'S POLICY PARADOX APPROACH

In Chapter 5, we introduced the work of Deborah Stone (2002) as an example of an interpretive approach to policy analysis that includes goals, problems, and solutions. To refresh your memory, Stone's approach is provided again in Box 6.1.

Box 6.1   Stone's Policy Paradox Approach

GOALS

Equity

How are services distributed, and who are the members and recipients?
How is power used to rank or distribute resources?
Is power used to oppress or discriminate?
What is provided (items of service linked to need)?
What is the process of receiving service (how)—competition, lotteries, elections, boundaries, values, and so forth?
Is there distributive justice?

Efficiency

What is the objective measure to judge efficiency?
What are the costs of obtaining services?
Who is the constituency (it is efficient for whom)?
What are the important inputs or outputs?
Is there duplication and when is duplication seen or judged to be important?
Is there allocative efficiency?

Security

What has primacy—economic, physical, or psychological considerations, or military security?
What are the minimums necessary to meet security needs? Those that are directly visible? For the future? For those at risk? For the community?
What is the status of the political validation of need and goal claims?

Where is power/hierarchy located within this policy and its oversight?
Which is preferred, security or efficiencies?

Liberty

What is the degree of lack of interference?
What is the degree of individual choice and action?
Which overriding value combination is preferred—liberty/security, liberty/equity?

PROBLEMS

Symbols

What words or symbolic devices are used to portray the policy problem?
What language is used to shape the drama of the stories?
What political strategy is used to construct and reveal the hidden stories?

Numbers

What symbolic devices are used in the numerical language?
How are counting and measuring used to create the problem story?

Causes

What symbols and numbers are used to portray cause?
What does the causal theory reveal about control?
What cause is linked to a result?

Interests

How is language used to portray the problem as a contest between competing interests?
Who are the villains and who are the heroes?
Where is the strength in the story of the problem?

Decisions

How are the preferred decisions being portrayed as rational choices?
How are numbers used to count up the costs and benefits of alternative pathways?
How are complexity and confusion being reduced to a single choice?

SOLUTIONS

Inducements

What rewards, punishments, incentives, or sanctions are being used to change behavior?

Rules

What commands are in place to act or not act?

(*continued*)

(continued)

Who are the people and what are the situations that determine permissions and entitlements?

What sanctions (inducements) back up the rule?

Facts

What strategies are used to persuade?

What cognitive strategies (rather than rewards and punishments) are used to provide information so that minds are made up in the desired direction?

Rights

What strategies are used to invoke government power?

Where is citizen enforcement to assure the desired solution?

Powers

What strategies are used to alter the decisions, to change the size of the decision-making body, to shift authority from one part of government to another, and so forth?

Who else is being included among the decision makers?

How has the political power been restructured?

Source: Adapted from *Policy Paradox: The Art of Political Decision Making*, by D. Stone, 2002, New York, NY: Norton.

First, consider how one might go about accomplishing the desired goal by applying Stone's (2002) approach in analyzing P.L. 111-13. In Chapter 5 we suggested,

> [I]f Madeline were confused about what problem was being served by the volunteerism solution, or if she were to wonder exactly which goals were being attended to by this public law, Stone's political approach, which allows a look at the paradoxes that seem to be present in the law, would be more than helpful. Madeline could interrogate the law to determine whether equity, efficiency, security, or liberty was the priority, and she could begin to understand why all of them might be in play. Stone would help her to look at the other paradoxes contained in the problem definitions and the selected solutions as well.

To accomplish this, let us first test the idea that the Stone approach is appropriate in this case. Then let us look at how one might proceed to accomplish the analysis.

TARGETING THE RESEARCH

Based on the Service, Engagement, and Volunteerism case, Madeline might easily have constructed a *policy research question* such as, What are the goals of this law, and why was volunteerism seen as the mechanism to solve the problem the policy seeks to address? Note that a rational analysis might have stopped with "What are the goals of this law?," taking the goals at face value. But Stone's approach is one that raises a number of probing questions about the goals. Madeline's bifurcated question would allow her to try to overcome some of the confusion about how the role of volunteerism, especially in her agency, has anything to do with the types of social problems that were implicitly and explicitly in evidence in the public law as signed by President Obama. Embedded in this question is a suspicion that politics, power, and multiple views about the nature of service, civic engagement, and volunteerism are at play in the final form of this particular policy. This research question can be addressed by the Stone approach because Stone's questions expand rather than narrow the analysis. This approach allows Madeline to probe, to ask "why," and to seek a deeper understanding of what this policy is about. Essentially a nonrational approach is a sense-making process.

Before jumping into the research effort itself, it is necessary to engage in more assessment in order to appropriately target the analysis. First, Madeline may identify the *form* of the policy that will be the focus of the analysis driven by the foregoing research question. Though Madeline is very close to the programmatic aspects of this policy in her day-to-day work, which might lead her to look at rules and regulations or the standards that might apply to practice guided by this policy in her agency, her research question is statutorial. The form is a federally mandated policy. She is interested in investigating the policy instrument—the statute, itself, as enacted by the federal government—so she will need to look for data outside the bounds of agency practice.

Next, Madeline would articulate the *level* at which the policy research question is being pitched. Though Madeline is highly interested in how this policy will play out at her agency and in her own professional work, her question at this stage is really about national level policy. She is interested in the aspects of this policy that will be operationalized through the various federal agencies being held accountable for the enactment of P.L. 111-13; therefore, what is going on at her agency or in her community, while important, will not be relevant data sources for this particular analytic process.

The Stone approach can be used across all aspects of the policy process. It can *focus* on formulation, product, implementation, or performance. Although the initial focus of this research question seems to be on the policy intent or goal at the formulation stage, the policy product or the choice of the policy instrument as articulated in the public law might also be important analytically. Since there are also aspects of measurement in the policy related to implementation actions and impact, attention to those aspects might also be important, making the Stone approach quite able to respond to what might be necessary for the type of research question that is presented.

Justification of the analytic approach involves critical thinking and decision making prior to the application of the analytic approach. The guidance provided by the Stone approach will allow the analyst to attend to information related to statutory law (the form) and national policy (the level). It allows broader questioning of both the statutorial policy product and the formulation process at the national level (a dual focus). Because of this, a policy analyst like Madeline will be able to look at both history and politics in order to understand the context that allowed or propelled the particular policy decisions represented in the public law. Most important is that the structure of this approach allows a look at goals, problems, and solutions in light of history and politics in order for the policy decisions to have meaning. As there seem to be some paradoxes in the content of the policy, this approach also allows the management of those paradoxes, making it a useful guide to researching the policy question at hand.

APPLYING THE APPROACH

While the questions that one might ask under the guidance of a particular approach to policy analysis are important, the feasibility of the enactment of a particular approach actually depends on whether or not the analyst knows where to find the needed information or data at each stage of the analytic process and has access to it. So rather than engage in a completely developed policy analysis in this section, we provide ideas about ways to construct the questions already present in the approach to target the particulars of the current analysis, given the policy research question. This allows us to look at each aspect of the approach, while also giving some suggestions about what might be useful data sources for the process.

Determining the Policy Goals   To determine the level of *equity* as a goal, it will be important to thoroughly review all aspects of the written public law to determine those who specifically are to be served. The language of the document will provide Madeline an indication both of the service that is to be provided and who the recipients should be. Because of the complexity of this law and the various identified service recipients and types of services, it would be wise to create a grid describing all potential participants and the services that can be received in order to determine issues of power and oppression. Some specific groups are identified, such as "underprivileged," "Native Hawaiians," "states," and those over 55 years old. Do these groups represent power or are they oppressed populations? Among those listed it would be important to attempt a power ranking. That power might come from a consideration of characteristics such as socioeconomic status, age, and education. There may be other language clues within the law that will give power identities.

Once the services and recipients have been identified, it is important to determine whether services are linked to need. The important aspect of this analysis will become clear when whose need is being discussed—those with the most or the least power. In the Act, what needs are articulated by whom? This will be further explicated when the services are linked to the way they are to be accessed. Where will there be competition, and where will services be easily available? How does that relate to the power analysis? From this, it should be apparent to Madeline whether distributive justice is a goal. Will those with less power be likely to gain power because of the services that they will be able to receive as a result of this law?

Within the language of the law, whether related to access, services, or evaluation, is there a mention of an objective measure of *efficiency*? Given the mandated evaluation, is there attention to efficiency? Going back to the service and eligibility grid, what costs are involved in receiving services? Costs may include resources other than money, such as time or effort. What is described for all recipients? Is it easier to provide or to receive services? Is there a connection to the power ranking in the equity analysis? If there is evidence of attention to efficiency, for whom is it intended to be efficient? In all the mention of services, which resources and actions are necessary to produce which products? Is there a possibility of duplication of efforts across services or recipients of services? Is duplication a problem at a partic- ular level of power? For example, is duplication of service at the locality level within a state seen to be a problem? Finally, Madeline needs to determine how services are allotted and whether efficiency is part of the design?

The assessment of *security* can also be accomplished through the language of the law. In considering the full document, Madeline should determine what seems to be most at interest—economic security or physical, psychological, or military security? What types of security might be attended to through the services to be provided? Is there any mention of what is sufficient to create the types of security of interest? If this is not explicitly stated and explicitly visible, what security issues might be behind the explicit choices represented in this law? Is there any evidence that future security is a consideration? Which of the recipients or recipient groups might be seen to be at risk either as a result of the service or if service is not provided?

There may also be a political dimension of this security consideration. Thus, investigating the hearings as documented in the *Congressional Record* that occurred before passage of the bill in both the House and the Senate will give Madeline an indication of political positioning regarding a validation of needs and goals regarding security and the other dimensions of policy goals. This assessment of hearing records, along with a review of the power and risk hierarchy created in earlier aspects of this analysis, will give some indication of the existence of a power hierarchy, if power is, indeed, a driving force regarding goal selection. With this analysis, it should be clear to Madeline whether security or efficiency is given precedence in the language of the law.

Liberty can also be assessed through the language of the public law. In this case it is important for Madeline to determine, through the discussion of the services and of those who are intended as recipients, the degree to which there is expected to be interference at some governmental level regarding decisions made in implementing the law. At issue here would be the investigation of the level of federal interference in the form of monitoring and evaluation of state and local levels of decision making. At the programmatic level, it would be important to assess the degree to which those to whom the law applies are forced to participate in the described services. Based on the language of the law, what degree of personal choice and action seems to be possible?

Once this information has been collected and assessed, it should be possible for Madeline to determine whether liberty is preferred over security or over equity. If it is impossible to determine a single preference among the four goals, statements justifying the existence of competing goals must become part of this analysis.

Determining the Problems the Policy Is Designed to Address In many cases, the exact problem may not be a stated part of the policy response. In other cases, the problem identified in the policy is not exactly the problem being addressed in the policy, so total reliance on the language of the policy might not aid Madeline in making sense about the intent of P.L. 111-13. The determination of the exact problem will largely be made through investigation of the discussions in the polity or in the public square.

Symbols in the form of words or symbolic devices will have been used to shape the public understanding of what constitutes the problem. To find these, it will be important for Madeline to look at what newspapers, online bloggers, TV commentators on all sides, public hearings, and other news sources were saying about the issues when the public law was first being considered and during the time of public commentary. It might be helpful to look at position statements and newsletters, Web sites, and other mechanisms of communication within and between the various advocacy groups with a stake in the problem this policy is designed to address. Certainly, it would be good to look at the position statements of the American Association of Retired Persons (AARP), but Madeline should also consider looking for anything that might have come from veterans' groups or child advocacy organizations interested in children aging out of the foster care system. Volunteer organizations at national and state levels might also be a good source of information, as well as any organization with a professional stake in the services that might be provided as a result of the bill.

Once the data sources have been located, it would be important to be certain that a range of positions are present before looking closely at the range of words being used to describe the problem. How loaded are the words? How dramatic are the stories being used to portray the situations that require attention? By looking at the range of positions and who has written these positions, in combination with what was spoken publicly in forums and hearings, it might also be possible for Madeline to uncover the strategies that were used to construct what is present while also revealing the hidden stories of the multiple stake-holding groups.

Using approximately the same data sources, Madeline should be able to identify how *numbers* were used to shape the problem. Was the focus of the numerical language on those with or without the problem? In short, Madeline should be able to tell how counting and measuring were used to construct the story of the problem that should be

addressed through this legislation. In the process, she may discover
that there is not just one problem.

Causes of the problem can also be found through the use of words
and numbers. The data sources already identified should provide
Madeline with sufficient information from the symbols to see how
the cause has been portrayed related to each problem that she identified. It will be important to see whether any of the causal elements can
be sufficiently articulated to create what can be called a theory about
the cause. Sometimes empirical evidence will be part of the symbolic
story line. If this evidence is present, can it be used to link the services
available in the policy to the results desired in the policy? Finally, it will
be important for Madeline to see whether those results can be linked to
the causes identified in the discussions about the problem.

Interests will also be identifiable, if Madeline has made a thorough
collection of positions by the multiple stakeholders to the problem
and its solution. A thorough analysis of the language used by all the
stakeholding groups should provide her with a sense of how the
problem has been differentially constructed by stakeholding groups.
Further, it should be possible to trace the various contests that existed
between the competing interests. In addition, it will probably be
possible to see how the problem-setting process involved policy interests from the community through to the national level.

To get a better understanding of the power involved, it will be
important for Madeline to determine who could be portrayed as the
"villains" and "heroes" in the story of the problem to determine
where the strength lies in the overall story. This will help her to
make sense about the *decisions* that were made in the construction of
the policy response. By looking both at the language of the law and
the material in the polity, it should be possible to see how the final
decisions about the policy content were portrayed as rational choices
(even if they were not). It will be possible to see how cost and benefits
were handled regarding all the potential policy solution alternatives. In
this way, the complexity and confusion that Madeline should be seeing
in the problem-setting process should make sense. In other words, it
should be clear why the solution choice or choices were made.

Determining the Selected Solution   In investigating the selected policy
solution(s), Madeline will return to the language of the law itself to
determine the existence and level of *inducements* present in the policy.
Through a thorough reading of the Act, it should be possible to list the
rewards, punishments, incentives, or sanctions that are being used. It is

also important to determine whose behavior these inducements are intended to change. Is the change in the provider or recipient of service, and at what levels of policy does it apply?

Madeline should be able to identify the *rules* that will be governing action or inaction related to implementation of the public law. Within the law itself, Madeline will find who the players are and in what situations permissions and entitlements will be enacted. Who is privileged and what positive or negative sanctions are built into the law to force or facilitate implementation? She should look closely at the information and analysis she already has obtained to see how the symbols and the problems play out in the portrayal of the solution.

Many of the solutions will be portrayed as *facts* that will be found in the polity contests that Madeline has already investigated. What strategies were used to persuade those with a stake that the chosen solution is the best? What strategies within the law exist to assure that the selected choice(s) will be enacted? Aside from rewards and punishments, what other cognitive persuasive strategies are present in the Act itself, and is there a relationship between this and what was found in the polity?

Madeline will be able to determine the *rights* present in the selected solution(s) by looking at what is stated in the Act to invoke government powers. She will be interested in those articulated at the federal, state, and local levels, because all may apply to her agency's subsequent programming. Because of the earlier analysis of the polity, she will also want to look at openings in the law for citizen participation and enforcement of the desired solutions. Where does the polity still have space to monitor and moderate the policy process and product?

Further interrogation of the Act itself should allow Madeline to analyze the presence or absence of the polity in the process by looking at the *powers* contained in it. What stated strategies exist to monitor and potentially alter the decisions present in the law? Is there information about how change can happen? Where are decisions to be made and at what levels of government and elsewhere? Is there evidence of expected shifts in authority from one part of the federal government to another or from one level of government to another? Who else will be included in the future decision-making process about the policy? Finally, as a result of this policy and the process to this point, have there been any changes in political power that will influence enactment of the law?

When Madeline has completed her analysis using the Stone (2002) approach, she will have a deep understanding of why the original bill took the form that it did as an enacted policy. In addition, she will have highlighted the paradoxes contained within the policy that should give her some ideas about where the challenges will be when it comes to the actual implementation of the services envisioned in the final Act. At her programmatic level, she should also have some clear ideas of the choices that her agency could make regarding services that could provide either great opportunities or great challenges when it comes to the evaluation process and the potential sanctions that might result.

CRITIQUE OF THE APPROACH

Based just on the length of the discussion of potential data sources needed to enact this approach, it should be clear that this is a very complicated way to engage in policy analysis. It requires a good deal of creativity to unearth relevant data sources and an even greater amount of critical thinking to appropriately analyze the data. However, the results should provide a complex picture of the process that resulted in the particular product with a good vision of the challenges present for those interested in implementation of the policy. In other words, most of the policy itself should make sense, even if the analyst is left with ideological disagreements with the final policy product. Finally, this analysis makes implementation choices clear at the programmatic level. It will show where the potential risks and benefits should be found, so that those engaging in implementation should be able to do so fully envisioning the opportunities and pitfalls that might be present.

Because this is an interpretive nonrational approach that is more attuned to power and politics than to cause and effect, this process does not provide precise predictive information. Nor does it specifically provide those interested in implementing the policy with the exact steps needed to successfully implement the policy to assure the desired results. In short, this approach does not simplify the policy process at any level. Unlike a rational approach, it will expose complexity rather than narrow the focus.

USING KINGDON'S POLICY PRIMEVAL SOUP OR GARBAGE CAN APPROACH

Another approach can be used in response to the issues that were recounted in Chapter 5, based on Kingdon's (1995) framework. Again to refresh your memory, Box 6.2 provides a reminder of the problems, politics, and participants (the three streams) that Kingdon identified, along with alternative specification, coupling and windows, and entrepreneurs.

Box 6.2 Kingdon's Policy Primeval Soup Approach

AGENDA SETTING

Problems

1. Why has this problem come to occupy the attention of governmental officials (or other decision makers) more than other problems?
2. Is or was there a focusing event (e.g., a disaster, crisis, personal experience, etc.)?
3. How did the condition become linked to a problem that gained public attention?

Politics

4. Which factors in the political stream facilitated addressing this problem?
5. How were decision makers and others persuaded to recognize this problem or settle on certain proposals?
6. What interest groups are involved in this process?

Participants

7. Who are the visible participants, and what roles do they play?
8. Who are the invisible participants, and what roles do they play?

ALTERNATIVE SPECIFICATION

9. How is the list of potential alternatives for policy choices narrowed to the ones that actually receive serious consideration?

COUPLING AND WINDOWS

10. How have streams of problems, policies, and politics become interrelated within a decision agenda?
11. Are problem windows or political windows open?

ENTREPRENEURS

12. Who are the entrepreneurs?
13. How are entrepreneurs softening up the system?
14. What are they doing to push proposals forward?

Source: Adapted from *Agenda, Alternatives, and Public Policies* (2nd edition, pp. 197–205), by J. W. Kingdon, 1995, New York, NY: Longman.

In Chapter 5 we stated,

> *[I]f Madeline had questions about alternative standpoints, context issues at the outset, or politics in action at the agenda-setting stage with P.L.111-13, she would investigate the stated problem and ask why it has come to the attention of decision makers at all stakeholding levels. She would identify the factors that have facilitated this effort to address the problem. This might include both financial and sociological issues. It would be important to identify all the players in favor and against the construction of the problem. Both overt and covert influences should be identified to understand what the alternatives were and what led to setting the agenda. Madeline, as a Director of Volunteers, would probably be aligned with certain stakeholders who advocate for the professionalization of volunteerism, raising a host of issues about where volunteerism and professional roles overlap.*

Here, Madeline is interested in unraveling everything that went into the construction of the bill in its final form so that she can make sense out of what will eventually be guiding her practice in her agency.

TARGETING THE RESEARCH

Returning to the Service, Engagement, and Volunteerism case and the concerns at issue previously, Madeline could have constructed another *policy research question* that would take her in another analytic direction. Another relevant question might be, What went into the decisions to move in the directions set by P.L. 111-13? By asking this question, she would be able to look at the complex set of circumstances and players that allowed the policy alternative as stated in this public law to be the acceptable choice. This research question could guide her investigation about just how this policy might impact her agency. In doing so, she may be able to uncover some surprising allies, while also making sense about how the bill emerged. This type of question can be addressed by applying Kingdon's approach.

Prior to launching into the application of the Kingdon approach, it is important to target the research by identifying the policy's form, level, and focus. As in the case of the application of the Stone approach, the *form* is the policy instrument, the statute. Again, the *level* remains the same. Madeline continues to have an interest at the national level of policy, though she may encounter influential players and circumstances at other governmental and community levels.

However, those data sources will be deemed important to this analysis only in terms of the degree to which they had influence at the national level.

Kingdon's approach is well suited for interrogation of the agenda-setting process. Its *focus* is on formulation. Madeline's policy research question is about how the policy got to be the way it is. She is interested in more than understanding the stated intent or goal of the policy product but wants to know in depth what influences and value conflicts were present to construct the policy as it was finally signed into law. This represents a broad view of the formulation aspect of the policy process.

Using Kingdon's approach allows interrogation of both the construction of the problem as well as the politics at play in the formulation process, along with the various players in the politics of influence at the national level. *Justification of the analytic approach* is clear, because that application of this approach will also allow Madeline to uncover and interrogate the alternative constructions of the social problem—the goals and solutions that were not chosen. This may ultimately lead to making more sense of the resultant policy product.

APPLICATION OF THE APPROACH

Madeline will find Kingdon adds new dimensions to her understanding of P.L. 111-13. In the following sections, we provide a look at each aspect of Kingdon's approach, while also giving some suggestions about what might be useful data sources for the process.

Determining Agenda Setting   Because Kingdon allows an identification and interrogation of several streams in the policy process, it is important to look at all three aspects as the first step in policy research guided by his approach. *Problems* that have gained the attention of government officials can be identified through various media sources, such as blogs, news outlets, and other formal means of capturing what is important to the polity. In addition to identifying how the particular problem identified in P.L. 111-13 gained attention, it is important to look at the empirical literature about population groups specifically targeted by this policy. What is being said about American citizens over 55 years of age, the particular "at risk" groups mentioned in the law, the general status of American youth?

It is also important to review the historical context around the time that the social problem began to capture media and other attention.

Were their particular crystallizing events or windows of opportunity opening on the national or local scene? Were there notable personal experiences that captured the attention of the public?

Remembering that a condition or situation has to be big enough, bad enough, or related to people powerful enough to make it a problem, it is also important to interrogate the *politics* involved in problem setting. Data sources can continue to be the media coverage, but the interrogation strategy should shift somewhat. Were there events within the political context that facilitated the need to address the problem? Elections of new candidates to office, particular politicians or advocacy organizations, could come to the forefront of the discussion. Determining exactly who began the discussion may be difficult to ascertain, but beyond the media it would be important to see what was said in public hearings on the subject at the national or local levels, to examine any government reports that might help to shape the country's understanding of the problem, and to review any advocacy group coverage of the issues. It would also be important to identify particular individuals and interest groups that demonstrated a stake in the problem, either seeing a problem or declaring that the situation was not a problem.

All important *participants* in the shaping of the problem may not be identifiable, because Madeline could not have been behind the scenes during the agenda-setting process. However, through the analysis so far, she should be able to identify the visible, explicit players and the roles that they played. Analysis would be looking for support actions, compromise efforts, and obstructions, as well as the range of ideas that evoked these responses. To identify the invisible participants may be possible after the fact by seeing the media commentary and the material written by those organizations (advocacy and otherwise) with a stake in the issues addressed in the bill.

Specifying Alternatives By looking at hearing minutes in both the House and the Senate along with the various ideas that might have been tested in the media outlets at the time, it should be possible to list the policy choices that were present and considered as viable ways to solve the identified problem(s) as stated in the bill itself. By tracking what was publicly discussed during the six months or so prior to the final construction of the bill, Madeline should be able to see how alternatives were narrowed. Another step in the process is to track how the decision happened, which actually may be easier to determine than the specific alternatives that were seriously considered.

Determining Couplings and Windows Madeline can track how some ideas disappeared from the public discussion using her media and other data sources by seeing how the identification of the problem(s); the current policies related to service, engagement, and volunteerism; and politics (and all the power players) came together to create the response represented in P.L. 111-13. In looking at the texts, there should be some identifiable "windows of opportunity" within the problem status, the current policies as constructed, and the politics at hand that made it possible to understand why at this time, this problem definition and this policy response became possible and others were rejected.

Identifying Entrepreneurs In reconstructing the history that led up to fashioning the bill as finally enacted, Madeline should be able to identify the important political players—Kingdon calls them "policy entrepreneurs"—who were able to take advantage of what was going on at the time. In reviewing the hearings and the questions and answers exchanged between the politicians and those presenting testimony, it should be clear how the governmental system was "softened" to allow certain policy strategies to push forward to acceptance over others. It would be interesting for Madeline to determine whether the process for this was rational and empirical or nonrational and affective. For example, it would be important to determine whether the state of Senator Kennedy's health played any part in what the entrepreneurs did. It would be interesting to see whether Kennedy, for whom the bill was named, was actually one of the entrepreneurs. Going back further into the history of hearings related to the bills that are being amended by this law would help Madeline to see what is being revisited with differing results and what seems to remain on certain entrepreneur agendas to be treated at another time.

When Madeline completes this analysis, she will have a good understanding about why the problem statements in the bill are as they are. She will have a solid understanding of the players in the agenda-setting process, the politics involved, and how the problem came to be defined as it was. She would also see which policy solutions surfaced for consideration and how certain positions were accepted, rejected, or modified. In short, she would have a good picture of how the policy came to be in its final form. She might also have some ideas about how it might become modified in the years to come, based not on effectiveness measures but on power and politics.

CRITIQUE OF THE APPROACH

Kingdon's approach is a very complicated way to engage in policy analysis with a decidedly political and power focus. Like Stone's approach, it requires a good deal of creativity to unearth relevant data sources and even a greater amount of critical thinking to appropriately analyze the data. The detective work required to find information about both the visible and the invisible participants and their roles may be particularly daunting. With appropriate tenacity, the analytic results should give a rich and complex picture of the political and contextual influences that shaped the policy product as it came to be. Further, this analysis may provide insight into subsequent modifications of the law.

On the other hand, this analysis does not make implementation choices clear at the programmatic level. Aside from understanding the political positioning of those with a stake in the problem and the selected solution choice, determining the range of acceptable implementation choices would still remain an interpretational challenge.

Like Stone's and all the other approaches used in this chapter, Kingdon's approach is an interpretive, nonrational approach. It is more attuned to power and politics than to cause and effect. If Madeline wanted precise predictive information, she would not find it through this approach. Kingdon's framework does not provide any guidance for the exact steps needed to successfully implement the policy to assure the desired results. It will, however, allow the analyst to understand why the particular results were the ones chosen over various other options. Again, like all nonrational approaches this one does not simplify the policy analytic process. Here the complexity is at the policy formulation level.

USING PRIGMORE AND ATHERTON'S POLICY ANALYSIS APPROACH

Prigmore and Atherton's (1986) policy analysis approach was introduced in Chapter 5 as an example of a framework that could be used to examine policy content (product). This nonrational approach can take Madeline in yet another direction in policy analysis. As a refresher, Prigmore and Atherton's Policy Analysis approach is reproduced in Box 6.3.

Box 6.3   Prigmore and Atherton's Policy Analysis

Consideration Related to Values

Is the policy compatible with contemporary "style"?
Is the policy compatible with important and enduring cultural values, particularly equity, fairness, and justice?
Is the policy compatible with social work's professional value and ethical system?

Dimensions of Influence

Is the policy acceptable to those in formal decision-making positions?
Does the policy satisfy relevant interest groups?

Knowledge Considerations

Is the policy based on knowledge that has been tested to some degree?
Is the policy workable? That is, can the programs that flow from the policy be carried out in the real world?
Does the policy create few problems for both the public and the intended beneficiaries?

Elements Related to Costs and Benefits

Is the policy reasonably effective?
Is the policy efficient?

Source: Social Welfare Policy (2nd edition, p. 46), by C. S. Prigmore and C. R. Atherton, 1986, Lexington, MA: Heath. Used by permission.

In Chapter 5 we stated,

[I]f Madeline had questions about the multiple values and meanings that had the most influence in the shaping of the policy content, Prigmore and Atherton's policy analysis approach would be helpful here. It would be important to examine the expectations of feasibility related to the reauthorization of the bill supporting volunteerism, and she would identify the predominant cultural values that served as a context for this particular reauthorization. As a social worker, she would be interested in determining the value congruence with the profession, along with determining who had influence in shaping the final policy product. Of particular interest would be the degree to which the selected solutions had been tested and whether or not all aspects of the policy are feasible with the potential to be effective in overcoming the social problem as defined in P.L. 111-13.

TARGETING THE RESEARCH

If Madeline were most interested in the values and meanings more than simply the politics involved with P.L. 111-13 and if she really wanted to know the values foreground of the policy, she might construct a *policy research question* in the following way: What are the values represented in P.L. 111-13 as evidenced by the policy itself? By asking this question, she could look closely at the language of the current policy as well as the language of all the policies that this public law was intended to revise. First, she will need to identify the values present. Then she can determine the degree to which these values are congruent with her profession in general and her agency in particular.

Again, the *form* of the policy of interest will be the statute itself, but the policy objectives and the administrative rules and regulations could also be of interest along with the budget decisions regarding the Act. Depending on the timing of her analysis, she may have only the statute itself available to her. Some of the policy objectives may be identifiable within the language of the law. Many others will be apparent when the administrative rules and regulations are fashioned by those agencies that have been tasked with the implementation of the policy. Budget information present in enabling legislation or from the Office of Management and Budget will also be of use as background to the language of the law itself.

The *level* of the analysis continues to be national, perhaps including federal agencies tasked with the responsibilities related to all aspects of the law. But, for this research question the *focus* is on the policy product—the policy instruments themselves. *Justification of the analytic approach* can be made on the basis of Prigmore and Atherton's capacity to analyze and provide data for judgments about how values play within the bill and whether or not values might overshadow other political or empirical considerations. This process will help Madeline to determine this policy's congruence with the values of the social work profession, especially related to the social justice aspects of the values and ethics of the profession.

APPLICATION OF THE APPROACH

Consideration of Values   To make the values of this policy explicit, first Madeline must review the full policy (and perhaps the budgetary information, as well as the rules and procedures related to imple- mentation that will come from the agencies in charge of implementa- tion) to identify and list the values that can be identified. First, the values can be identified by the language that is used. Is the language inclusive, exclusionary, controlling, or punitive? Second, it would be important to look at the values represented by the behaviors anticipated by the law and who is identified and tasked with particular expectations?

Once the values have been identified, then Madeline, based on her knowledge of what is going on at the national scene through her attention to the media outlets, will need to assess whether this policy is compatible with contemporary national positions. It might also be important in the future for her to determine whether the values are congruent with what she knows about the values at her state and community levels. Prigmore and Atherton suggest an analysis of congruence with the cultural values of equity, fairness, and justice, which will indeed be congruent with the values of Madeline's profession but may not be congruent with state, local, or agency values.

Dimensions of Influence Based on what she can find through media outlets that recorded the public discussions prior to the final shaping of the policy and through the committee hearing documentation, as well as the minutes of the House and Senate debates on the bill, it should be clear to whom this bill is acceptable and to whom it is not. Formal decision makers are those who vote on the bill, so it will be important to see who voted for and against the bill in its final form. It might also be important to track committee votes as well as the amendments that were offered along the way, not only to explicitly understand the personal and political values being presented but to identify the influence that was present in the shaping of the final form. In addition, hearing information, along with printed material prepared by interest groups and other advocacy elements, should be interrogated, not only for the values present but to determine the degree to which the policy as approved is satisfactory to which interest groups and to which interest groups it is not. This will provide greater clues to other dimensions of influence in shaping this policy.

Knowledge Considerations To enact this aspect of the policy analytic process, it will be important for Madeline to have some idea about the literature surrounding service, engagement, and volunteerism. This is important in determining whether the elements of the policy are based on empirical evidence, which would suggest that what is offered in this law has some chance of solving the problem as identified in the law.

Information about intervention research related to the stated problems will help Madeline to determine whether the policy as constructed can be feasibly implemented in her place of work. In assessing the program elements of the policy, Madeline, from her practitioner's position, will probably be able to identify implementations problems that might accrue for the public in general and for the intended beneficiaries. She will need to look closely at the Act to identify all the beneficiaries. Identifying who is present as a beneficiary and who is absent will help underscore certain values positions. Determining who might have problems at implementation and who might not will also underscore what is valued and what might not be.

Elements Related to Costs and Benefits   Costs and benefits can be assessed both empirically and from a values perspective. This section of the approach may not be able to be undertaken until full implementation of the policy, but previews based on empirical evidence and Madeline's practice wisdom will be possible. Can the policy be effective? Does it have a chance to impact the problem(s) as defined in the Act? For whom will it be effective? What values are present with the answer to this question? The same is true for the efficiency question—efficient for whom? More importantly, how do effectiveness and efficiency interrelate in this policy? Do these words convey different meanings to different groups?

This analysis, when completed, could provide much information at various levels that will help both Madeline and her agency anticipate the professional and personal challenges and opportunities present in this bill. Madeline will have a clear understanding about how the nonrational aspects of values and ideology were at play, sometimes in recognition of and at other times ignoring evidence. Making sense of the final product is possible, so that professional choices about the opportunities and challenges of enacting the bill can be clarified.

CRITIQUE OF THE APPROACH

In Prigmore and Atherton's approach, much of the analysis rests on understanding and articulating values perspectives at a number of levels. Even-handed identification of these values and inclusion of all perspectives may be difficult. It may also be a bit confusing to discover that the elements related to costs and benefits have nothing to do with empirical evidence and everything to do with values and ideology. This might lead to a great deal of frustration for the analyst who wants the "so what" of the analysis to lead to clear decisions about the feasibility of the policy. Like all other interpretive, nonrational approaches, only sense-making, not prescriptions for success are possible.

USING GUBA'S POLICY-IN-ACTION APPROACH

In Chapter 5, we introduced yet another nonrational policy analysis approach that is particularly helpful in studying implementation. Guba's Policy-in-Action Aspect of Policy Types Taxonomy (1984) is reproduced in Box 6.4 and can be added to Madeline's toolbox.

Box 6.4 Guba's Policy-in-Action Aspect of Policy Types Taxonomy

- What constitutes the sanctioned behavior?
  - Is it formal?
  - Was it established (or "sanctified") over time?
- What are the norms of conduct?
  - Are they related to the goals or intents of the policy?
  - Are they related to the policy decisions? Rules?
  - Are they related to any guides to discretionary action? Guidelines?
  - Are they related to a problem-solving strategy? Sets of tactics?
- What are the impacts of the policy-making system on the action?
  - What actions at other levels impact the expectations, norms, and effects of the policy?
  - What decisions at other levels impact expectations, norms, and effects?
  - What behaviors in bureaucracies at all levels impact the point of policy action being investigated?

Source: Adapted from "The Effects of Definitions of Policy on the Nature and Outcomes of Policy Analysis," by E. G. Guba, 1984, *Educational Leadership, 42,* 63–70.

In Chapter 5 we stated,

[I]f Madeline had questions about the meaning of mounting the policy response or the politics that narrowed or expanded the shape and direction of the program at its enactment stage, particularly in her agency, we would first wait until the program supported by P.L. 111-13 was fully mounted (even though there is a one year timeline for evaluation). To use the policy-in-action she would identify the practices being supported both formally and implicitly, which would include the norms of conduct within the agency between employees, volunteers, and the

clients they serve and how those are related to the intent and rules of P.L. 111-13. It would also be important to interrogate how the federal, state, and local processes are being impacted and are impacting the work.

TARGETING THE RESEARCH

Expanding a bit on the Service, Engagement, and Volunteerism case, let us imagine that a state plan was developed that focused on expanding volunteers to work with at-risk adolescents. A three-year plan was developed to eliminate the drop-out and unemployment problems of the young people who were aging out of foster care. This was the main direction of the efforts at both the state and the local community levels. because Madeline's state had one of the highest levels of children and youth in long-term foster care in the nation. Because her agency had a great deal of experience recruiting and retaining the more mature volunteer, they easily expanded the program for which they had already received federal funding to include individuals 55 years and over. Since the agency wanted to expand its approach to service learning, Madeline also was tasked with recruiting veterans. Using both types of volunteers, Madeline's agency proposed and was funded for a multilevel service delivery program for adolescents aging out of foster care. Male and female mentors were on hand to help them with staying in school. There was mentoring for young people getting ready for college, with mentors being matched with the young people based on what the young people needed and what the volunteer was interested in doing. Several specialized volunteers (some of whom had been military recruiters) worked directly with young people to lead them to volunteer in community and neighborhood projects and, when appropriate, to choose one of the volunteer programs that were supported by P.L. 111-13. To do all this, the agency expanded its geographical catchment area both for recruiting volunteers and for accepting clients. As they were preparing for the year three program proposal to the state, Madeline's *policy research question* is What has been the agency experience in implementing P.L. 111-13?

This question allows a rather complex look at the public law according to the various *forms* it has taken from the time the statute was signed into law. It would allow a look at the policy objectives as they have become operationalized in Madeline's agency. This would certainly include the rules and regulations that are governing their work, the sources of which would be the federal agency in charge of the aspects of the law they are implementing as well as the specific directives that have come from the state and local levels and at the agency level. This would also include the program as proposed and the budget as received to fund program activities. Madeline would be interested in both the formal, written policies that pertain at all the *levels* as well as those informal policies that have influenced the way the agency's practice has evolved. Though it might be important to look at standards of practice and her professional code of ethics, she will have time only to look at the experience of moving the policy into action. Therefore, the *focus* of this policy analysis is policy implementation, with a particular interest at the programmatic level.

Guba's policy-in-action approach can be *justified* because of the purpose of the analysis. Madeline is interested in understanding the experience of implementation. In many ways she is interested in the implementation at all levels, because those levels impact what can and cannot be funded and subsequently undertaken at her agency level. She wants to understand how the program became the way it is now, in advance of moving forward into another round of funding. The policy-in-action approach is well suited to this sort of interrogation.

APPLICATION OF THE APPROACH

Data sources for this approach will consist of the policy itself, what is written about the policy, and what is observable about behaviors related to the policy. This may involve direct discussions with certain individuals important to implementation decisions at all the levels of interest.

What Constitutes the Sanctioned Behavior? To understand what is positively sanctioned behavior, it would be easy to look at what was funded at Madeline's agency. What part of the program proposal was modified prior to funding? Where were the enhancements that were never part of the agency's original proposal? If possible, it would also be instructive to identify what was not funded locally or at the state level. This would mean getting information regarding other agency's efforts in response to requests for proposals (RFPs).

To ascertain the level of formal sanction, it would be important to compare the program design with the administrative rules and procedures as well as the original language of the public law. It would also be important to compare the original program that was funded in year one to how it was in year two to determine whether the sanctioned behaviors held over time. If they had not held, discussions with decision makers at various levels might be helpful.

What Are the Norms of Conduct?   When looking at the norms of conduct of the agency professionals, the volunteers, and the young people served by them, Madeline must look at how each stakeholding group behaves. Once that behavior has been described, she can analyze how those behaviors might or might not be related to the goals or intent of P.L.111-13. Returning to the analysis of sanctions could be helpful in understanding findings in this area.

Whether behaviors are or are not related to the goals or intent of the policy at the federal level, another level of analysis would interrogate how policy decisions at the agency, locality, state, or federal levels might relate to program operations. Tracking changes in direction via official communication about the program would be useful. Also useful would be the content of the two years of state-level RFPs. It might be at this point that gatekeepers at the local or state levels could provide insight into expectations and changes that might have been implemented since the public law was signed. Formal interviews might help.

To get a full picture of the expectations about how stakeholders in her agency's program are expected to behave, it would be important to examine the level at which there is choice in how service is delivered or received. In this case, it might also be useful to look at guidelines that have evolved at any of the levels, including what might have come from the agency's board of directors. The context of these decisions about guidelines will have more meaning if Madeline can determine whether any changes in norms were related to problems that emerged or tactics that were necessary to satisfy other policy or particular program stakeholders. To get a sense of this, Madeline would need to return to her investigation of media sources, but this time she would need to look at media coverage that occurred since the bill was signed into law.

What Are the Impacts of the Policy-Making System on the Action?   A look at media-related information, along with interviews with those in the policy-making system, should give Madeline important clues to the changes that she might be seeing in the program from year one, through year two, to what is being expected at this time in response to the RFP that has just been received from the state. The budgetary decisions must also be interrogated, along with other decisions that have been taken at the federal, state, and local administrative levels as well as in her agency. By looking at all levels, she will see how actions and decisions outside the agency have impacted the work of the agency and the general expectations surrounding that work.

This analysis will help Madeline understand why the program currently looks the way it does and how it must be shaped to secure future funding. This may help the agency decide if it wants to continue its participation in policy implementation. It will help her to determine the difference between what she knows were the intentions of the original federal policy and what was deemed necessary and possible as the policy was implemented from the federal level, through the state, to her own agency. In many ways, this analysis could give her clues about the difference between "best practices" as envisioned by the original bill and the "best possible practices" that emerged during implementation. It should help her to see how other policy forces and policy determiners (including herself) have influenced the implementation process and the multilevel relationships that have been shaped by the bill. It might also give her some ideas about places for advocacy-level "push-backs" that might allow her program and her agency to get closer to the original intent of the policy.

CRITIQUE OF THE APPROACH

Guba's approach provides a process analysis of implementation. Because the process can be fully understood only by looking at the various implementation points of the policy, the analysis is cumbersome, and necessary data points may be all but impossible to access. If a full picture can be constructed, the human side of the implementation process will become clearer, and sense-making about evolving mandates and expectations may occur. It might not give rise to agreement with the sanctions, but the basis of those decisions and their implications should become more transparent.

Because this is a nonrational approach, any attempts to uncover and understand rational, cost/benefit decisions will be impossible. Values and ideology will be understood. Effectiveness and efficiencies related to implementation decisions will remain undiscovered.

USING AN IMPACT-ANALYSIS APPROACH

The final important aspect of policy practice and policy research is at the "so what" level. What did the policy produce related to the social problem that the policy was intended to address? In Chapter 5, we introduced some possible questions to ask about interpretive-level impact, and we reintroduce those in Box 6.5.

Box 6.5 Possible Questions to Ask About Interpretive-Level Impact

- Who would be the stakeholders who experience the policy in addition to those who were "carriers" of the social problem that the policy sought to address?
- Who might be beneficiaries? Victims? Where is there evidence of coercion and control or of consciousness raising and empowerment?
- What might be related to the experience that has something to do with how the policy became enacted at the street level? How is that enactment different than the original policy intent?
- What values are at play in the experience of the policy? How do those correspond to the values undergirding the original intent?
- Given the various constructions, what are the similarities and differences among the stakeholders on the answers to the preceding question? Where is consensus about the meaning of the experience of the policy?
- Where are there mismatches about the conditions that gave rise to the policy and the policy itself?
- What are the stakeholders' reactions to your results?

In Chapter 5 we stated,

[I]f Madeline was interested in understanding the meaning of the experience of those with a stake in the policy, she would assess all those impacted by the policy beyond those who are "disadvantaged," noting both beneficiaries and victims at the individual and institutional levels. Based on this, efforts would be made to identify the values at play in the implementation of the policy and their congruence with policy intent. The idea is to identify and understand all the standpoints that are present. Consensus and the lack of it should be articulated along with the needs that remain as a result of the mismatch between the original need and the policy itself. It would also be instructive for analysis in the future to capture stakeholders' reactions to this type of analysis.

TARGETING THE RESEARCH

Madeline has a great interest in what happened as a result of this policy, but she is limited in time and resources, so she will "simply" look at the experiences of those with a stake in her agency's implementation of P.L. 111-13 at the programmatic level. *The research question*, then, could be,

What is the meaning of P.L. 111-13 as implemented in my agency's program funded as a result of this policy? The policy *form* is programmatic and will look at the agency rules and regulations related to their implementation of the policy. In this case, then, the interest is in the organizational *level* of policy. The *focus* of Madeline's research is on impact or performance. In other words, she is interested in seeing the results of the operationalization of the public law at her agency level, and she is interested in the multiple perspectives of all those who have a stake in the operationalization of this policy by her agency. *Justification of the analytic approach* rests on the idea that Madeline wishes to understand the experiences of the various stakeholders to the program, not the output or the outcomes of that program made possible through P.L. 111-13. She wishes to assess impact from a values perspective and is interested in matching the intent of the policy with the implementation undertaken by her agency. From that she wishes to ascertain whether the results of that implementation for all involved with the problem can be linked to the process of resolving the social problem(s) identified in the policy. This approach can do that.

APPLICATION OF THE APPROACH

Actual impact analysis enacted in a nonrational way cannot be accomplished in the usual ways that impact analysis is understood due to the general inability of these approaches to assess a causal link between problem resolution and policy/program activities. Instead, nonrational approaches such as this one allow for an understanding of the experience of the problem-solving process at the individual and organizational levels. The assessment of impact is at the meaning level. It provides a way to understand the program that resulted from the policy and the program's efforts to solve the social problem of the policy at the individual level. This is what Madeline is interested in investigating.

Stakeholders An important stage in the application of this analysis is to identify all the stakeholders involved in the agency's implementation of P.L. 111-13 at the programmatic level. To do this, Madeline must identify all individuals and organizations that might have something to say about the result of her agency's work. She could start internal to the agency by identifying board members, administrators, professional practitioners, volunteers, and those who are served by the practitioners and volunteers. The volunteers of interest would be those who are older than 55 and those who are veterans. The individuals served would be all the young people who are or were in transition from foster care to living independently.

Since these young people have a family and community context, Madeline could identify biological family as well as foster family members as having a stake. Representatives of all the systems serving these children while they are out of their home might also be included, such as the educational, health, mental health, religious, and justice systems. Concerned community members might have a stake in the program's success or failure, as do competitor agencies. Funders are also stakeholders.

Beneficiaries and Victims   Once the list has been built, it is important to identify who might be considered beneficiaries and/or victims of the program and, thus, of the policy. If Madeline is unable to make this categorization based on experience, she may need to engage in some direct interviews to achieve a deeper understanding of perspectives on beneficiaries and victims. This would be particularly needed for any part of the stakeholding population that might feel as though they had experienced coercion or control because of the program. This might be on the part of the practitioners, the volunteers, or the young people who might not have been able to act as they wished as the program emerged. It would also be important for Madeline to discern during these interviews whether or not consciousness raising or empowerment were identified as results of the program. Were any stakeholders more aware of the complexity of the issues involved? Were individuals or the agency as a whole able to act on their own behalf to improve the policy-enacting situation?

Enactment Experience   Program reports and other narrative records of the history of implementation will provide reasonable resources for understanding exactly how the program unfolded. But it will be important to hear from the program enactors (practitioners, volunteers, service recipients) about their experience in providing and receiving the service. How did they feel about what happened? Of particular interest would be an analysis of these data to ascertain how the enactment of the program might differ from the original intent of the policy. Information about intent can be found in the *Congressional Record* and the public law itself. A comparative analysis of these differing levels of stakeholders would be informative.

Values at Play   In the analysis of the discourse of those interviewed, it will be important for Madeline to analyze the presence or absence of values in what was reported. The narrative of stakeholders will generally contain both implicit and explicit values in statements or judgments made. Madeline will then need to determine how or in what ways these identified values correspond or not with the values undergirding the original intent. This means that the intent found in the *Congressional Record* and in the public law itself must be analyzed for explicit and implicit values in order to make the comparison.

Similarities and Differences in Perspectives   Further analysis of interview material should include both within and between stakeholding group comparisons of answers regarding all of the preceding questions. In undertaking this analysis, it will be important for Madeline to identify where the various groups disagree and where there is consensus. Lack of agreement and the meaning of that lack should be further interrogated, perhaps with further interviews, in order to create a full picture of the meaning of the experience of the policy. This can be accomplished through a narrative analysis.

Mismatches between Condition and Policy   Analysis of the individual narratives will most likely provide a historical as well as a contextual view of the lived experience of those connected to Madeline's agency's program. Further analysis of stakeholders' words should provide a sense of the presence or absence of mismatches between the conditions found in her agency's context and the experiences of the individuals served by the agency. She should be able to identify what the program was able to accomplish in implementing this national-level policy at a programmatic level.

Results would probably be presented in a narrative case study format, showcasing the multiple perspectives of all the stakeholding groups. The story would probably give a rather visceral picture of what policy enactment was like from all stakeholding perspectives. In the telling of the story, the meaning of the experience from all perspectives should be clear, as should be the many paradoxes that exist because of the differing perspectives.

Stakeholder Reactions   The final measure of impact using this analytic approach will be the reactions of all the stakeholders to the case study itself. Certainly, it would be important that each of the stakeholding perspectives be accurately captured and reconstructed, which would require checking with participants to assure accuracy. Another measure of impact for Madeline will be how stakeholders react to their own perspective as well as to the perspective of others as contained in the case report. In this way, Madeline's analysis could be characterized as another aspect of the policy intervention geared to further consciousness raising about the problem, the selected policy response, and the consequence of the policy postimplementation.

CRITIQUE OF THE APPROACH

This approach does not have the capacity to measure traditional impact (specific outcomes) expected by rational analysts, nor does it look at efficiencies or effectiveness measures. Instead, it is capable of unearthing the human side of the policy implementation process by way of various perspectives on the overall experience. This approach, while being rather complex, is also quite intimate in that the personal perspectives of very different individuals will be articulated. This analysis will underscore the affective dimension of the experience of policy "up close and personal," while also making clear the complexity of that experience, given all the standpoints involved in the experience. Given the complexity, it is difficult for the analysis to produce either a wholly positive or wholly negative assessment of the process and its impact, so those wishing to use impact analysis for "yes" or "no" decision making regarding a policy will be left without a definitive direction for such a decision. On the other hand, the paradoxes that are made clear can help to identify useful directions for future action.

DISCUSSION

Nonrational approaches to policy analysis are nonlinear and nonreductionist, requiring a holistic stance in the analytic space. Although our discussion of approaches throughout this chapter may appear to have similar starting points in the application of the approaches, this was only our effort to make each approach as clear as possible. In the real world of policy analysis, nonrational approaches allow the analyst to start wherever it is possible. Data availability generally is the starting point. Clearly, all aspects of the selected approach must be used to interrogate the policy for the policy question to be answered, but the process tends to unfold in a back-and-forth discursive manner that leads the analyst full circle doing what is possible when it is possible.

The types of policy research questions that are usefully answered by application of a nonrational approach are those that represent multiple understandings or meanings. Questions that allow meaning making rather than the discovery of cause are appropriate because of the fluidity of the analysis and the types of decisions that result. Questions that relate to processes based on influence and decisions that are built on paradox and politics are also well suited for non-rational policy analysis. Policy questions asking for cause, prediction, objective costs, or efficiencies are not appropriate, due to the paradigmatic perspective that these questions represent. They are more easily and productively handled by linear, rational models built on positivist assumptions.

From this chapter's discussion, most of the skills necessary in order to effectively and productively engage in nonrational policy analysis should be clear. The policy analyst using a nonrational approach will principally need qualitative research skills. Managing word data will be a primary undertaking. Quantitative research will be only descriptively useful to understand context. The nonrational analyst should be a creative, tenacious detective to uncover needed information and engage important stakeholders. Circular logic is helpful for continuing an emergent process that requires both critical and creative thinking. Good boundary management skills are also useful to assure that identified personal ideologies and biases are kept in check during the discursive process of listening to competing perspectives required for productive analysis. Finally, the analyst should be a writer capable of writing reports that embody the thickness and complexity represented in the analytic process. This type of writing should be closer to that found in meaningful narratives than what is typically found in scientific reporting.

A final point should be made in the critique of nonrational policy analysis. This type of analysis provides deep, individualized or context-based meaning. It cannot be the basis for generalizable work that provides transferable evidence to support hypotheses about what the problem is and what should be done about it. It can only highlight the various processes that resulted from diverse participation representing differing levels of power, need, and political ideology. These approaches are excellent tools for making sense of aspects of policymaking that heretofore seemed to have made no sense.

CONCLUSION

Generally speaking, the best defense of a nonrational approach to policy analysis lies in its ability to demonstrate that the particular policy research and analysis question can be appropriately answered through the application of the chosen approach. Being able to articulate why the approach is also well targeted to the form, level, and focus of the question is also helpful.

Further defense of what is done in the analytic process can be made on the basis of the rigor of the analysis. The well-schooled analyst will knowingly assert that the underlying assumptions of the policy question establish a paradigmatic location for the analysis. This, of course, is done by evaluating the aims or goal of the analysis for fit. In doing so, the analyst must be certain that there is no mixing of assumptions that suggests an incorrect understanding about what can be accomplished by a nonrational policy analysis approach. The analyst should apply the standards for the analysis design and quality or rigor that is consistent with the paradigm.

This approach is subjectivist. No generalization is possible, just deep understanding of the context-imbedded aspects and the multiple perspectives of those with a stake in the policy. This sort of analysis recognizes that diverse participants with differing levels of power and involvement in politics are part of policy development in all forms, levels, and foci. The policy analysis that is produced will represent multiple perspectives. It will be pragmatic both in the analysis and the results, recognizing the pluralism that is present in all policy processes. It will capture the competing perspectives; when done well, it will, through a circular reasoning process, result in a more sophisticated understanding of the complexity of the issues involved and the ideological reasoning at play from problem setting to policy impact.

DISCUSSION QUESTIONS

1. Many people are not comfortable with nonrational modes of thinking because of the difference between them and the way they have been taught or the way they naturally think. Where is your comfort zone for nonrationality? What is necessary for you to skillfully engage in this approach to policy analysis research?

2. Look at all the approaches to policy analysis discussed in both Chapters 5 and 6. Identify what theories (multiple streams, social construction, or advocacy coalition theory) are guiding each. Can

you identify dimension of those theories present that were not discussed? Are there also other theories influencing the structures of the nonrational approach to policy analysis discussed?

3. Your research question will determine the approach needed. Based on a policy with which you are familiar, write a policy research question that would require a nonrational approach. Why does this question fit with a nonrational approach?

4. The approaches highlighted in this chapter are not standardized tools. Thus, there may be other questions that one might ask that are equally helpful to the analytical process. If you were constructing a nonrational policy analysis framework to examine a policy approved by a local human service agency's board of directors, are there particular questions that you would want to include? Provide a rationale for your choices.

5. Nonrational policy analysis approaches tend to broaden rather than narrow the complexity of a situation. When do you think it is important to broaden and be inclusive of all perspectives in the analysis process? If you were working in a very rational environment, in which getting to generalizable information was highly valued, how might you persuade your colleagues to use a nonrational approach?

6. Pose an interpretive question about a policy with which you are familiar. Practice targeting your research by identifying the form, level (and scope), and focus of your analysis. Then select an appropriate framework and analyze the policy. After you finish, talk about what was learned in the process, what you would do differently in the future, and what were the benefits and challenges you encountered.

CHAPTER 7

Critical Policy Analysis

I N CHAPTER 2, we introduced the critical paradigm with a worldview that is one of mass oppression, ceasing only through transformational class-level conflict aimed at rearranging or restructuring the social order. This paradigm also includes a worldview of individual oppression and limitation wherein the social goal is one of individual liberation in service of individual potentiality. This postmodern view is generally seen to be more radical than the other two paradigms already introduced. It tends to fit with the political (or partisan) uses of policy analysis, rather than the substantive (or informative) uses (Jenkins-Smith & Weimer, 1986, p. 485) that we have covered so far. This chapter shows that radical views can be either progressive or conservative in attempting to replace the current social order with an alternative order more congruent with a particular ideology; however because of the cases we have been using to illustrate the use of policy models, our discussion and applications generally come from a progressive rather than conservative radical perspective.

Regardless of location on a political ideology spectrum, a more radical approach to policy is introduced in this chapter, based on the assumption that policy analysis leads to policy change intended to be transformative, producing structural change with implications at the collective or individual levels. In this chapter and in Chapter 8, you will see the implications of an ideologically driven analysis process that uses both rational and nonrational approaches to policy analysis. We begin with a discussion of reason and radicality along with a short history of the development of a critical approach to systematic knowledge building. We focus on some important issues that arise when a perspective accepts and encourages conflict as part of the policy process.

In identifying the congruent goals of radical approaches to analysis, it will be noted that most policy analysis frameworks are not designed at such a critical level. In fact, our search of the literature identified few radical policy frameworks, although the practice rhetoric of some professions such as social work would suggest the possibility of radical change agency regarding policy. To overcome this limitation in our argument about the relationship between research and policy analysis, we will introduce analytic approaches adapted from some of the major sociopolitical criticism streams as a way to demonstrate how even value-laden positions can produce systematic guidelines for analysis. We close with a focus on mechanisms used to assess whether the benefit of conflict or radical action or inaction outweighs the cost when considering policy change. At the conclusion of this and the following chapter, you will be able to engage in an even-handed analysis of what is gained and what is lost in applying critical policy analysis.

REASON IN RADICALITY

The radical, critical perspective is built on critical thinking skills. Critical thinking "involves a careful appraisal of claims, a fair-minded consideration of alternative views, and a willingness to change your mind in light of evidence that refutes a cherished position" (Gambrill & Gibbs, 2009, p. 51). From earlier discussion, it should be clear that critical thinking requires an examination of assumptions, goals, questions, and evidence involved in whatever is being interrogated. It includes appraisal of claims and discovery of mistakes in order to achieve a deep, complex understanding of the issues involved. Many theorists (see for example Gambrill & Gibbs, 2009; Kroeger & Thuesen, 1998; Paul & Elder, 2002; Ruggiero, 2001) suggest that critical thinking is also dialogic and dialectical, dealing with differing opinions and achieving clarity about how those support or contradict personal opinions and patterns of thinking. Baars (1991) describes a critical framework as "a collection of questions, problems, and analyses that have been excluded from the established mainstream" (p. 220).

A dialogic and dialectic process of critical thinking takes advantage of both rational and nonrational thought. "Critique is a legitimate and often powerful mode of policy analysis with roots dating back to the earliest philosophers (e.g., the skeptical frame of analysis of Socrates and later Descartes)" (Lejano, 2006, p. 115). The main focus of the radical position is pointing out errors in thinking. Through both linear, rational thought and more circular, nonrational thought false consciousness is transformed into true consciousness. Here, it is expected that whatever reasoning is necessary to engender empowerment and overcome oppression is acceptable. Keep in mind that the perception of oppression can come from any position on the ideological spectrum and occurs when an alternative to that positioning has the power to establish the "mainstream" ideology at the time; however, most postmodernist critique comes from a rather progressive perspective. For example, one should be able to see how a progressive perspective would be perceived to be oppressive to those holding fundamentalist Christian or Muslim beliefs.

ASSUMPTIONS OF THE CRITICAL PARADIGM

Returning to Guba's paradigmatic framework in Figure 2.1 in Chapter 2, the critical perspective is both objectivist and subjectivist. It is objectivist in that it takes a critical realist perspective. There is critique of a "real" reality "out there." It is subjectivist in that values mediate the paradigmatic position and the inquiry that results.

This perspective is value-laden. The important questions for any type of inquiry from this perspective are what values and whose? Studies, including policy analyses, will vary depending on the values of the inquiry. Is the goal to empower or disempower? Either way, fundamental structural change through conflict is the expectation. Policy analysis from this perspective is ideological. Consequently, doing any policy analysis from this perspective is a political act. It will be pragmatic and oriented toward rearranging the social order. In a critical analysis that differs from those seen so far, this type of political inquiry uses social activism and conflict for class or individual action.

The critical perspective challenges positivism/postpositivism for its neutrality. Positivism/postpositivism ignores the role of values in knowledge building and underemphasizes the oppressive nature of the search for truth (even if it is unattainable). Positivism/postpositivism is inattentive to political social facts and political controversies that by their nature infuse values into any analysis. Positivism/postpositivism favors value-free understanding, social control, and social engineering. In contrast, the critical perspective typically advocates for the underprivileged to the powerful, educates the underprivileged, and organizes the revolution (Fay, 1987). Though less critical of interpretivism/constructivism because of the consciousness raising that results from meaning making, the conservativism regarding the interpretivist acceptance of incremental change represents a real detriment to fundamental, transformative change promoted by the critical paradigm.

For the critical perspective, there is no separation of research or science and political activities. There is an expectation that critical policy analysis can create individual and societal transformation. The goal is praxis, or knowledge-driven action (Lather, 1986). The critical approach deals with conceptions of power and its implications. It looks at structural relations associated with such social elements as class, ethnicity, and gender. It interrogates privilege, that power that exists and circulates to produce subjugation and oppression. For the analysis to be effective, however, consciousness is not sufficient; fundamental change is the measure of effectiveness. Box 7.1 provides a list of the major assumptions of the critical approach.

Box 7.1 Critical Policy Analysis Assumptions

- It is important to criticize both the argument (questioning methods, reasoning, procedures, logic, rules) and the results (knowledge, truth, nature of problem, ideology).
- Modified realist—there is objectivity, but reasoning is part of historical process, so data, perceptions, attitudes, and beliefs are in a social and cultural horizon such that history shapes them all.
- Analysis must include social and historical concerns about the problem and the production of knowledge.
- Belief in human potential and understanding how boundaries and structures shape perceptions and how they are shaped through struggle is essential.
- Policy analysis is part of participation in a political, not just an intellectual movement, with efforts being made to transform social relations in a particular way.

Policy analysis using this approach is enacted with skepticism regarding accepted notions, conventions, and social practices. This type of analysis, to be successful, must elevate the contradictions and social domination that can be identified through the lens of a particular ideological perspective. Notice how these assumptions aim at radical transformation of policy and society by means of conflict. Look at the strategies of this type of analysis in Box 7.2 to see how it can be considered critical realist and pragmatic as well as both subjectivist and objectivist.

Policy analysis from this approach must engender class or structural changes from objective, generalizable data. Interestingly, it can also engender individual, subjective changes at the intersection of art,

---

Box 7.2   Critical Policy Analysis Strategies

- Be critical—employ skepticism, social regulation, distribution of resources, and power.
- Be pragmatic—empirical, conceptual, and experiential.
- Systematically inquire into contradictions of policy and practice.
- Use dialogic process.
- Eliminate false consciousness.
- Energize and facilitate transformation.

---

spirituality, and scientific ways of knowing because of its focus on practical action-oriented knowledge that enlightens and catalyzes political and social change.

CRITICAL APPROACHES TO POLICY ANALYSIS

Theories that inform this critical worldview are attentive to the embeddedness of reality in history and ideology. They tend to operate out of their own ideology and aim for a dialectical synthesis of various views of reality and science. Value dispositions are keys to shaping the theoretical approaches to understanding and managing reality. In the following discussion of the types of theories that guide critical policy analysis, look at the range of criticism presented, ideological orientation or value-ladenness, and the role of skepticism in each. Take particular notice of voice, the language of empowerment, and the role of hermeneutics for understanding complexity. Exactly how critical are these theories, and how congruent do they seem to be with the critical paradigm?

Theories about policy are about change, but they differ in the amount of change for which they account. "Each of the theories comes to grips with policy change slightly differently" (Schlager, 2007, p. 309). For example, in Chapter 3 we highlighted prescriptive theories including rational choice, decision, and game theories. Each is helpful in explaining the policy process and the gradual changes that occur as new policies are formulated and implemented within existing systems. Similarly, in Chapter 5, we highlighted descriptive multiple streams, social construction, and advocacy coalition theories that described how policies emerge amid the interactions and dynamics of individuals and groups. These theories are usually focused on gradual changes that do not affect structural, systemic change, although they could certainly inform broader changes. In this section, we highlight three schools of interrelated critical theories that attempt to provide insight into broader-scale, even radical change that is congruent with a critical paradigm: critical theories, theories of distributive justice, and power and conflict theories.

Critical Theories

"Critical theory provides criticisms and alternatives to traditional, mainstream social theory, philosophy, and science" (Mullaly, 2007, p. 214). It is at a dialogic or dialectical level that critical approaches to policy analysis are linked with a long line of critical theorists such as Marx, Weber, and Durkheim. Critical theorists are motivated by concerns for oppressed people; they critique domination; and they are driven by the goal of liberation (Kellner, 1989). For example, Marx's criticism of capitalism focused on how human labor had been transformed from a creative activity to a unit of production, replacing the worth of a human being with the abstract concept of human work. Marx was questioning a worldview that commodified labor from human worth to monetary value (Marx, 1887). This was a radical notion. Similarly, Weber focused his critique on rationalization, a process in which society was systematically transformed into "the single-minded pursuit of some prespecified end without so much reflection on the end itself . . . Such processes worked out not only on the material plane, but in the very meanings attached to human activity" (Lejano, 2006, p. 117). The significance of Weber's work in critiquing rationalization was profound for its time.

The Frankfurt School of critical theory (Adorno, Fromm, Horkheimer, Marcuse, and others), French structuralism, literary poststructuralism, cultural Marxism, and certain types of feminist theory (e.g., Calasanti, 2004; Gilligan, 1982; Pascall, 1986) have formed the radical underpinnings of critical approaches to thought. Dominant, male models of reasoning, as well as Eurocentric portrayals of history, in which the Enlightenment and Renaissance were viewed as major turning points in human history, were criticized for having left women, as well as revolutionary changes in other parts of the world, entirely out of the decision-making context (Nussbaum, 2006). "More broadly, hegemonic practices or bodies of thought operate by constructing the 'other,' i.e., people, groups, or places that constitute the periphery, and proceeding to systematically create a privileged position for them in the center of policy, discourse, and practice" (Lejano, 2006, p. 119).

Unlike social science theories that are constructed according to certain canons of inquiry, critical theories are constructed under different premises. First, a critical theory assumes that persons who are oppressed cannot overcome their exploitation if they do not know how exploited they are. Thus, they must liberate the individual from the norms of oppression that they have likely internalized, and the sources of domination must be unmasked in the process. Second, critical theories have a practical intent in raising issues and engaging conflict to demonstrate how the present situation needs to change and in pointing out the injustices within the current system. This means that an alternative vision of what could be must be provided. And third, there must be a practical dimension to the theory in that the insights and tools generated by the theory should be used to empower others. In short, the theorists become advocates for changing society (Leonard, 1990).

By now, you have probably figured out that there is not one single critical theory but a collection of critical theories. Agger (1998, p. 4) identified the characteristics that make a theory part of this critical theory group:

- Within the theory, there is opposition to positivism because the world is not value-free or purely objective.
- The theory distinguishes between an oppressive past or present and a future free of exploitation and domination.
- There is a focus on domination as a structural factor that affects people's daily lives within existing social institutions.
- The theory recognizes that people internalize oppression or false consciousness.
- It argues that social change begins at the grass-roots level and rejects determinism in favor of personal and collective power.
- The link between human agency and social structure is viewed as dialectical.
- The theory holds people responsible for their own liberation.

As you can see, critical theories are congruent with the assumptions of the critical paradigm. Many feminist theories and theories on race would be considered part of critical theory, since they question current power dynamics and seek to liberate both men and women from gender or racial roles. An example of how this theoretical perspective plays out in policy could be seen in the history of the development of the Equal Rights Amendment (ERA), where efforts were made to critique a male power structure such that female human agency was understood to be impinged upon with women's ultimate potential thwarted because of lack of equal opportunity. The dialectic around the enactment of this amendment to the Bill of Rights hinged upon one part of the feminist perspective, seeing false consciousness and internalized oppression on the part of women who did not favor ERA. From a critical interpretation, the amendment failed because certain segments of the population did not choose to be responsible for their own liberation.

THEORIES OF DISTRIBUTIVE JUSTICE

A second set of theories that are particularly relevant to a critical approach are those that focus on justice. Aristotle distinguished between two forms of justice—*corrective* in the form of punishment and retribution and *distributive* in the form of resource allocation. Eighteenth-century philosopher David Hume viewed distributive justice as an extension of property rights (which left out women and people who did not own property), but Herbert Spencer defined justice in terms of what people have a right to or deserve if they contribute to society. Theorists who align justice with property ownership or acquisition are inclined not to buy into the concept of redistribution, whereas those that do often take a more critical stance. The concept of equality (and inequality) is central to any dialogue about justice and obviously plays out in different ways, depending on the theory to which one subscribes (Reamer, 1993, pp. 26–27).

John Rawls's classic *A Theory of Justice* (1971) stimulated a great deal of thought about distributive justice. Building on the concept of the social contract that establishes a just society, Rawls proposed that if individuals operated under a "veil of ignorance" in which they did not know who was advantaged and who was disadvantaged, they would create a moral principle that protected the disadvantaged; they would be benevolent. Rawls focused on a contractual approach in which a just society embodied a set of basic freedoms and rights. The two basic principles were (1) the "maximin principle" according to which every person would have at least the primary goods (e.g., financial and material), a minimum below which nobody is allowed to fall; and (2) there should be a "fair equality" of opportunity. In a just society, Rawls argued, there could be some differences in wealth and assets, but only if those who are not as well off benefited in some way. Rawls reacted to utilitarian philosophers who assumed that a just society is concerned with equity of distribution defined as maximizing the total of a group's utility, satisfaction, or happiness. He viewed as unfair any theoretical approach that benefited the greatest number of people but still did harm to citizens who were not in the majority.

Rawls's theory has served as a starting point for other theorists who counter some of his arguments and look for new ways to envision the welfare state. One such critic is Martha Nussbaum (2006), who dedicates her book to Rawls and honors his work in trying to "answer hard foundational questions with rigor and pleasing detail" (p. 5). She approaches his theory in both a "critical and constructive" manner, hoping to add to Rawls's conceptual advances.

Nussbaum (2006) points out that there are unsolved social problems that justice theories have not been able to address, and she draws on a capabilities approach developed by Sen (1992) that attempts to move beyond current thinking. Theories of justice have been tied to the concept of the social contract, characteristically viewed as a relationship between individuals and the nation-state as the basic unit. But in a global world, justice transcends national boundaries and traditional issues related to discrimination and exclusion within those boundaries. Great asymmetries of power and capacity require the extension of reciprocity and respect to persons with a variety of impairments, needs, and dependencies and require a reconceptualization of what is "normal." Movement away from tired conceptualizations of the state is also needed.

Nussbaum focuses her theoretical perspective on capabilities, recognizing that people have variable abilities to convert goods into valuable functionings. Nussbaum pushes beyond Sen and Rawls, widening the safety net and identifying what she considers to be central capabilities: life; bodily health; bodily integrity; senses, imagination, and thought; emotions; practical reason; affiliation; other species; play; and control over one's environment. Combining Nussbaum's capabilities perspective with the concept of social responsibility, three unresolved problems of social justice emerge: (1) doing justice to people with physical and mental impairments, (2) extending justice to all world citizens, and (3) facing the issues of justice involved in our treatment of nonhuman animals. We extend this discussion in Chapter 8, because Nussbaum's work offers a contemporary segue between the premises of justice theory and the process of enacting a critical policy analysis (Morris, 2002).

An excellent example of how theories of distributive justice are at play in local policy making is seen in the recent "living wage" efforts. This is an example of attempting to widen the safety net by asking local governments and businesses to accept the social responsibility to pay their employees what is necessary to have a quality of life in the locality. This does not mean the equal pay for equal work that was embedded in the Equal Rights Amendment (ERA) but declaring a mandate that employers pay workers enough for housing, food, transportation, health care, education, and so forth so that they can maintain independent control over their own environments.

POWER AND CONFLICT THEORIES

A third theoretical school relevant to the critical paradigm concerns the dynamics of power and politics. Rejecting assumptions that organizations and groups act in rational ways, power theorists focus on the complexity of systems in which individuals, groups, and coalitions interact with each other based on having their own "interests, beliefs, values, preferences, perspectives, and perceptions" in a continual competition for scarce resources (Shafritz & Ott, 2001, p. 298). In this scenario, conflict is inevitable and expected. Influence is the primary tool used to access power and political activities.

Power dependency theory, originally developed by Blau (1964), is particularly helpful in understanding political processes. Based on the concept of social exchange, Blau raises the basic question about how social life becomes organized into increasingly complex associations composed of interdependent structures. Of particular concern to students of social welfare is his examination of the power dependency that is created when social welfare organizations are funded by (and thus obligated to) external funders who are separate from the recipients of service. The separation of funding source and service consumer creates a dynamic in which providers are constrained by policies that accompany their funding streams and impact (often constraining) their relationship to service users.

Adam and Kriesi (2007) provide an excellent overview of policy networking, which was strongly influenced by interorganizational theory as well as research on interest groups and agenda setting. Particularly relevant to power and politics is a matrix they developed that links the distribution of power (concentrated or fragmented) to the type of interaction (conflict, bargaining, cooperation). For example, when power is concentrated and the interaction between actors occurs, there is a moderate potential for rapid change; whereas, when there is fragmented power, conflict brings a high potential for rapid change (and sense of risk). Network analysis "conceptualizes policy making as a process involving a diversity of actors who are mutually inter-dependent" (Adam & Kriesi, 2007, p. 146).

A radical approach to power is conflict theory, in which the struggle between the "haves" and "have-nots" is characterized as an ongoing quest for equality. Hardina (2002) provides a summary of the primary assumptions of conflict theory. First the haves and have-nots are in competition for societal resources. Second, the haves are more powerful and advantaged than the have-nots. Third, a great deal of the oppression felt by various groups is based on the "isms" that plague society. Fourth, the control of the sources of power and resources (government and other decision-making authorities) is in the hands of the haves. Fifth, there are advocates who work with oppressed groups to acquire power and gain access to resources. Sixth, there are strategies that these advocates use to increase the power and access of disadvantaged groups (p. 55).

Like multiple streams and advocacy coalition theories discussed as interpretive theories, punctuated-equilibrium (P-E) theory assesses contextual factors and events that lead to change. In fact, all three theories have something to offer in terms of understanding how various levels of change occur. But it is P-E theory that pushes a bit farther in trying to explain why major, transformational changes as well as incremental change occur to alter the structure of political, economic, and cultural systems. Like advocacy coalition theory, P-E theory recognizes the importance of long-established patterns that often precede a major change, even though P-E theory acknowledges that these major changes may appear to have happened in an earth-shatteringly short period of time. P-E theory leads "us to expect that these punctuations will happen and that the magnitude of change will be related to its frequency of occurrence, but it will not help us to make specific predictions for particular policy issues" (Schlager, 2007, p. 310).

P-E developed out of theories of conflict expansion and agenda setting in which disadvantaged groups managed to break through the inertia of conservative institutions and the status quo, so that major change occurred. These "bursts of change" often come from policy subsystems that have mobilized around specific policy issues. The subsystems "may be called iron triangles, issue niches, policy subsystems, or issues networks" (True, Jones, & Baumgartner, 2007, p. 158). Bursts of change are not viewed as coming from rapid shifts in choice, but in "serial shifts" in which an image is contested, a policy monopoly is under attack, and a wave of growing criticism or enthu-siasm propels the issue onto the public arena. This could be seen as describing a linear, causal chain that produces revolutionary impact.

One could look at some of the world revolutionary history to see examples of different dimensions of power and conflict theories. Any student of American, Russian, Latin American, or African history will be able to see power and conflict dynamics as important elements producing revolutionary impact. However, it would be important to understand that power and conflict theories can also aid in understanding and managing what happens in current life. The actions of fundamentalist conservatives, antitax groups, white supremacists, and those with a state's rights perspective collectively called the "tea party movement" enacted many elements of power and conflict theories before, during, and after health care reform was signed into law. Their goal was overthrow of the federal governmental structure.

Three schools of theories have been highlighted here because they reveal the conceptualization of critical thought. Collections of critical theories are those that ask the provocative, challenging questions of the status quo, whereas theories of distributive justice pose the hard questions related to the distribution (and redistribution) of resources within democratic societies. While all critical theories are radical, theories of distributive justice run the gamut from highly conservative views that advocate against redistribution to highly transformative views that advocate for the inclusion of entire groups excluded from the dominant society. All these justice theories (both conservative/ preservative and progressive) pertain to the critical paradigm, and it is important to recognize the divergence among these perspectives. Similarly, there are a number of theories that have power and conflict as their primary focus, and we have selectively introduced a few. The major point is that the reader should be aware of this plethora of theories that attempt to provide conceptual frameworks for critically analyzing the status quo, the relationship of living beings to the societal contexts in which they live, what they can expect from those societies, and the dynamics of power and conflict in transformative change.

CRITICAL APPROACHES

Our argument about the advantages to the policy-analysis process when one considers it a type of research stumbles a bit within the critical worldview because these "bursts" of major structural change or radical reform are extremely complicated. When one looks at this radical perspective, one sees a kind of philosophical and theoretical fullness, but it is challenging to locate approaches that are useful without being so reductionist as to bleed out the very complexity one is trying to understand. Therefore, to press forward in this research/ policy conceptualization, we provide examples that we think have reasonable possibilities for being useful—systematic critical approaches aimed at radically transforming policy and society through conflict.

Our first example is one that many of you have seen in other contexts than policy analysis. Just a quick "Google" of Marx will show that criticism based on Marxist thought is present not just in philosophy and politics but in literary criticism, radical education, and certain strains of feminism, just to name a few. Heavily informed by Hegelian thought, Marx's special brand of analysis is called historical or dialectical materialism (Marx & Engels, 1998). Marx and Engels's approach grows from an analysis of the contradictions in material conditions (rather than what Hegel did with contradictions among ideas). The approach is outlined in Figure 7.1.

The thesis is a proposition. The antithesis is the negation of the thesis, a reaction to the proposition. The synthesis solves the conflict that is created in the clash between the thesis and antithesis by bringing together their common truths and forming a new proposition. This

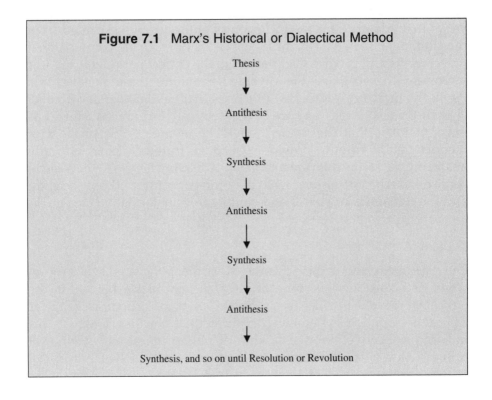

Figure 7.1 Marx's Historical or Dialectical Method

Thesis

Antithesis

Synthesis

Antithesis

Synthesis

Antithesis

Synthesis, and so on until Resolution or Revolution

new proposition is set against its own opposite in a similar, nonlinear, dialectical way until full resolution is achieved. For both Hegel and Marx, this process represented the struggle between actual and potential worlds. For the critical policy analyst it represents the struggle between the actual political/policy reality and a potential revolutionary alternative.

The idea is that change occurs through the clash of opposites. From that clash comes higher consciousness, which leads to resolution, or in this case, revolution. The clash is created by dichotomously defining opposites (e.g., the bourgeoisie and the proletariat). Following the format, for the purpose of policy analysis, the statement of the social problem is termed the thesis. In traditional, rational policy analysis, this statement of the problem (the thesis) is accepted at face value and the policy would be derived and analyzed in an effort to address the situation as it has been accepted.

In this approach to critical policy analysis, the effort is made to negate the thesis by considering the opposite of the original position regarding the social problem. This is possible because social constructions of social problems bring with them a form of incompleteness that gives rise to the conflicting alternative construction of the social problem. This new construction of the social problem becomes the antithesis. If the constructions are carefully crafted, they should be in direct collision and conflict should ensue. It is through this clash of opposites in a critical and dialectical back-and-forth debate that a new conceptualization of the problem should be created, rather than having one side or the other win in the definitional war. It can be pictured as a clash between black and white; rather than having either black or white "win," gray is created. Generally, this back and forth is productive rather than warlike when the participants in the analysis become aware of the comparative (hermeneutic) manner in which analysis and judgment are undertaken. Synthesis occurs when that hermeneutic circular process becomes a more evenhanded interpretation of the problem, based on the disclosure of the contradictions in the arguments on both sides.

Synthesis then becomes a previously unrecognized definition of the social problem, moving it in a direction that contains elements of both earlier definitions (the thesis and antithesis) because the contradictions have been overcome. In philosophical terms, this is called a "fusion," or politically it can be said to be a "resolution." The idea is to create something that is more than what was understood by either definition of the social problem in a forward-, not backward-looking way. This effort at dichotomously defining ideological positions can continue, if necessary, throughout the policy-making process.

At first blush, this sort of policy analysis would seem to create incremental change responses through this clash of opposites, but the actual critical "end game" of this process, following Marx (1977), is the continuation of this dialectical analysis until such higher-level analysis is achieved and such higher consciousness is present that truth is arrived at. This "truth" cannot be affected by slow changes or incremental reforms but only by fundamental change—a revolution. This approach to analysis, then, assumes that policy analysis should not be reformist, but revolutionary.

Return to our case example on Service, Engagement, and Volunteerism. Suppose Madeline were to establish the thesis of P.L. 111-13 as "the disadvantaged can be served effectively by volunteers," and then she moves to the negation of this thesis by saying that volunteers as part of the sociopolitical structure do not effectively serve the disadvantaged but assure that they remain disadvantaged. Madeline would begin the dialectical process by trying to move those holding these opposite positions into a synthesis. The content of the synthesis would depend on the quality of the participation of opposing stakeholders. The process would move back and forth until a revolution of the disadvantaged would establish an alternative and more empowering approach to equalize advantage.

Our next example is a social work framework that takes a feminist perspective (McPhail, 2003). It is one of the few models in social work that assesses policy through a gendered lens. You will notice that there are aspects of the analysis that are quite linear based on economic principles but rather than only attending to the "efficiencies" that were present in the positivist/postpositivist rational models, it is value-driven to assess both meaning and power for women. The dimensions of the framework are said by the author not to be complete but should act as starting points for making women's issues visible (p. 55). Although it is a complex approach to policy analysis, it can be useful in gender analysis of problem identification, policy design, implementation, and experience. Box 7.3 contains the feminist policy framework.

The idea of this analysis is to specifically focus on the particular issues pertaining to women, rather than having women's voices drowned out by overlooking feminist values and roles even when looking at economics and other contexts. It contains many guides to assessing symbolic aspects in the policy to determine whether fundamental change is intended or possible. While the framework was

Box 7.3 McPhail's Feminist Policy Framework: Through a Gendered Lens

A. Values
1. Do feminist values undergird the policy? Which feminism, which values?
2. Are value conflicts involved in the problem representations either between different feminist perspectives or between feminist and mainstream values?

B. State-Market Control
1. Are women's unpaid labor and work of caring considered and valued, or taken for granted?
2. Does the policy contain elements of social control of women?
3. Does the policy replace the patriarchal male with the patriarchal state?
4. How does the policy mediate gender relationships between the state, market, and family? For instance, does the policy increase women's dependence upon the state or men?

C. Multiple Identities
1. How does gender in this policy interact with race or ethnicity, sexual identity, class, religion, national origin, disability, or other identity categories?
2. Are white, middle-class, heterosexual women the assumed standard for all women?
3. Does the policy address the multiple identities of women? The multiple oppressions a single woman may face?

D. Equality
1. Does the policy achieve gender equality? Are there equality of results or disparate impacts?
2. Does the policy treat people differently in order to treat them equally well? Does the policy consider gender differences in order to create more equality?
3. If the positions of women and men were reversed, would this policy be acceptable to men?

E. Special Treatment or Protection
1. Does any special treatment of women cause unintended or restrictive consequences?
2. Is there an implicit or explicit double standard?
3. Does being labeled different and special cause a backlash that can be used to constrain rather than to liberate women?

F. Gender Neutrality
1. Does presumed gender neutrality hide the reality of the gendered nature of the problem or solution?

G. Context
1. Are women clearly visible in the policy? Does the policy take into account the historical, legal, social, cultural, and political context of women's lives and lived experiences both now and in the past?

(continued)

(*continued*)
2. Is the policy defined as a traditional "women's issue" (i.e., "pink policy")? How is a policy that is not traditionally defined as a "women's issue" still a "women's issue"?
3. Is the male experience used as a standard? Are results extrapolated from male experience and then applied to women?
4. Have the programs, policies, methodologies, assumptions, and theories been examined for male bias?
5. Is women's biology treated as normal rather than as an exception to a male-defined norm?

H. Language
1. Does the language infer male dominance or female invisibility?
2. Are gendered expectations and language encoded in the policy?

I. Equality and Rights and Care and Responsibility
1. Is there a balance of rights and responsibilities for women and men in this policy?
2. Does the policy sustain the pattern of men being viewed as public actors and women as private actors, or does the policy challenge this dichotomization?
3. Does the policy bring men, corporations, and the government into caring and responsible roles? Is responsibility pushed uphill and redistributed?
4. Does the policy pit the needs of women against the needs of their fetus or children?
5. Are women penalized for either their roles as wives, mothers, or caregivers or their refusal to adopt these roles?

J. Material or Symbolic Reforms
1. Is the policy merely symbolic, or does it come with teeth? Are there provisions for funding, enforcement, and evaluation?
2. Are interest groups involved in overseeing the policy implementation?
3. Is litigation possible to refine and expand the law's interpretation?
4. What is the strength of authority of the agency administering the policy?
5. Is there room to transform a symbolic reform into a material reform? How?

K. Role Change and Role Equity
1. Is the goal of the policy role equity or role change?
2. Does the type of change proposed affect the chance of successful passage?

L. Power Analysis
1. Are women involved in making, shaping, and implementation of the policy? In which ways were they involved? How were they included or excluded? Were the representatives of women selected by women?
2. Does the policy work to empower women?
3. Who has the power to define the problem? What are competing representations?

4. How does this policy affect the balance of power? Are there winners and losers? Is a win-win solution a possibility?

M. Other

1. Is the social construction of the problem recognized? What are alternate representations of the problem?
2. Does this policy constitute backlash for previous women's policy gains?
3. How does feminist scholarship inform the issue?
4. What women's organizations were involved in the policy formulation and implementation? Was there consensus or disagreement?
5. Where are the policy silences? What are the problems for women that are denied the status of problem of others? What policy is *not* being proposed, discussed, and implemented?
6. How does the policy compare to similar policies transnationally? Are there alternative models that we can both learn from and borrow from?
7. Does the policy blame, stigmatize, regulate, or punish women?

Source: "A Feminist Policy Analysis Framework: Through a Gendered Lens," by B. A. McPhail, 2003, *The Social Policy Journal*, 2(2/3), 39–61. Used with permission.

designed to provide a gendered lens in analysis, we believe that the analytic guidance provided could also apply to other minority experiences including such aspects as race and class. We also think the same analytic approach could be used for men in a paralleling process with the comparison of the results capturing the different effects of the social policy on men and women. This sort of disaggregated analysis, if driven ideologically, could result in the same type of dialectical analysis and revolutionary results aimed for in the Marxist approach discussed previously.

In the Service, Engagement, and Volunteerism case example, the implications for men and women are deeply embedded in a system that has typically disregarded volunteer work as the domain of women who do not "work" and has dismissed their efforts as less worthy than the efforts of men who have been employed in the labor force. This would lead Madeline to some identification of the impact of the general objectives of P.L. 111-13 through a gender lens that could identify negative implications of the policy on women. Madeleine would then interrogate the policy by looking at the implications of the policy design for women and the implementation of the policy at all levels. Once the full Serve America Act was implemented, the experience of women at all levels of policy would need to be part of her data collection and analysis.

EXAMPLES FOCUSING ON DIFFERENT UNITS OF ANALYSIS

The easiest way to shore up our argument about policy analysis and research has been to take note of those approaches that are derived from particular paradigmatic assumptions and embrace a particular strategy for policy analysis. In the case of the critical paradigm, the perspective is of critical realism and pragmatism with both subjectivist and objectivist orientations. Methods of analysis that are ideologically oriented with transformational change goals are appropriate. Generalizability is suspect, due to the context-embeddedness of the sociopolitical aspects of the social problem and the policy response. Usefulness of the change orientation rather than rigor of the process is important here.

In the critical approach to policy analysis, anything that has the ability to radically transform policy and society through conflict would be acceptable. Most of the radical approaches to policy analysis have been theoretically or ideologically driven, often leaving few precise guidelines for this type of policy-analysis process. The focus is on change products rather than the analytic process. You may see some differences here as compared with the preceding chapters, which looked at specifics in the presentation of the approaches that target differing levels of critical analysis. As in the other chapters, see if you can identify which theories are guiding the approach discussed.

Formulation Example   This focus of analysis looks at the process of how the policy is shaped. It looks at the intent or goals of policy. As a critical approach, the interrogation would be of the forces in favor of the policy and those against the policy, it also involves looking at the various constructions of the social problem that the policy is set to address. Interrogating the socially acceptable and the unacceptable approaches in the context of the sociopolitical history would help to raise consciousness about "Why this?" and "Why now?"

Chow and Austin (2008) conceptualized a guide for developing a culturally responsive social service agency (pp. 47–49), a portion of which we have adapted in Box 7.4 as an exemplar of analyzing cultural responsiveness in policy formulation at the organizational level. Many of the theories discussed in this chapter focus on societal change, but transformative change can occur within organizations and communities as well.

Box 7.4   Chow and Austin's Analyzing Cultural Responsiveness in Policy Formulation at the Organizational Level

Culturally Responsive Organizational Processes

- Does the process value diversity and embrace culture as a resource?
- Are participants aware of the dynamics, risks, and potential conflicts when different cultures intersect?
- Is expanding knowledge of various cultures and cultural issues incorporated in the process?
- Do the process and the formulation of the policy fit with the culture of the community to be served?
- Does the process demonstrate capability of being both program focused (responsive to public policy and funding streams) and family focused (respectful and inclusive of families, strength-based interventions, participatory involvement of clients, consumer-oriented, and use of support networks and natural helpers)?

Agency–Community Relations

- Does the process engage an array of advocacy groups representing different cultural and ethnic communities?
- Does the process celebrate existing community strengths in order to empower disenfranchised populations to assess and monitor culturally responsive policies and procedures?
- Are participants linked horizontally to client communities and community networks, and vertically to professional, legislative, and funding sources (including local, national, and international networks)?
- Does the process promote consciousness raising among participants about how structural power, privilege, and oppression operate inside and outside the community?
- Do participants recognize through dialogue with community groups that the policy changes needed to create a culturally responsive organization can threaten the core culture of an agency, foster resistance, and radically transform the status quo?
- Is the formulation process proficient in receiving and integrating divergent forms of input from all parts of the community and within the organization?

Source: Adapted from "The Culturally Responsive Social Service Agency: An Application of an Evolving Definitiion to a Case Study," by J. C-C. Chow and M. J. Austin, 2008, *Administration in Social Work, 32*(4), 39–64.

In Box 7.4 are found questions one could use to analyze the process intended to move toward culturally sensitive policies within a human service organization. Note the inclusive nature of the questions, and pay particular attention to "Do participants recognize through dialogue with community groups that the policy changes needed to create a culturally responsive organization can threaten the core culture of the agency, foster resistance, and radically transform the status quo?" This "burst of change" could alter life as agency workers have known it within their place of employment.

An approach to policy formulation at the organizational level pertains to our case in a number of ways. If Madeline were interested in the cultural responsiveness of the implementation of the policy at her agency, she would be interested in ascertaining the degree to which the local and neighborhood culture is a part of the program design. This would include how diverse perspectives were included in the interpretation and the formulation of the program in response to the federal policy. Madeline would look for use of community-based resources in real, rather than symbolic ways, with an eye to determining whether the implementation process results in consciousness raising at all levels of policy participation.

The tea parties that occurred in the summer of 2009 just before Congress was due to consider the options for reforming health care in the United States (previously mentioned in the power and conflict theories section) are certainly an example of what activism can be enacted at the policy-formulation stage of policy development. Another example of formulation is the development of a living-wage approach for city government and for all government contracts, and this process could be analyzed using Chow and Austin. The use of this type of framework for analysis would enable the analyst to move past simply whether living wage employment occurred to whether the cultures of the organizations changed as a result of modifying the socioeconomic environment within them.

Product Example   The critical investigation of the policy product would look at content and choices demonstrated in the formal policy. In examining a product, it is necessary to look at what was included and what was absent, as well as at the sociopolitical, cultural, and structural issues related to what is and is not acceptable in the current historical context. The choices about what was included and what was absent from the policy options are important considerations. In Box 7.5, Lejano (2006) provides a set of critical questions that an analyst might use to approach a policy product.

Box 7.5 Lejano's Normative Policy Analysis

1. Standards

   Does the policy have elements within it that can be considered in the light of providing a minimum standard of quality for those affected by the policy?

   Can we begin discussing the levels of quality the policy can ensure at this point in time and what degrees of quality we can aspire to in the future?

   Can we express these standards in the form of rules?

   Can we have a discussion of how these (explicit or implicit) rules might be constructed?

   Is there a hierarchy of values that the policy needs to consider, and how are different values prioritized in this situation?

2. Distribution

   What is the distribution of costs, benefits, opportunities, obligations, and others, associated with the policy?

   Are burdens and gains inequitably distributed?

   Should the policy have a redistribute component?

3. Structural relationships

   Does the policy foster a structure of sociopolitical relationships that privilege some groups or individuals and systematically marginalize others?

   How does the policy create this structuring?

   Does the policy undo existing social structures and privilege the presently disenfranchised?

   Does the policy reflect virtues of care and empowerment?

4. Process

   Does the policy allow access of all concerned to the policy process?

   Does the policy create additional support for participation or representation of the traditionally underrepresented?

Source: Frameworks for Policy Analysis: Merging Text and Context (pp. 151–152), by R. P. Lejano, 2006, New York, NY: Routledge. Used with permission.

Lejano's (2006) example in Box 7.5 is based on what he calls an ethical approach and is informed by theories of justice. He compares this approach to rational models in which the intent is to narrow the questions and focus the analysis. He observes that "while the sharp analytic of the rational model leads easily to a systematic operational definition of efficiency, the less sharply defined . . . ethics [approach] provides a richer analytical ground of policy questions around which to focus the questioning" (p. 152). He adds that questions such as the ones posed in his approach to a policy product will likely raise additional questions in the process. But to him, this does not mean that the approach needs to become stalled in endless questioning and analysis. This approach supports action on a policy. It moves forward with values, virtues, and morals as screens for decision makers. Lejano contends that policy analyses that do not raise a moral dimension (such as questions of right and wrong) are inadequate. He confirms that moral questions are often missing or avoided, because moral questions are those about which people strongly feel and that brings forth strong (even vociferous) disagreement (2006, p. 163). When guided by rational approaches, analysts may want to avoid such conflict. From a critical perspective it is absolutely necessary to raise the questions and engage in the conflict.

In the Service, Engagement, and Volunteerism example, if Madeline had questions about minimum standards of quality and what values are represented in P.L. 111-13, she might be interested in using this approach. In doing so, distribution of costs, benefits, opportunities, and obligations for both the volunteers and those being served must be assessed for inequality. She would have questions about power redistribution being central to changes in the structural relationships between the "disadvantaged" and the young people, veterans, and seniors providing volunteer services. The idea would be to determine the degree to which this policy allows access to all concerned at all levels of the policy process, including the inclusion of the traditionally underrepresented.

Lejano would be particularly useful to both the liberal and conservative sides of the health care reform controversy, since both are concerned with power redistribution. Each perspective has differing redistribution desires. Application of Lejano to the full text of the Act would give both sides important information about the strategies necessary to meet their ultimate goals, those that were not achieved in the compromise package that was finally signed into law.

Implementation Example   Recall that for there to be a critical theory, there must be a vision of a different future. This means that critical approaches to implementation are driven by visionary goals of a better world, but when it comes to implementation this is highly challenging. Moser (1993) has a vision of an equitable society for women and men, but she readily admits that the "most important problem faced by planning practitioners is their inability to translate gender policy into practice . . . the complex reality of planning processes is difficult to separate out the many components which determine the implementation process" (p. 9). Moser's approach to policy analysis allows the

---

Box 7.6 Moser's Approach to Gender Policy Implementation

- Gender role identification
  - ◦ Reproductive work: inside the organization, in the household.
  - ◦ Productive work: providing/receiving goods and services inside/outside.
  - ◦ Community work: social events and services: inside/outside.
- Gender needs assessment
  - ◦ Practical gender needs: needed assistance in activities inside/outside.
  - ◦ Strategic gender needs: assistance to transform balance of power between men and women inside/outside.
- Disaggregating control of resources and decision making within the policy action
  - ◦ Who controls what?
  - ◦ Who decides what?
  - ◦ How?
- Planning for balancing the triple role
  - ◦ Does the policy action increase a woman's workload in one of her roles inside/outside to the detriment of other roles?
  - ◦ Is there a need for intersectoral/interagency planning to avoid problems?

Source: Adapted from *Gender Planning and Development: Theory, Practice, and Training,* by C. Moser, 1993, London: Routledge.

---

interrogation of the role of women as implementers as well as beneficiaries to the policy action. Her approach appears in Box 7.6.

As you look at Box 7.6, note how Moser has developed a rather circular guide for interrogation in which connections become apparent and questions more complex for consciousness raising. For example, probing about gender role identification and how gender plays out within the multiple, overlapping arenas in which women work, may raise more questions rather than prematurely narrowing the analysis. Notice the influence of power and conflict theories in Moser's reference to transforming "the balance of power" and the action dimension that this represents. This is also embedded within her questions about disaggregating control of resources and decision making in the implementation process.

Gender role questions become central to this analysis approach so that the implicit and explicit assumptions about gender roles inside and outside the organization implementing the policy are articulated. In the

Service, Engagement, and Volunteerism case, gender questions could serve Madeline as the basis for assessing whether the disadvantaged and the volunteers have differing practical and strategic gender needs that might have a relationship with the control of resources represented by this policy. The main concern in this analysis is how identification of areas of the policy at any level increase women's workloads to the detriment of their other roles and, if so, to force options inside agencies or between agencies to avoid those problems.

The living-wage movement mentioned previously is an excellent example of how a gendered policy analysis framework is critically important in examining policy implementation. Privatization, contracting out, and a host of other factors have contributed to labor force stress among women and immigrant workers. Implementing a living wage has an impact on families, many of which are headed by women and many of which are living in poverty. Monitoring the implementation of a living-wage policy, using Moser to determine how it affects women, would allow both assessing the policy's performance and determining how the policy needs to be amended.

Impact Example   The following example comes from Jerome Schiele's (2000) work built on Afrocentrism. We are using a small aspect of his Afrocentric framework for policy analysis to underscore the critically analytic strength of an approach built on an Afrocentric epistemology. According to the author, a "description of the Afrocentric paradigm generally, is hampered and even distorted somewhat by the medium of the English language" (p. 173), but even with this challenge, we are showing a few of the ideas that could characterize an Afrocentric framework for policy analysis, because the approach is quite different from others we have introduced. We think this approach has impressive consciousness-raising potential both for the vulnerable and the well intentioned. Those wishing to see the full nonrational approach should read Chapter 8 of Schiele's text (pp. 171–197). Here, we focus on its impact on vulnerable groups, especially African Americans. The focus of the analysis is the degree to which exploitation, Eurocentrism, and disrespect are outcomes rather than empowerment, opportunities, and respectful inclusion. Notice how both positives and negatives are considered. Features of Schiele's framework can be found in Box 7.7.

This approach illustrates intended or unintended negative implications of policy for those with less mainstream power. It taps into just how Eurocentric American policy tends to be. Though there is an appearance of evenhandedness in the questions guiding the analysis,

Box 7.7 Schiele's Features of the Afrocentric Framework of Policy Analysis

Implications of Policy for Vulnerable Groups

- To what extent does the policy exacerbate the exploitation of the labor of working people?
- To what extent does the policy facilitate or hinder the conditions of the marginalized?
- To what extent does the policy enhance or hamper opportunities for nonprofessionals and others without power?
- To what degree does the policy exclude or include interpretations and cultural values from the groups targeted by the policy?
- To what degree does the policy include provisions that protect African Americans from physical harm, harassment, intimidation, or stigmatization?
- To what extent does the policy reinforce and promote continued Eurocentric domination?
- To what degree does the policy offer additional opportunities for African Americans?
- To what extent does the policy support the strengths and resources within African American communities and families through the inclusion of African Americans in its formulation and implementation?

Source: Adapted from *Human Services and the Afrocentric Paradigm* (pp. 175-177), by J. H. Schiele, 2000, New York, NY: The Haworth Press.

notice how closely aligned the questions are to the three schools of critical theories when looking at policy impact.

In the Service, Engagement, and Volunteerism case, if Madeline were struck by some of the inconsistencies in the policy and wanted to understand why they were present, this policy approach will allow an identification and interrogation of the basic assumptions upon which the policy was built by its supporters. She would test these assumptions against the reality of those with a stake in the social problem and this particular policy response built on volunteerism. Her goal would be uncovering or otherwise identifying alternative assumptions about serving the disadvantaged that would be more logical, consistent, or realistic. Just how different are the assumptions guiding the policy from the values of the vulnerable groups it is intended to help? The idea would be to identify alternatives that would avoid domination and other control elements for all involved; from doing this, radical change would result.

Picking up on the living-wage example discussed under implementation, it is the impact of this policy that will ultimately determine whose economic and social quality of life has changed. Impact can be determined by labor force statistics that provide comparative information on how various groups are doing now that a living wage has been mandated. But use of Schiele's framework would go past impact description to deep understanding of important aspects of impact related to race, including changes in patterns of consumption when workers can afford to maintain a living standard that was simply not possible before the policy's implementation. Race-based comparative documentation could help to identify where the policy falls short and which groups are not benefiting from its impact. This, in turn, will provide data for continuing the fight to transform the system so that no group is left out.

HOW TO ASSESS THE DEGREE TO WHICH AN ANALYSIS APPROACH IS CRITICAL

Policy analysis enacted from a critical perspective has as a goal the radical transformation of policy and society through conflict. Questions regarding disenfranchisement, empowerment, suppression of ideas, and oppression are all appropriate to guide critical policy analysis. Specific questions might be: Why is this social problem constructed as it is and what is being overlooked or suppressed? What structural forces are causing the problem? What is preventing the problem from being recognized now? What are the forces that are working against elimination of the problem? What power, driven by what ideology, established the current policy agenda? What are the structural outcomes of the policy at the class or individual level? These questions are built on the critical paradigm's concern for rearranging the social order, engendering empowerment, and overcoming oppression through conflict. Embedded in each question is an unstated ideological push that will shape the analytic process and the product that results. The ideological precipitants are important drivers for the process, for shaping the position about what comes next as a result of the analytic process, and for determining the level of conflict that could result once the analytic product is made available.

A particularly interesting example of how ideological precipitants are central to critical policy analysis is the use of policy analysis as a retrograde tactic in politics (Brewer, 1973). This process uses analysis to delay political decisions. It actually does not matter what approach to analysis is being used. What matters is the repeated demand for further information about or justification of a particular initiative. This type of analysis can also strategically criticize analytic processes and products that have come before, especially those that are supportive of the policy. The aim is promoting a reversal in the policy. This critical approach is intended to establish the analysis as the focus of conflict in subsequent cycles of policy shaping and review in order to establish a rationale for the delay in the iterative process of policy decision making. Hopefully, you can see that ideology drives this, but it really doesn't matter whether it is conservative, preservative, or progressive. What matters is the distance between the particular ideology and the policy in question. Certainly after the election of Barack Obama we have seen great examples of this in the rhetoric exchanged between the Republicans and the Democrats at both the national and state levels.

If we applied a critical perspective to our case example on Service, Engagement, and Volunteerism, the goal of the questions would be to empower the disempowered by enlightening them about the false consciousness that has informed their behavior up until now. These questions would be approached pragmatically. Whatever source of information that can be derived systematically so as not to be rejected as biased would be used as a means of persuasion about what has been discovered regarding unequal distribution of resources and power and the social regulation that has resulted. In our case, the goal would be to upset the status quo related to how volunteerism is being touted as a panacea for social problems that cannot be left to the voluntary sector alone. The analysis would be seen as successful if there was intense critical opposition on the part of multiple stakeholders that resulted in a change in the basic conceptualization of voluntary–public relationships.

QUESTIONS RELEVANT FOR ASSESSING THE CRITICALITY OF APPROACH

As may be clear by now, both the approach and the process are important in critical policy analysis. An analyst could use a rational or nonrational approach from a positivist/postpositivist or interpretive/constructivist perspective if the goal of the process was to establish the groundwork for radical transformation of policy. The point would be that the analytic process would need to be ideologically driven, not attending to the best answer or the most meaning, but focusing on change in the current social order. Therefore, almost any approach can be a critical approach if the goal of the analysis is doing what is necessary to effect change through conflict.

In addition, some approaches in and of themselves are critical, built on the assumptions of the critical paradigm. The following are screening questions to ask to determine the degree to which an approach can be said to be critical in its orientation:

- Does it take a skeptical stance regarding the social problem or policy response?
- Is it focused on the historical, structural, and value bases of the social problem or policy response?
- Does it interrogate contradictions and distortions therein?
- Do the questions and the analytic results reflect the values and priorities of a particular ideological tradition?
- Is consciousness raising or enlightenment possible as a result of the process or the product of analysis?
- Is there an emancipatory action orientation inherent in the process or product of analysis?
- Is political or social change possible as a result of the analysis?

Once the analyst has determined that either the precipitant for the analysis or the approach to analysis is a critical one, there is still another profoundly important area of consideration before making the final decision to engage in critical policy analysis. It is wise to know the gains and losses involved in using a critical approach.

GAINS AND LOSSES WHEN CRITICAL APPROACHES
ARE USED TO ANALYZE POLICY

Critical policy analysis is an overtly political act. As a result, there is a type of seduction present when one considers the realm of ultimate possibilities resulting from one's efforts at ideologically driven change. Sometimes the passion behind the ideas of the positive change possibilities serves to overshadow the real risks involved in so overtly grappling with power and embedded power structures. One must be very circumspect about the decision to engage in this sort of policy analysis activity. One should not overlook the risks involved to oneself or others in making such a decision. On the other hand, true emancipation is not possible without some degree of risk. The following issues should be thoroughly investigated before beginning a critical process, because the analyst will ultimately lose control of the reverberations from the critical consciousness that will result from a well-constructed critical policy analysis.

Gains and Benefits   Critical approaches are powerful because they challenge the status quo. Anytime one challenges existing interests resistance will occur, but when one has resistance one has the undivided attention of the resistors. Laser-beam focus on the issues at hand can result, or at least important information regarding the context of the policy and the challenges therein will be clarified. Thus, recognizing the power of asking provocative questions cannot be underestimated as a viable change strategy.

Critical approaches, if well articulated, will allow for practical action-oriented knowledge to be produced through a consciousness-raising process. This productive hermeneutic dialectic enables and stimulates action, but it also leads to unanticipated changes that may not have been included in the original vision. The creativity that can result from this circling and recircling cannot be overlooked, nor can its shape or type be predicted. Some sort of powerful action, most of it uncontrollable by the analyst, will result. Essentially, the critical approach establishes the role of the analyst as an interested and facilitative observer with a social conscience able to have a "practical political impact" (Fay, 1987, p. 2) and "to change the world, not to describe it" (Popkewitz, 1984, p. 45). This positioning provides great meaning to the work of the policy analyst, but it also brings with it a great deal of social, personal, and professional responsibility.

Costs and Losses   One of the most ardent criticisms of a critical approach is that it raises many questions that cannot be easily addressed and becomes a game of raising one's awareness of how much change is needed, without providing an easy direction for how to make change happen. For some, this raises the question of whether it is better to be ignorant or to have one's eyes open, only to find out that no one knows exactly what to do about highly discriminatory or inequitable conditions. Lejano (2006) sums it up when he talks about the analysis as undoing "falsities in thinking. It is after all, a negative dialectic in which we simply tear down the illusory. What we put up in its stead is another question. It is left to other modes of analysis to posit ways to bridge the gaps" (p. 132). Critical consciousness is never a comfortable state, not for the analyst or for those engaged in the dialectic.

Just as the power nature of a critical analysis is a positive strength, there will be many who are discomforted with power. Most human service practitioners see power as negative, without understanding that power itself has no valence; it is how one uses power that gives it its "goodness" or "badness." Thus, the analyst throughout the critical process has an awesome responsibility that requires a great deal of targeted focus, time, and commitment. Regardless of how the process goes, given the magnitude of the change, accompanied by the inability to control what results from the process or product, there will be unintended consequences with which the instigator (the analyst) must be willing to live.

When a critical approach is undertaken, what worked before and what knowledge has been said to have accumulated is critiqued, rejected, or at least not reified. Whatever is known is held tentatively and judged to be useful only if it spurs action. Maintaining awareness that the sociopolitical context is in flux is a great challenge. Assuming the responsibility that the modifications that ensue are a result of the analytic process is also daunting. The consciousness and responsibility are challenging enough, but the analyst and those involved in the process will not have the security of knowing for sure what should be nor will they have any particular way of achieving it. Even with ideological certainty at the outset, what results will be uncontrollable. In the process representation, negotiation, persuasion, and even intimidation (intentional and subintentional) may result. All have ethical considerations that should not be ignored. In sum, revolution as a result of mass action is exciting, threatening, and dangerous.

CONCLUSION

In this chapter, we introduced critical approaches to policy analysis. There was a short history of philosophy of science to document how critical reason and logic are different from classical, traditional approaches to rationality in Western thought as well as from non-rational approaches that focus on incremental change in that these approaches will utilize both rational and nonrational reasoning when needed. A brief overview of sample theories was introduced, along with an exploration of the dimensions of critical approaches to policy analysis, providing examples of approaches that are situated in a critical paradigmatic perspective. The understanding of the possibilities and the challenges of critical approaches of policy analysis were further explored by looking at examples that target differing units of policy analysis.

The following chapter is built on the assumptions and approaches introduced here but will have an applied focus. You will see how to actually use critical approaches to achieve policy analysis goals that fit within a critical perspective. At the conclusion of this section

(Chapters 7 and 8), you should be able to assess the paradigmatic perspective of a particular policy analysis approach to determine whether it fits within a critical worldview in its approach to policy analysis, to identify the unit(s) of analysis that are the focus of the particular approach, and to know what is necessary to determine how to enact analysis using a critical approach. In addition, by the time you have completed Chapter 8, you should have at your fingertips a full range of research options using policy analysis guidelines, so that upon completion of the text you will recognize and be able to utilize multiple ways of analyzing policy.

DISCUSSION QUESTIONS

1. Early in this chapter, we argued that both linear and circular thought are congruent with the critical paradigm. First, discuss how it might be possible to use linear and circular thinking at the same time. Then, identify at least three ways that this approach to thinking is congruent with a critical ontology or frame of reference.

2. Review the theories that were discussed in Chapter 7. Why would you consider them to be critical theories? What are the benefits of critical positioning guiding work? What are the costs of the critical passion these theories provide?

3. Look at critical, distributive justice, and power and conflict theories in order to identify how they are similar and different. Now, using the media (radio, TV, the Internet, or other news source), see if you can identify policies at the formulation, product, implementation, or impact levels that can be better understood using one or all of these theories as a guide.

4. Critical, distributive justice, and power and conflict theories are relevant at multiple levels of practice. Select a policy issue within an organizational setting. How do these theories inform your thinking about this issue? Select a policy issue within a community with which you are familiar. How do these theories inform your thinking about this issue? If you are having difficulties embracing these radical theories as guidance for action, try to determine reasons other than fear of consequences that might be preventing your evenhanded analysis of their usefulness.

5. What do you see as the strengths and challenges of using critical approaches to policy analysis, especially with issues impacting nondominant groups?

CHAPTER 8

Applications in Critical Policy Analysis

I N CHAPTER 7, we provided background for understanding the underlying assumptions of a critical approach using both rationality and nonrationality, and we introduced a number of frameworks that are in harmony with those assumptions. All the approaches presented in Chapter 8 fit within a critical perspective as well as within a general ideology that views the sources of both individual and social oppression to be within social structures. To be congruent with this political ideology, existing social structures must be replaced with alternative structures. Being more radical than the rational or nonrational policy analysis approaches we discussed in previous chapters, this perspective forgoes incremental change in favor of transformative or revolutionary change as the only way to achieve the structural modifications necessary to realize the ideologically driven goals of policy.

This perspective on policy analysis does not just provide a critique of the status quo but is radically driven to use policy analysis as a revolutionary resource. The Service, Engagement, and Volunteerism case discussed in Chapter 7 and in previous chapters is used extensively in this chapter to demonstrate how radical policy questions alter the analytic process. How these various approaches can be applied differentially in the process of enacting a critical policy analysis is the primary focus of this chapter. Again, it is important to keep in mind that based on how the case was constructed, the ideology driving these critical analyses will be progressive. Other ideologies can also impel the application of the critical models of analysis. The only difference would be in the sort of data that would be sought. In the case of a more progressive ideology, data will be sought to support more liberal interpretations of social justice, but other interpretations could be the basis of systematic critical policy analysis just as well. As promised in earlier chapters, what follows will pick up on Nussbaum's (2006) concerns about nuanced attention to differing capacities and capabilities when considering social justice. Both the able and those with impairments are implicated in P.L. 111-13. The various exercises in policy analysis that follow should showcase the challenges in policy responses to social problems when people have differing capabilities and opportunities.

This chapter's focus is on the "doing" of critical policy analysis as a type of research. As with the other chapters that discussed the application of different policy analysis approaches, here we start by identifying the purpose of the policy analysis, which also determines the critical paradigmatic perspective for the research aspect of the process. In this case justice, power, and conflict will play a part in the application of the approaches. This chapter will take you through another analytic process that results in the determination of an appropriate critical approach. Given the real and imagined risks involved in pushing policy analysis to a critical, revolutionary point, discussion will focus on both the systematic aspects of considering this research and the implications of critical research as a consciousness-raising intervention.

After completing this chapter, you should be able to identify or construct a policy research question that fits within the critical perspective. Anchored in the identification of the purpose of the research, you will be able to select critical policy analysis strategies and defend the use of those strategies to answer the policy research question. As a result of determining the form, level (and scope), and focus of the social policy, you should be able to select and defend the selection of a particular critical approach to policy analysis. In this chapter, you will learn how to engage in various types of critical policy analysis through the application of several critical approaches. More importantly, you will develop the type of critical judgment necessary to determine when and where the risks related to this more radical positioning might outweigh the opportunities that this sort of systematic consciousness-raising might produce. The chapter ends with a discussion of what critical approaches can and cannot offer when you undertake policy analysis. Finally, you will be able to consider the consequences for helping professionals and the clients they serve when social justice rhetoric becomes operationalized through systematic policy analysis.

Recall that critical approaches to policy analysis are value-laden along a continuum from conservative to progressive. Critical approaches challenge both positivism/postpositivism and interpretivism/constructivism, viewing these paradigms as limited when it comes to achieving fundamental change. This critical perspective sees no separation of research or systematic inquiry from practice or political change activities. It operates from a position of skepticism regarding power, accepted norms, conventions, and social practices because of their assumed dominating capacities. As a means of consciousness raising, critical approaches criticize both the policy argument and any results that accrue through analysis. Critical approaches are modified realist in that there is objectivity but reasoning is historically situated so data, perceptions, attitudes, and beliefs are part of the production of knowledge. The critical policy analytic process, more than any other described up to this point, is action oriented because of a solid belief in human potentiality coming to fruition through struggle due to greater consciousness.

Critical approaches tend to build their analysis and action orientation on the following strategies: being critical, being pragmatic, systematically inquiring into contradictions of policy and practice, using dialogic methods, eliminating false consciousness, and energizing and facilitating transformation. The focus of the critical approach must match the reason for engaging in critical policy analysis in order to produce useful findings. Consciousness about all these aspects of a policy analytic process, in addition to the appropriate and thorough application of a particular approach in the analysis, makes policy analysis a type of research. In this case, however, the change agency dimension of the research enterprise must also be considered for fit, and risk assessment must be part of determining appropriateness and feasibility.

To arrive at a clearer understanding of the practicalities of enacting a critical approach to policy analysis, let us expand our interrogation of P.L. 111-13 using most of the approaches introduced in Chapter 7. In the sections that follow, we will demonstrate the essential elements requiring critical decision making that lead to critical policy analysis and to the selection of a particular approach to policy analysis within the critical perspective. For each approach we will provide guidance about how one might go about applying the approach selected. Given the interventive nature of critical policy analysis, in addition to the complexities of fully applying these approaches, neither products nor consequences of the critical approaches will be presented. Instead, as in the other chapters on the application of approaches, based on the kinds of questions contained in the selected approaches, we will suggest where one might go to find answers in order to complete an analysis of P.L. 111-13 as discussed in our case and guided by a particular critical approach. This should enable you to know what can and cannot be accomplished by a particular critical approach to policy analysis, as well as the risks and benefits present with each. Since it is as important to know how to select an appropriate resource for analysis as it is to know how to apply it, each section will detail the decision making that suggests why the approach is appropriate for the desired analysis before demonstrating the potential data sources for the type of inter-rogation that would be useful when applying the approach to a particular policy question.

USING MARX'S HISTORICAL OR DIALECTICAL METHOD

In Chapter 7, we introduced the work of Marx to frame a critical approach. To refresh your memory, Marx's approach is provided again in Figure 8.1.

Let us look at how one might go about accomplishing critical policy analysis if one applies the historical or dialectical method in analyzing

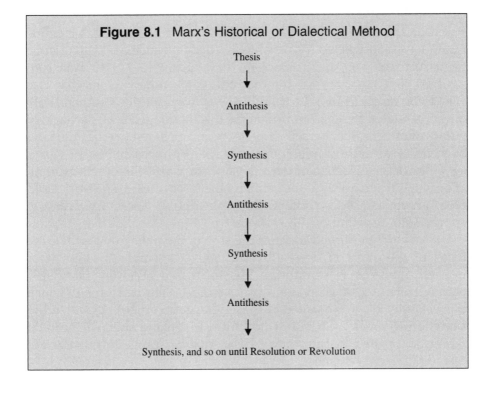

Figure 8.1 Marx's Historical or Dialectical Method

Thesis

Antithesis

Synthesis

Antithesis

Synthesis

Antithesis

Synthesis, and so on until Resolution or Revolution

P.L. 111-13. In the previous chapter, we envisioned a potential application by supposing that if

> *Madeline were to establish the thesis of P.L. 111-13 as "the disadvantaged can be
> served effectively by volunteers," and then she moves to the negation of this
> thesis by saying that volunteers as part of the sociopolitical structure do not
> effectively serve the disadvantaged but assure that they remain disadvantaged.
> Madeline would begin the dialectical process by trying to move those holding
> these opposite positions into a synthesis. The content of the synthesis would
> depend on the quality of the participation of opposing stakeholders. The process
> would move back and forth until a revolution of the disadvantaged would
> establish an alternative and more empowering approach to equalize advantage.*

Clearly, Madeline will face many contextual challenges in enacting this
sort of analysis, but before we tackle those let us first test the idea that
the Marxian approach is appropriate in this case. Then, we consider
how one might proceed with the analysis in ways that would accomplish the desired ends.

Targeting the Research

Based on the Service, Engagement, and Volunteerism case, Madeline
might have constructed a *policy research question* such as, "What is the
primary reason or social problem for which P.L. 111-13 was constructed, and what are the alternatives or opposite reasons that also
exist to be resolved by P.L. 111-13? She is interested in a rather "hot"
question related to social control of the disadvantaged and, perhaps, of
older volunteers. She, herself, may not be in a position to enact the kind
of critical analysis envisioned by the Marxian approach, but she can at
least clarify the direction of the analysis before assessing the feasibility
of enacting the analysis alone or with others. This research effort could
be controversial, if not conflictual, so it is doubly necessary to assure
appropriate targeting of the analysis.

First, Madeline should identify the *form* of the policy that will be the
focus of the analysis driven by the above research question. Her
research question is statutorial. The form is a federally mandated
policy. Her interest is in investigating the policy instrument which
is the statute, itself, as enacted by the federal government. As with other
analytic processes addressing this form of policy, she will need to
pursue data (and participants in the analytic process) outside the
bounds of agency practice.

Next, Madeline should articulate the *level* at which the policy research question is being pitched. Though Madeline is highly interested in the policy impact at her agency and in her own professional work, her question at this stage is really about policy at the national level. She is interested in the aspects of this policy that will be operationalized through the various federal agencies being held accountable for the enactment of P.L. 111-13, so actions at her agency or in her community, while important, may not be relevant data sources for this particular analytic process, at least not initially.

Like several other policy analysis approaches, the historical or dialectical method can be used across all aspects of the policy process. It can *focus* on formulation, product, implementation, or performance. While the initial focus of this research question seems to be on the policy intent or goal at the formulation stage, the policy product or the choice of the policy instrument as articulated in the public law will probably be important analytically and strategically. Since there are also aspects related to implementation actions and impact, attention to those aspects might be important for pushing for the resolution or revolution envisioned by both Madeline's concerns and the Marxian approach, making it quite able to respond to what might be necessary for the type of research question that is presented.

Justification of the analytic approach involves critical thinking and decision making in advance of the application of the analytic approach. The guidance provided by Marx will allow the analyst to attend to information related to statutory law (the form) and national policy (the level). It allows broader questioning of both the statutorial policy product and the formulation process at the national level (a dual focus). Because of this, a policy analyst like Madeline will be able to look at both history and politics in order to understand the context that allowed or propelled the particular policy decisions represented in the public law. Because she is interested in efforts to enact a more useful policy, this analytic process, when enacted, could lead to both a critical analysis of what is and a new conceptualization of the problem with very different proposed results. This approach allows Madeline to act both as analyst and change agent, if the possibilities of the analysis outweigh the risks.

Madeline spent a good deal of time thinking about whether she had the skills and the resources to engage in this research project. She engaged in a thorough *feasibility assessment*. As she thought more and more about what she was seeing at the national, state, and local levels, she was aware that whole populations were disempowered and not part of the civic engagement envisioned in the public law. She was not sure whether this was an intended or unintended result, but she was worried that her part in the process only touched a bit of the complexity of the public law. She felt she could engage critically with her gerontological colleagues and service recipients, but this sort of analysis was much bigger than that. She reached out to several national and community activists who shared her concern but from the standpoint of those engaged in youth development and services to the poor. They jumped on the chance to take critical action. Their funders, unlike Madeline's board, expected more assertiveness. So after taking leadership in the first stage of the critical analytic process, she stepped aside to become less active (and perhaps more subversive) because maintaining her position in the agency depended on it.

APPLYING THE APPROACH

In earlier discussions, we hope we made it clear that while the questions that one might ask under the guidance of a particular approach to policy analysis are important, the feasibility of the enactment of a particular approach is actually most related to whether or not the analyst knows and has access to the needed information or data at each stage of the analytic process. With critical approaches, data identification and access is important; however, just as important is strategic thinking regarding the consequences of enacting the approach. This is also a major aspect of feasibility assessment in critical policy analysis. Both need to be pursued and understood in order to avoid wastefulness. More importantly, feasibility assessment is needed to protect the vulnerable, which might even include the analyst herself.

In our application discussion of critical approaches, rather than engage in a completely developed policy analysis, which is beyond the scope of a text like this one, we have two purposes. First, we provide ideas about ways to construct the answers to the questions present in the approach to target the particulars of the current analysis, given the policy research question. Second, we look at who should be involved and in what ways in the enactment of the critical policy analysis. In doing so, it should become clear that useful data sources, while important, are not sufficient for successful enactment of critical policy analysis as research.

Determining the Thesis   In the analytic plan, Madeline will be taking the first steps and then handing the effort over to her advocate colleagues.

Her responsibility is to thoroughly support the thesis *"the disadvantaged can be served effectively by volunteers."* Data sources for support of such an assertion might be found in the empirical literature. A thorough literature search could be undertaken, including searching the conceptual and historical literature as a means of tracing the ideology attached to volunteerism and work with the disadvantaged. In addition, she might look at the literature on users of services to see how service organizations in general target disadvantaged populations.

To assure a solid link to the current policy, a review of the hearing records of all committees involved in the creation of P.L. 111-13 would also be useful. This review would ascertain who directly or indirectly took the position previously described, as well as searching documents for the explicit language that supports the position. Any research that was identified should be located and reviewed in the same way.

Present-day sources in support of this position might be found electronically. In fact, Madeline got the idea for her thesis through her active use of the blogosphere. Locating blogs that take the position under discussion (as well as alternative positions to be used in the creation of the antithesis) would be helpful in the development of a full-blown dialectical process. Identifying the individuals with supporting and opposing positions will be an aid when handing off the next stage to her colleagues. YouTube and Twitter would be good sources to support the thesis, as well as Web sites that were particularly active during the public discussion of P.L. 111-13 or that represent generally conservative ideologies, such as those demonstrated during the public debate on health care reform. The idea is to identify and locate all the public players that shaped the polity's position—that volunteerism can improve the status of the disadvantaged.

Once the information has been gathered and synthesized, Madeline can provide an ideologically and perhaps empirically-based position statement, one that includes names and contact points nationally of those who have taken this position. In order to assume a critical perspective, it will be as important for Madeline and her colleagues to understand the rationale that guided the assertion that volunteerism could be used to serve disadvantaged people. In fact, they will need to know those arguments that supported this policy intent as well as their own alternative arguments, so that they are prepared to debate the issues.

Determining the Antithesis   As Madeline engaged in this analysis, she also was able to begin to support the negation of the thesis. From many of the same types of information sources used to support the thesis, she began to find data to support that argument that *volunteers as part of the sociopolitical structure do not effectively serve the disadvantaged but assure that they remain as such*. Historical and empirical information regarding program effectiveness, testimony at the Congressional hearings, other media coverage, as well as material found in more liberal or radical blog spaces, Web sites, Facebook, and Twitter provide data sources to fill out this opposite positioning. Again as previously, data sources and those taking the position are identified as part of the position statement that Madeline will hand off to her more advocacy-oriented colleagues, who certainly hold a position more closely associated with the thesis than the antithesis.

Madeline found a wealth of literature that disputes the concept of charity that implies a supraordinate/subordinate relationship in which the givers (volunteers in this case) engage in nonreciprocal relationships (e.g., Hick, Fook, & Pozzuto, 2005; Margolin, 1997; McKnight, 1995; Specht & Courtney, 1994). Feminist writers provided alternative ways of thinking about volunteerism and the potential imposition of well-intentioned volunteers who take on disadvantaged persons as projects or superimpose their values on others. The potential of institutionalized dominant views through volunteerism has been criticized for generations; thus, Madeline has no trouble locating resources that accuse volunteer and other services provided by well-meaning staff of subjugating entire population groups.

Accomplishing Synthesis   Because there has been limited financial support for this national (and grassroots) policy analysis, no direct action has been undertaken. Few forums for actively and assertively fighting about positioning (like the "tea baggers" did in health care reform) are available at the beginning of this reform process. Madeline realizes that to oppose any aspect of this policy would be like destroying apple pie and motherhood, because volunteerism is so much a part of the nation's psyche. However, a public forum can be structured electronically, and that is exactly what Dawn (the youth advocate) and Jerome (the poverty advocate) decide to design and facilitate. Using the information provided by Madeline, they construct a blog laying out the two opposing positions. They send emails to all the stakeholders, identified by Madeline, and invite them to participate in a national discussion about the strengths and challenges embedded in P.L. 111-13.

Then they sit back and watch the sparks fly. Monitoring and managing the controversial discussion is difficult because the goal is to keep everyone in the discussion, while not establishing rules that are too restraining. The discussion becomes hot and heavy for about six months. Madeline even enters into the conversation, at first timidly, but later more assertively as data from her agency's program evaluation become available. Others add empirical data along with their own ideological views. Staffers of different Congresspersons participate. They are able to include state representatives from at least three regions of the United States. Some state employees are probably present, but none identify themselves in that way.

Dawn and Jerome know they are making inroads into the public discussion when several commentators on MSNBC make note of their blog and the Web sites that some of the participants have developed in support of and in reaction to the ideas expressed in the blog. There is a listserv set up and managed by someone wanting to influence the language of needed future amendments to P.L. 111-13. What is becoming clear is that within both the thesis and the antithesis are good ideas that make the concept of civic engagement more expansive. A few traditional media outlets cover the material that is generated, and even Rachel Maddow mentions it on her cable show. National advocates on both sides vow to take their position statements to Washington in whatever ways they can.

Proceeding to Antithesis, Synthesis, and So On, until Resolution or Revolution   If this critical analysis is pushed forward into action, a number of things could happen. P.L. 111-13 could be dramatically changed to be more sensitive to the values it projects and to the diverse populations affected by its mandates. But even more importantly, if change agents reconceptualize the concept of volunteerism (and this will take time), images of volunteers will no longer be seen as doing "to" or "for" the disadvantaged (a charitable perspective). Volunteers will be seen as collaborators with those receiving services. And those receiving services will be encouraged to provide services as well.

To this end, Madeline, Dawn, and Jerome begin to locate studies that pose radical approaches to civic engagement. For example, they locate a study that raises the possibility of tapping children and youth as volunteers (Shannon, 2009). "The most significant barriers [to tapping volunteers 8 to 12] are related to perceptions others have related to what younger youth can do as volunteers" (p. 828). Rather than seeing children as simply the recipients of what adult volunteers provide, this study shows an alternative that they could enter into the blog as an exemplar. Their goal overall is to reduce ageism through recognizing the strengths young people can bring to the civic engagement table. But they know that what they want must be entered into the dialectic just as every other position is until the revolutionary direction is established.

CRITIQUE OF THE APPROACH

A Marxian approach provides a process out of which a multitude of products can emerge. It is particularly helpful in asking the analyst to think about the thesis that undergirds the original policy so that she or he is as informed as possible about why this policy came into being. For the critical policy analyst, it might be seen as a waste of time to delve deeply into the reasons behind a policy with which the analyst doesn't necessarily agree (or may openly oppose). But with any radical change, it is important for the analyst to be totally informed so that in making the counterarguments that must be made, one is totally aware of all sides of the argument. Not much detail is provided in this policy analysis approach, because it is more of a process that is dependent on what emerges. Clearly, the results of the process may not be very controllable. However, it might open up new possibilities as the analyst engages dialectically. There is also the potential for real conflict, with some individuals becoming frustrated by the endless questioning process, leading them to declare that the analytic process is simply cause oriented without having adequate factual backing. Consequently, it is important to have the facts at hand to make one's case and to be prepared to be challenged by those who don't share the same cause orientation.

ANALYZING CULTURAL RESPONSIVENESS IN POLICY FORMULATION AT THE ORGANIZATIONAL LEVEL

Based on Chow and Austin's (2008) framework, another approach can be used in response to the issues that were recounted in Chapter 7. Again to refresh your memory, Box 8.1 provides guidance for the assessment of cultural responsiveness.

In Chapter 7 we stated,

> [I]f Madeline were interested in the cultural responsiveness of the implementation of the policy at her agency she would be interested in ascertaining the degree to which the local and neighborhood culture is a part of the program design. This would include how diverse perspectives were included in the interpretation and the formulation of the program in response to the federal policy. Madeline would look for use of community-based resources in real, rather than symbolic ways, with an eye to determining whether the implementation process results in consciousness raising at all levels of policy participation.

Box 8.1 Chow and Austin's Analyzing Cultural Responsiveness in Policy Formulation at the Organizational Level

Culturally Responsive Organizational Processes

- Does the process value diversity and embrace culture as a resource?
- Are participants aware of the dynamics, risks, and potential conflicts when different cultures intersect?
- Is expanding knowledge of various cultures and cultural issues incorporated in the process?
- Do the process and the formulation of the policy fit with the culture of the community to be served?
- Does the process demonstrate capability of being both program focused (responsive to public policy and funding streams), family focused (respectful and inclusive of families, strength-based interventions, participatory involvement of clients), and consumer-oriented; does it make use of support networks and natural helpers?

Agency–Community Relations

- Does the process engage an array of advocacy groups representing different cultural and ethnic communities?
- Does the process celebrate existing community strengths in order to empower disenfranchised populations to assess and monitor culturally responsive policies and procedures?
- Are participants linked horizontally to client communities and community networks, and vertically to professional, legislative, and funding sources (including local, national, and international networks)?
- Does the process promote consciousness raising among participants about how structural power, privilege, and oppression operate inside and outside the community?
- Do participants recognize through dialogue with community groups that the policy changes needed to create a culturally responsive organization can threaten the core culture of an agency, foster resistance, and radically transform the status quo?
- Is the formulation process proficient in receiving and integrating divergent forms of input from all parts of the community and within the organization?

Source: Adapted from "The Culturally Responsive Social Service Agency: An Application of an Evolving Definition to a Case Study," by J. C-C. Chow and M. J. Austin, 2008, *Administration in Social Work, 32*(4), 47–48.

Chow and Austin's (2008) critical policy analysis approach can be used to examine policy formulation, but more is involved in targeting this type of critical policy research.

TARGETING THE RESEARCH

Returning to the Service, Engagement, and Volunteerism case and the concerns at issue above, Madeline might have constructed a *policy research question* that could take her in another critically analytic direction. A relevant question might be, To what degree have the local and neighborhood cultures been considered in the agency's policies regarding the program implementation due to P.L. 111-13? This research question could expand her investigation about just how this policy might impact her agency, the clients, and the community that is served. It is a test of how contextualized program formulation has been in response to the federal policy and if not, why not. Her goal is to be certain that the planning for the program is culturally inclusive and responsive so that P.L. 111-13 implementation at the local level is a target. This type of question can be addressed by applying Chow and Austin's (2008) approach.

The next step in selection of the approach is to assure that it is appropriately targeted by identifying the form, level, and focus of the policy. In this case, the *form* of the social policy would be the rules and regulations developed by the agency at the organizational and/or community *level* to implement the federal law. Madeline may be informed by policy at the national level, though she is interested in the players and circumstances at the agency and community levels. The data sources, the analysis, and any action that results will be primarily at the local or neighborhood level. However, if major challenges are uncovered, influence at the national level may be a change-focused analytic outcome.

Chow and Austin's approach is well suited for interrogation of cultural responsiveness, because its *focus* is on policy formulation at the organizational level. Madeline's policy research question is about how the agency's policy got to be the way it is and whether or not it is culturally responsive. She is interested in more than understanding the intent or goal of the policy at the national level. She is interested in particular cultural aspects of agency-level formulation as a result of national action.

Chow and Austin's framework allows for a close look at processes at the organizational level, including diversity. The framework also interrogates how the organization contextualizes its efforts. Madeline will be testing agency cultural responsiveness and key community players' active and effective participation with the organization and their community. *Justification of the analytic approach* is clear when considering that application of this approach will allow Madeline to determine whether diverse perspectives were considered and included in program design and whether community participation was both real and influential in the planning process and can be seen in the planning result. Has the agency changed as a result of this formulation process? What might come next will depend on how the analytic process unfolds, what is found, and what participants think about those findings.

From a *feasibility assessment* perspective, it would appear that within the context of her organization this sort of interrogation will not put Madeline at risk. Because of the long-standing commitment of the agency to community responsiveness, it is clear that the agency's administration and the board of directors are truly interested in ascertaining how well the formulation process has gone and whether it has been embraced in the neighborhood. In this case, it would appear that Madeline and her agency are well targeted to take the risk to engage in this consciousness-raising project. Other agencies with less attention to the cultural contexts within which they work might not be as supportive if their employees want to engage in this sort of analysis.

APPLICATION OF THE APPROACH

Data for this analysis will be found both inside and outside the agency. The analysis will require both formal and informal data gathering, using both quantitative and qualitative methods. Also, because this approach is attentive to process and the process of critical policy practice is ongoing, there is a potential of creating more questions than answers in the analytic process.

Assessing Organizational Processes for Cultural Responsiveness   To determine the degree to which the organizationally based policy-making process values diversity and embraces culture as resources to programming, descriptive statistics about who has been involved in the planning will be important. Those data should include all the formal participants at the agency and board levels along with others who have a stake in the program, who have been included in program discussions and meetings both inside and outside the organization. Meeting minutes should be analyzed for themes demonstrating attention to diversity and culture. Attention to language usage would be important to determine whether the attention has been positively or negatively characterized.

To look at the formal history, meeting minutes should be analyzed to determine who is speaking and in what way. Minutes and other documents can be used to determine whether a diverse group is aware of the dynamics, risks, and conflicts that have been or may become part of the implementation process. At this point, it might be useful to directly interview some of the participants about their awareness and how they might have expanded their own or the agency's knowledge about the different cultures represented by those in the plan as both providers and recipients of service. Special attention to formal and informal data sources should help to determine whether the program as designed actually fits with the culture of the communities to be served. Determining this would require a good deal of information about the catchment areas and the potential providers and recipients of services that can come only from a thorough ethnographic understanding of the context. Since Madeline both lives in the area and has worked there for many years, she should have this knowledge; the challenge, however, is to make her knowledge explicit as a frame for interrogating the policy as it is currently embodied in the program.

Finally, using the policy implementation as proposed in the written program, Madeline should engage in an interrogation that includes determining whether what has been enacted fits agency and funding stream expectations. Then it is also important to determine whether it is consumer oriented. In this case, consumers would be both the volunteers needed for mounting the program as designed and the projected youth recipients of the program. She needs to determine whether the specific cultural issues of all involved are being planned for and whether there is sufficient flexibility for responsiveness. Direct interviews are called for in this case. Finally, even if solid participation is evident in the planning process, has it been built into the implementation and evaluation of the program plan?

Assessing Agency–Community Relations   To ascertain whether the relevant advocacy groups have been engaged in the process, Madeline will first need to determine whether there are formalized advocacy groups in the catchment area and who are represented by these groups, before looking at participant lists and meeting minutes to see if their influence was felt. If no formal advocacy groups exist, it would be useful to look through newspapers and local media to identify spokespersons and to determine whether these individuals have been invited and included in discussions.

The meeting notes for planning sessions should be interrogated not just for who participated but for who spoke and the kind of language used to record what was said. Madeline should be looking for examples of how existing community strengths were being identified and plan-fully used in the preparation of the program plan. When participant lists are created, an additional analysis would be useful. Because the participants will represent various constituencies, it will be useful to see whether horizontal connections with the client community and the community networks are present, as well as vertical connections with formal power structures including professional "experts," legislators, and funding sources.

By conducting individual interviews and assessing meeting records, Madeline can tap into the consciousness-raising aspects of the planning process. It will be important to determine whether or not participants became more aware of the complexity of the issues involved in being culturally responsive. But more importantly, did participants become more aware of how some of the structural issues might be impeding the planning efforts? Formally or informally, have all those with a stake in the planning process looked at how structural power, privilege, and oppression operate inside the agency and outside in the community and, for that matter, in the locality as a whole?

Once these analyses have been undertaken and the results under-stood, the next step is feeding the information back to all involved in the planning process. Community representatives and community groups should receive the information, and for the policy analytic process to get to its most critical potential, these community groups should ascertain whether the agency is operating in a way that is acceptable to them. If not, the agency in the form of sensitive practitioners such as Madeline and the decision makers in the ad-ministration and on the board must hear the details about how the agency is off the mark.

The end of this process may threaten the core of the agency's culture. Some decision makers at all levels may resist the efforts of nonprofes-sionals to tell them how to be culturally sensitive and responsive. The push-back may put the agency into a turmoil that might result in its radical reconfiguration and may impact how it will engage in the implementation of P.L. 111-13. The organization may be restructured so that it can consistently incorporate divergent forms of input from various sources in the community and within the agency. The planning process may become an emergent, rather than a linear one (see Netting, O'Connor, & Fauri, 2008 for a discussion of emergent approaches to planning).

CRITIQUE OF THE APPROACH

This framework focuses on cultural responsiveness at the organization or agency level. It requires the analyst to gain a deep understanding of the community's cultural context in order to maintain the appropriate information sources about implementation. Chow and Austin pose specific questions designed to help the analyst fully understand the dynamics of implementation, which may or may not be deemed culturally responsive.

When questions of cultural responsiveness are raised, there is likely to be some negative information that might be received defensively by well-intentioned organizations. The information may not be of interest at all to agencies unconcerned about the more interpretive elements of cultural responsiveness. This framework is designed to push the envelope with the expectation that structural changes may be required to fully address the issues raised. The first task of the analyst will likely be to convince persons who are comfortable in their various roles to consider the possibility that business as usual is just not acceptable. Resistance may come if staff and volunteers do not see cultural responsiveness as an important analytic aspect of policy or programming or if they think they have "done enough." In addition, to fully conduct this type of analysis, everyone (including program participants) must be part of the process, given that it is actually program participants who will know whether the organization is culturally responsive. This approach, then, rejects a traditional expert model in analysis and change by literally restructuring the way in which information is gathered and from whom. This may be transformative for persons who find the process empowering but threatening for others who already hold powerful positions within the organization.

USING LEJANO'S NORMATIVE POLICY ANALYSIS

In Chapter 7, we introduced a critical policy analysis approach that is particularly helpful in studying a policy instrument choice. Lejano's (2006) normative policy analysis is provided in Box 8.2 as a reminder and as an aid to the discussion that follows.

Box 8.2   Lejano's Normative Policy Analysis

1. Standards
   Does the policy have elements within it that can be considered in the light of providing a minimum standard of quality for those affected by the policy?
   Can we begin discussing the levels of quality the policy can ensure at this point in time and what degrees of quality we can aspire to in the future?
   Can we express these standards in the form of rules?
   Can we have a discussion of how these (explicit or implicit) rules might be constructed?
   Is there a hierarchy of values that the policy needs to consider, and how are different values prioritized in this situation?
2. Distribution
   What is the distribution of costs, benefits, opportunities, obligations, and others associated with the policy?
   Are burdens and gains inequitably distributed?
   Should the policy have a redistribute component?
3. Structural relationships
   Does the policy foster a structure of sociopolitical relationships that privilege some groups or individuals and systematically marginalize others?
   How does the policy create this structuring?
   Does the policy undo existing social structures and privilege the presently disenfranchised?
   Does the policy reflect virtues of care and empowerment?
4. Process
   Does the policy allow access of all concerned to the policy process?
   Does the policy create additional support for participation or representation of the traditionally underrepresented?

Source: Frameworks for Policy Analysis: Merging Text and Context (pp. 151–152), by R. P. Lejano, 2006, New York, NY: Routledge. Used with permission.

In Chapter 7 we stated,

[I]f Madeline had questions about minimum standards of quality and what values are represented in P.L. 111-13 she might be interested in using this approach. In doing so, distribution of costs, benefits, opportunities, and obligations for both the volunteers and those being served must be assessed for inequality. She would have questions about power redistribution being central to changes in the structural relationships between the "disadvantaged" and the young people, veterans, and seniors providing volunteer services. The idea would be to determine the degree to which this policy allows access to all

concerned at all levels of the policy process including the inclusion of the traditionally underrepresented.

To move systematically through an analysis of the policy choice to create a critical interrogation as well as to establish the context for potential change, additional assessment of Lejano's model is necessary before it can be applied

TARGETING THE RESEARCH

Continuing the Service, Engagement, and Volunteerism case, let us push further analysis of the state plan and its implementation at the agency level. Recall that the state plan focused on expanding the number of volunteers to work with at-risk adolescents, setting a three-year goal to eliminate the drop-out and unemployment problems that arise when young people age out of foster care. Madeline's agency expanded its program to include veterans and other individuals 55 years old and over in a multilevel service delivery program for adolescents aging out of foster care. Male and female mentors helped youth stay in school; they also targeted young people preparing for college, with mentors being matched to the young people based on what the youth needed and what the volunteer was interested in doing. Several specialized volunteers (some of whom had been military recruiters) worked directly with young people to move them to volunteer in community and neighborhood projects and, when appropriate, to choose one of the volunteer programs that were supported by P.L. 111-13. The agency expanded its geographical catchment area for recruiting volunteers and for accepting clients. In preparation for the year-three program proposal to the state, Madeline's *policy research question* is, Has the agency implemented its program under P.L. 111-13 in a socially just or moral way?

This question allows a rather complex interrogation of the public law according to the various *forms* it has taken from the time of signing the statute into law. It would allow a look at the state-level policy objectives as they have become operationalized in Madeline's agency, including the rules and regulations that govern their work. The sources of these would be the federal agency in charge of the aspects of the law they are implementing along with the specific directives that have come from the state and local levels and at the agency level. This would also include the program as enacted and the budget as received to fund the program activities. Madeline would be interested in both the formal, written policies that pertain at all the *levels* as well as informal policies that have influenced the way the agency's practice has evolved. It might be important to look at standards of practice and her professional code of ethics, but she is actually interested in the distributive-justice aspects of the quality of the policy process within her state and her agency. Therefore, the *focus* of this policy analysis is on policy implementation, with a particular interest at her agency's programmatic level.

Use of Lejano's normative policy analysis can be *justified* because of the purpose of the analysis. Madeline is interested in policy implementation and the ethics therein. She wants to understand how the program's structure and relationships enhance or impede distributive justice, which is the point of Lejano's approach. *Feasibility assessment* involves consideration of whom or what might be put at risk with this sort of interrogation. Because her agency is so well known and has funding stability, any negative findings would not put it at risk. Because Madeline has the support of her administrator and board of directors, there is no apparent risk for her. State-level bureaucrats may become uncomfortable with the blatant transparency of the process and may not be happy with any critique that may result, but they would be unable to sanction the agency, its employees, its volunteers, or the clients it serves. They themselves could be at risk, but this is not an election year. There may be push-back in the community, but all in all, the benefits of the process and what might result appear greater than the risks at hand.

APPLICATION OF THE APPROACH

Data sources for this approach will consist of the rules and procedures that shape the agency's program that were derived from the state policy. This approach will require the collection of both quantitative and qualitative data. When problems are identified, the process will certainly involve direct discussions with certain individuals important to implementation decisions at all the levels of interest, as well as with others with a stake in the policy process.

Assessing Standards   The very concept of standards gives Madeline pause. Standards sound very rational and prescriptive and are often established as oppressive universals. But she realizes that Lejano's questions offer a new way of conceptualizing standards as inherently tied to values, often multiple values. As she considers the questions guiding the analysis, she searches for examples of standards used to guide volunteer management and realizes that there are multiple ways to oversee or guide volunteer activities. She reads in the volunteerism literature about the concept of psychological contracting (Farmer & Fedor, 1999), in which people bring their own values to the situation and approach their roles with very individualized internal contracts that are rarely articulated. However, these psychological contracts can determine whether the fit between whatever standards are set will work or people will leave and look for connections elsewhere (Macduff, Netting, & O'Connor, 2009).

As a result, she locates no guiding standards for her program and is left with more questions than answers. Two important questions that require further consideration are: How would one establish a minimum standard of quality that would meet everyone's needs? and How does one define quality in volunteer management? To answer these questions, she will need to talk directly with the recipients of volunteer services, the volunteers themselves, and the various program managers to contextualize these issues to her agency and her program. She will see which rules each group recognizes and whether or not different values are prioritized differently by those affected by P.L. 111-13.

Assessing Distribution of Burdens and Gains   The concept of redistribution makes Madeline think about how some people benefit from this policy and how others don't receive any benefit at all. She will need to look closely at the language of the public law to identify not only what is present, but what has been left out, in order to begin to identify who actually benefits and who does not. Madeline realizes that in posing questions of distribution, Lejano raises issues about the morality of policies that carry implicit assumptions about people's access to resources and their ability to perform traditional volunteer roles.

Using the management information data from the agency, she could create a profile of the volunteers. She is interested in determining whether the volunteer work is being undertaken only by the able-bodied. She also could look at her recruitment and retention plans and the documentation of activities in that regard to determine whether all potential volunteers have had access to the information—not only about the need for volunteers but about the gains that accrue as a result of volunteering. She wants to determine whether her program does everything necessary to help all citizens in her catchment area to engage civically in volunteerism. She needs evidence to support the idea that the agency is helping all eligible citizens to live up to the societal expectations embodied in the public law and to determine whether redistribution within any dimension might be needed.

Identifying and Assessing Structural Relationships   Guided by the literature on critical gerontology, Madeline looks to the work of such scholars as Martinson and Minkler (2006) to identify the structural relationships that should be interrogated. In doing so, she identifies a problem in the concepts of civic engagement and volunteerism. She notes in her linguistic analysis of P.L. 111-13 that they appear to be interchangeable. The consequence seems to be that visible roles in civic life (e.g., voting, community activism) become privileged while more informal roles (e.g., care giving, informal connections) are largely ignored. The Serve America Act privileges specific kinds of volunteerism. Martinson and Minkler point out that the call for engagement is often a political ruse to capture volunteer time when social programs remain underfunded. Madeline decides to look at the history of her agency's funding pattern to test the idea that "older adults are called on to be useful and to counter budgetary shortfalls through volunteering while their own safety nets are disintegrating" (p. 320). Extending her interviews with the recipients of volunteer services, the volunteers themselves, and the various program managers about their experiences seems necessary, because Madeline begins to realize that those programs that seek societal change on a broader basis are not highlighted in this policy. She wonders whether the participants in her analysis are aware of how current sociopolitical relationships are being maintained.

Assessing the Policy Process   To determine access to the policy process, Madeline reviews numerous press releases, studies about how volunteering can improve health, hype over civic engagement and service learning opportunities, and a host of other Web sources to identify who might be included in the dialogue and in the policy changes that could give her volunteer programs even more credibility. To make the analysis critical, Madeline begins to list the groups that are missing in the civic engagement movement—for example, people who have lost their jobs in the economic downturn, persons who have chronic conditions that impair their functional ability, or children with disabilities. In analyzing the language of P.L. 111-13 Madeline finds that the policy is silent regarding support for participation or representation of the traditionally underrepresented. Again, she determines that an extension of her interview protocol is warranted to see whether those involved in her agency realize that not only are these policies targeted to the productive, the successful, and the well, but the voices of persons below the political radar screen have been subjugated—not only at the federal level but perhaps in her agency.

Critique of the Approach

Lejano's framework is designed to raise even more questions than it poses. He suggests "the less sharply defined [approach] to ethics provides a richer analytical ground of policy questions around which to focus the questioning" (p. 152). This critical approach creates opportunities for further deliberation, rather than focused answers. It pushes inclusivity by asking about who is left out as much as who is a part of the policy process. Its complexity can become somewhat overwhelming if there is no attempt to focus the analysis, because processing can go on indefinitely if the analyst does not guide the process so as to determine what action can be taken to move toward change rather than engaging in constant ongoing dialogue.

USING MOSER'S APPROACH TO GENDER POLICY IMPLEMENTATION

Another model introduced in Chapter 7 is Moser's (1993) ideological approach to gender and policy implementation, which is intended to result in a more equitable status for women. In Box 8.3, we have included Moser's approach again to aid the discussion.

Box 8.3 Moser's Approach to Gender Policy Implementation

- Gender role identification
  - Reproductive work: inside the organization, in the household.
  - Productive work: providing or receiving goods and services inside or outside.
  - Community work: social events and services, inside or outside.
- Gender needs assessment
  - Practical gender needs: needed assistance in activities inside or outside.
  - Strategic gender needs: assistance to transform balance of power between men and women inside or outside.

- Disaggregating control of resources and decision making within the policy action
  - Who controls what, and how?
  - Who decides what, and how?
- Planning for balancing the triple role
  - Does the policy action increase a woman's workload in one of her roles inside or outside to the detriment of other roles?
  - Is there a need for intersectoral or interagency planning to avoid problems?

Source: Adapted from *Gender Planning and Development: Theory, Practice, and Training,* by C. Moser, 1993, London: Routledge.

Recall in Chapter 7 we suggested that,

[G]ender questions could serve Madeline as the basis for assessing whether the disadvantaged and the volunteers have differing practical and strategic gender needs that might have a relationship with the control of resources represented by this policy. The main concern in this analysis is how identification of areas of the policy at any level increase women's workloads to the detriment of their other roles and, if so, to force options inside agencies or between agencies to avoid those problems.

The intent of the analytic approach is clear, but what should be clarified are the dimensions that will allow appropriate targeting of the policy analysis process.

TARGETING THE RESEARCH

Continuing within the expansion on the Service, Engagement, and Volunteerism case, as discussed previously, let us imagine that Madeline's concern comes in year two. The time is nearing to construct the proposal for year-three funding and Madeline is beginning to wonder about service distribution and volunteer recruitment along gender lines. While there have been great efforts to recruit both male and female veterans as well as other volunteers 55 years and older, participation of women is uneven. This is also true for those being served. Mostly young men are being served. Madeline understands that some of this may just be artifacts of military life, aging, and who moves from foster care to independence; but she is suspicious that something else is at play. She also is quite aware that there is only one male employee in the agency, while most of the board members are male business people. Given her suspicions Madeline's *policy research question* is, What has been the agency's attention to gender roles in implementing P.L. 111-13?

Madeline is interested in agency-level issues, but those issues are informed and impacted by the various *forms* the public law has taken from the time of signing the statute into law. Her focus will be on the policy objectives as they have become operationalized in her agency, but to fully understand the implementation issues, the rules and regulations that are governing the agency's work would also be important. As with many of the other examples, the information sources would be the federal agencies in charge of the aspects of the law they are implementing as well as the specific directives that have come from the state and local levels and at the agency programmatic level. Madeline would be interested in both the formal, written policies that pertain at all these *levels* as well as those informal policies that have influenced the way the agency's practice has evolved. The *focus* of this policy analysis is policy implementation, with a particular interest at the programmatic level. At a minimum, this will inform her as she prepares part of the third-year funding proposal; but other fundamental changes might also be pursued.

Justification of the approach may in some ways be difficult if neither the administration nor the board sees a reason for a gender analysis. Without some sort of administrative sanction, there is a chance that this sort of inquiry into policy implementation would represent too much potential for criticism just at the time for third-year review and funding. If that were the case, *feasibility* would be at issue, even if Moser's approach is precisely suited for the purpose of the analysis. If it were not possible for Madeline to enact the analysis, she might seek support from local, regional, and national feminist organizations along with military organizations acting on behalf of "women warriors." The challenge in this strategy would be legally releasing agency internal documents and information. Freedom of Information Act requests could provide contract-based information related to funding from both state and federal sources; the analysis would be possible, but not as easily undertaken. For the purpose of this exercise, let us imagine that several female board members are extremely interested in the gender issue and are supportive of the effort notwithstanding the hesitation of the male board members, so Madeline thinks it is possible to proceed. She sees the internal and external risks to herself personally and professionally, as well as to her agency, and is certain that this policy analysis is worth it on social justice grounds alone.

APPLICATION OF THE APPROACH

As we suggested in Chapter 7, this particular analytic process can be used to focus on gender from a feminist ideological perspective. It can be modified to allow an analysis of any oppressed class, because the analytic elements actually look at power differentials. Work levels as defined in the approach now appear to have meaning across gender perspectives and may be useful when analyzing the particulars of minority experiences, regardless of gender. Finally, a comparative analysis between genders might also be quite instructive. For the purposes of this application, we will look only at female gender role issues.

Identifying Gender Roles   Madeline will need to use both the management information data and participant observation data regarding what is considered "reproductive" work. Here, the question would be about actual reproduction via pregnancy, but also what are the expectations for women within the organization and the particular program. The same sources of data would be used to determine the "productive" work of providing and receiving services. Are women principally the providers or the recipients of service? What about the relationships outside the agency? The same data sources, along with the possible inclusion of meeting minutes related to recruitment and other "community" work, should be interrogated to determine if there are certain assumptions about who is expected to do what. This may also include an analysis of who is recording all the data being used for analysis. This might suggest a general "housekeeping" role identification that might be female gender related.

Assessing Gender Needs   The major data sources for the assessment of gender needs may be the women who are providing and receiving services under the program enacted under P.L. 111-13. Madeline could construct a questionnaire to see whether there are practical needs that should be addressed for service providers, including female volunteers, to competently engage in program activities. The same questions could be posed to the female recipients of services in order for them to be able to participate in service activities. In the process of structured interviewing or questionnaire completion, all would engage in identification of needed assistance in order to transform the balance of power both within and outside the agency. In some cases, the interrogation of this male/female power can lead to outside advocacy and actions leading to change. In Madeline's case, the results will set the stage internally for the next phase of the analysis.

Disaggregating Control of Resources and Decision Making within the Policy Action   Through observation, management information sources, and analysis of formal meeting minutes including activities of the board of directors, Madeline should be able to determine who controls what regarding the agency and the program related to P.L. 111-13. She needs to identify who decides what in both domains and how those decisions are made. Determining the "how" may require direct questioning of those involved in both formal and informal decision making.

Planning for Balancing Reproductive, Productive, and Community Work
Based on the foregoing analysis, Madeline should look at the program plan as currently explicated in order to determine whether women's workloads (providers and recipients) are increased as a result of what is expected in the plan. Particular attention should be placed on all three levels of women's work related to gender role identification. For background literature and alternative perspectives in which to reframe gender identity and work roles, Madeline may want to access feminist studies that provide new insights and ways of thinking about how to balance reproductive, productive, and community work (e.g., Ashcraft & Mumby, 2004; Belenky, Bond, & Weinstock, 1997; Bordt, 1997; Ferree & Martin,1995; Kravetz, 2004; Metzendorf, 2005).

Assessing Need for Intersectoral and Interagency Planning   Findings may indicate the need to expand the agency conversation both internally and externally in order to avoid unintended negative consequences related to the plan as currently proposed and funded. From a feminist perspective, she might explore nontraditional planning options. Radical planning approaches assume that the system in which planning is occurring is oppressive and that collaboration among all stakeholding groups is rarely possible, due to power inequities. Depending on her findings, Madeline may want to push for more empowerment-focused planning (Hardina, 2002) in her agency to assure that oppressed groups share in the fruits of the system or engage in planning for systemic level change.

CRITIQUE OF THE APPROACH

This framework is focused on implementation with a gendered assessment. Because of the narrowness of a gender orientation, the Moser approach could miss details related to other groups that have been neglected in the process. Thus, the policy analyst will want to consider the strengths and limitations of a gender lens, potentially using this with other frameworks that target different population groups for comparative purposes or altering the focus to include more than gender.

USING SCHIELE'S AFROCENTRIC FRAMEWORK OF POLICY ANALYSIS

The final aspect of critical policy research and policy action involves attention to policy impact. From the critical perspective, there is interest in assessing whether the policy did eliminate or remediate the social problem it was intended to address or whether it incurred unintended negative consequence. If negative implications for vulnerable groups persist, the idea is to provide the impetus to take action so that fundamental change can occur. In Chapter 7, we introduced some features of Schiele's (2000) Afrocentric approach to assessing impact for vulnerable groups; we reintroduce those in Box 8.4.

Box 8.4   Schiele's Features of the Afrocentric Framework of Policy Analysis

Implications of Policy for Vulnerable Groups

- To what extent does the policy exacerbate the exploitation of the labor of working people?
- To what extent does the policy facilitate or hinder the conditions of the marginalized?
- To what extent does the policy enhance or hamper opportunities for nonprofessionals and others without power?
- To what degree does the policy exclude or include interpretations and cultural values from the groups targeted by the policy?
- To what degree does the policy include provisions that protect African Americans from physical harm, harassment, intimidation, and stigmatization?
- To what extent does the policy reinforce and promote continued Eurocentric domination?
- To what degree does the policy offer additional opportunities for African Americans?
- To what extent does the policy support the strengths and resources within African-American communities and families through the inclusion of African Americans in its formulation and implementation?

Source: Adapted from *Human Services and the Afrocentric Paradigm* (pp. 175–177), from J. H. Schiele, 2000, New York, NY: The Haworth Press.

In Chapter 7 we stated,

[I]f Madeline were struck by some of the inconsistencies in the policy and wanted to understand why they were present, this policy approach will allow an identification and interrogation of the basic assumptions upon which the policy was built by its supporters. She would test these assumptions against the reality of those with a stake in the social problem and this particular policy response built on volunteerism. Her goal would be uncovering or otherwise identifying alternative assumptions about serving the disadvantaged that would be more logical, consistent, or realistic. Just how different are the assumptions guiding the policy from the values of the vulnerable groups it is intended to help? The idea would be to identify alternatives that would avoid domination and other control elements for all involved; from doing this, radical change would result.

As with the application of the other critical approaches, it is important to ascertain the appropriateness of the selected approach for the question at hand as well as determining the feasibility of engaging in such a critical or "hot" analysis.

TARGETING THE RESEARCH

Madeline has a great interest in what happened as a result of this policy, particularly related to inconsistencies in results. Over the years of implementation, she has become more and more active in a listserv constructed by members of local agencies all over the nation who have been implementing P.L. 111-13. She even participated in a meeting of service providers that was held in conjunction with the annual meeting of the Gerontological Society of America. She chuckles when she remembers how confused some conference-goers were when many sessions were filled with young people, military personnel, and others all interested in volunteer recruitment and retention but less interested in the needs of the aging population. She has also been struck by how "white" all the issues have been and how few African Americans have joined the dialogue about implementing the provisions of the Act. Because of the questions that are swirling around in the media and in cyberspace prior to the Act's reauthorization, she has the following *research question*: Where are the African-American perspectives when considering the sources of inconsistencies that have resulted in uneven results in the impact of P.L. 111-13?

The policy *form* is statutorial, but Madeline will also be looking at policy objectives and rules and regulations at the national, state, and agency levels throughout the nation. Madeline's interest, and the interests of the listserv members are at the national, state, and local organizational *levels* of policy, because foundational assumptions can be found at all levels. The *focus* of Madeline's research is on impact or performance; but with the objective of identifying intended or unintended domination, reduction of service, alienation, or reification of any sort, particularly related to African Americans. *Justification of the analytic approach* rests on the idea that Madeline and her colleagues are interested in impacts other than those provided through evidence-based programming (EBP) to ascertain whether or not some of the policy and program inconsistencies were actually intentional. If they were, she and other advocates want to be ready to push alternatives in the reauthorization process that will achieve better, more inclusive, and more consistent outcomes in civic engagement. This approach can accomplish this.

The *feasibility* question remains. Alone, Madeline does not have the resources or the sanction to enact this sort of policy inquiry. She must rely on others with greater insider information, but she is confident that she has sufficient agency information to add to the process. There is a risk in moving forward without administrative and board permission, especially with the racial issues that may be involved, but she feels she is part of a movement and it is worth the risk.

APPLICATION OF THE APPROACH

Schiele's analysis looks at impacts of a social justice type for vulnerable populations, especially African Americans. Much of the analytic effort is to identify intended and unintended consequences that have resulted in oppressive conditions for some elements of the policy stakeholding population. Imbedded in this approach is a hypothesis that the assumptions underpinning the actual policy are generally the source of the oppressive off-targeting particularly due to Eurocentric domination. The goal of this type of impact analysis is a change in perspective that will lead to a revised policy option more apt to have positive, empowering results for those without power.

Assess Exploitation For Madeline to begin this analysis, she would need to read all the historical material related to the framing of the policy. The *Federal Register* would be useful. It would be important to see who said what and what particular claims were being made. Creating an analytic grid would be important for finding the major foundational assumptions. What she will be looking for specifically are stated or unstated assumptions about the labor of working people, since the focus of the policy is on unpaid volunteerism. Extension of the assumptions could be made through checking media reports at the time for claims about the policy. In all cases, it would be important to identify the ideologies undergirding the claims as a step towards the next aspect of the analysis regarding marginalization.

Data sources for support of assertions might be found in the empirical literature. A thorough literature search could be undertaken, including searching the conceptual and historical literature as a means of tracing the ideology attached to volunteerism and the disadvantaged—for example, the award-winning, funded study (Tang, Morrow-Howell, & Hong, 2009) on diversity among older populations of volunteers. She would be looking for information exhibiting class and race sensitivity. Madeline notes that although this article recognizes the critical perspective and cites a number of studies that raise concerns, it is an excellent example that supports the original intentions of the policy with no recognition of potential exploitation. Evenhanded analysis requires that she find alternative perspectives as well that might critique unpaid labor. This would also be the place where some quantitative data regarding social and economic status of both the providers and the receivers of volunteer services would be assessed.

Assess Marginalization   Madeline would then interrogate the identified original claims, the general discourse, and the empirical evidence looking for information about what might facilitate or hinder the conditions of the marginalized. For her purposes this would mean the poor, minorities, and probably women. This test could involve a simple thematic analysis, but attention to language usage would also be important. Her earlier literature review provided her with data from critical gerontologists who have followed the progress of the civic-engagement movement during the past decade, so Madeline would have access to empirical evidence that will allow her to determine what might have positive or negative impacts on the general conditions of those she has identified as vulnerable.

Assess Opportunities for Those without Power   Next she would look at what has happened as a result of the policy for nonprofessionals and others without power. Have volunteerism and other aspects of civic engagement eliminated or extended job possibilities? Some of this information could come from agency data about service delivery, and some might come from direct interviews with volunteers. Madeline could assess at all levels, but because she is noting inconsistencies at the local level, focus there would probably be the most informative, and it would be the most feasible area. Given the information identified in earlier steps, Madeline must search for data situations that are both consistent with and different from those findings. Data sources will depend upon what she sees related to exploitation and marginalization.

She should also interrogate her agency program outcomes for what is present or overlooked regarding vulnerable groups. Most likely local socioeconomic data from the most recent census (in it are data gathered after implementation of the policy), general business trend data from media sources, housing information, education information, and homelessness and violence and general police data would be informative, because this information relates to opportunities for nonprofessionals and others who lack political and economic power. The point is to determine whether opportunities have increased for both the volunteers and those served by them now that the policy has been implemented in programmatic form by her agency.

Determine Presence of Interpretations and Cultural Values of Policy Targets   Given her findings, Madeline should be able to propose alternatives for the agency program, but she would need to be focused on the national policy to be more consistent with local needs. The result could drive a policy about civic engagement more logically while being more realistic in view of the current ideological climate and resources. This is based on the assumption that the policy and her agency should be clear about the role of the cultural values of the groups targeted by the policy. If programs nationally are silent about the special issues faced by vulnerable populations, it might be possible at least for Madeline to provide change recommendations to her agency based on her analytic findings. However, the analysis reaches its most critical aspects in the stages that follow.

Assess Protections against Physical Harm, Harassment, Intimidation, and Stigmatization   If many of her cohorts are engaging in this same analysis at their local levels, the absence of cultural sensitivity may be identified throughout programming. Schiele (2000) asks the analyst to take the analysis one step further to assess policy protections, especially for African Americans. The first level of analysis for this will be the language of the Act, the second level will be the language of the formal state and local responses, and the last level will be programmatic to identify specific protections. It will be important to engage in linguistic analysis to ascertain any intended or unintended stigmatization that might be present, either through the language of the policy's rules and procedures, or in mandates for implementation. It will be important to identify and record any overt experiences of harm. These might be available through the news media or at her program level through incident reports.

Assess for Eurocentric Domination   Earlier analysis of content and language of both the policy and the programs that have resulted can also help Madeline to determine the degree to which the policy and its implementation are Eurocentric in their focus. As a white American, she may need the cultural interpretation of her minority colleagues for this. Care should be taken to search for maximum perspectives from minority colleagues for this analysis, insofar as no individual minority person is capable of speaking for the minority groups he or she represents. Attention should also be given to class issues that may be present and overlooked by well-educated minority professionals, so a variety of social and economic positions should be tapped for their perspectives.

Assess for African American Opportunities   The same informants for the Eurocentric analysis may also be useful in determining the degree to which opportunities are present for African Americans at any level as a result of the policy. Madeline would do well to rely on her colleagues' views regarding what in the policy and its implementation at her agency level either impedes or enhances possibilities for African Americans. Token attention to opportunities should not be allowed to stand for sufficient opportunities.

Assess for Respect for and Inclusion of African Americans in Formulation and Implementation   In many cases the answers to this aspect of the analysis will have been made clear in the analytic process, particularly in the last several steps in Schiele's framework. Madeline should have been able to identify the degree to which African American voices were heard in the original shaping of the bill. Through the analysis, she will begin to understand how some of the inconsistencies she has experienced at all levels may be related to lack of race and class sensitivity.

Once her assessment is complete, she can compare the current program and the national policy to what she is recommending by assessing both for their reflection of critical thought about implications for vulnerable groups. In stating her recommendations, she will be particularly interested in avoiding language that suggests intended or unintended consequences of domination, diminishment, alienation, intimidation, or stigmatization of people without economic or political power, especially African Americans. Once this aspect of the analysis is complete, she will need to determine what actions should be taken by her alone or in concert with others and at what level. In some ways this particular analysis could lead Madeline to engage in further work using the Marxian approach presented at the beginning of this chapter.

CRITIQUE OF THE APPROACH

Schiele's approach is based on identification of exploitation, lack of opportunity, disrespect, and other types of domination that rise out of Eurocentric thought. Much of what is assessed does not conform to the questions deemed important for evidence-based or outcome-based assessment. This value-driven approach is derived from having lived with the consequences of policy based on the assumptions that Afrocentric issues and issues pertinent to African Americans and other vulnerable populations rarely are paramount in Eurocentric processes, even in the most well-intentioned. When one is deliberately addressing race and class problems, it is important to recognize that data sources may be difficult to locate. Talking directly to those who were instrumental in the origination of the bill will be a challenge, especially when confronting intended and unintended oppressive tendencies. Linguistic or hermeneutic analysis of hearing minutes might be sufficient. An alternative would be to locate critical scholars and activists who have exposed discontinuities between policy intent and impact for vulnerable groups. This approach when applied appropriately will enlighten and reveal what needs to be transformed. But because there is no guidance regarding action following upon analysis, other methods will be needed to guide critical action to change the system and fully pursue the critical perspective.

DISCUSSION

Critical approaches to policy analysis are both nonlinear and nonreductionist regarding values, while also being linear and reductionist in the analysis and in asserting the assumed causal linkage between the analytic process and the fundamental changes that should result. The approaches discussed in this chapter have differing foci and strengths;

but just as in the preceding chapters on application, certain analytic steps should be undertaken prior to the application of the selected critical approach. Added to the consideration here for the first time was the central notion of feasibility through risk assessment. Feasibility assessment in program evaluation (Chambers, Wedel, & Rodwell, 1992) generally looks at the availability of data as well as at vulnerabilities. For critical policy analysis it is assumed that the data are available, at least in some form, so that feasibility assessment can become risk analysis.

In our narrative, we may have simplified the issues at hand for actual risk determination, but a general critical thinking and decision-making process should have been clear. We want to also make clear that we are not arguing that risk should be avoided. We are suggesting that choices should be made about whether or not the risks outweigh the benefits. In other words, any policy analyst wishing to engage in the critical policy analysis process as research should be conscious of which battles to pick, picking only those where there is a possibility of winning. We always tell our students that as advocates they should know which mountains are important enough to die on and which ones should not be climbed until another day.

The types of policy research questions that are usefully answered by application of a critical approach are ones that are heavily value-laden. Questions that are "hot" for someone because of the structural issues and consequences involved are of interest, especially if understanding the issues is not sufficient. Critical approaches set the stage for fundamental, transformative change, as opposed to the incremental change possible with purely rational and nonrational approaches. From the critical perspective, the analyst uses whatever works to move the systematic analytic process to action. This means both rational and nonrational approaches may be appropriated in a rather pragmatic fashion.

So, in addition to the skill sets identified for the successful application of both of the more conservative approaches, the policy analyst using a critical approach will principally need courage and excellent strategic and critical thinking skills. Both verbal and numerical data will need to be analyzed. More importantly, power and its use and misuse must be understood and utilized. Critical policy analysis, more than the other approaches, requires excellent interpersonal skills as well as good community organizing and advocacy skills. Critical policy analysis entails the systematic research properties of the other two approaches, but by its nature, it is also a kind of action-oriented practice not for the faint hearted.

In these times of heated national policy debates, critical policy analysis has been much maligned by people on all parts of the political and/or ideological spectrum. Critical policy analysis upsets the status quo and creates opportunities for fundamental change. Critical policy analysis makes people uncomfortable and involves conflict. If the policy analyst does not have a wide interpersonal comfort zone or if the analyst needs to be appreciated and respected, critical policy analysis should not be undertaken because of the potential for doing more harm than good for the analyst, personally and professionally, and for those with whom the analyst works.

CONCLUSION

When we began this chapter, we structured the decision-making process about the selection of a particular critical approach to include a justification of the use of each approach. This was provided only to aid an analyst's decision making. Justification or defense of the use of a critical approach will be of little interest to those engaged in critical policy analysis. Those using these approaches might not even be interested in the systematic nature of the processes we have discussed here, preferring to be more mission or passion driven in the analysis. We believe that the cognitive processing that was introduced here will move passion to strategic thinking and research rigor to useful analytic information. Given this, the change actions that are hoped for as a result of critical analysis will have greater chances of success.

DISCUSSION QUESTIONS

1. Many people are not comfortable with critical modes of thinking because of the difference between them and the way they have been taught or the way they naturally think. Where is your comfort zone for criticality? What is necessary for you to skillfully engage in this approach to policy analysis research?
2. Look at all the approaches to policy analysis discussed in both Chapters 7 and 8. Identify the theories (critical, distributive justice, power and conflict) guiding each. Can you identify dimensions of those theories that were not discussed? Are there other theories influencing the structures of the critical approach to policy analysis discussed?
3. Your research question will determine the approach needed. Based on a policy with which you are familiar, write a policy

research question that would require a critical approach. Why does this question fit with a critical approach?

4. The approaches highlighted in this chapter are not standardized tools. Thus, there may be other questions that one might ask that are equally helpful to the analytical process. If you were constructing a critical policy analysis framework to examine a policy approved by a local human service agency's board of directors, are there particular questions that you would want to include? Provide a rationale for your choices. In using a critical framework, what personal or professional concerns might you have?

5. Critical policy analysis approaches tend to broaden rather than narrow the complexity of a situation while also adding a clear element of threat or risk. When do you think it is important to broaden and be inclusive of all perspectives in the analysis process? If you were working in a very rational environment, in which getting to generalizable information was highly valued, how might you persuade your colleagues to use a critical rather than a rational approach?

6. Pose a critical question about a policy with which you are familiar. Practice targeting your research by identifying the form, level (and scope), and focus of your analysis. Then select an appropriate framework and analyze the policy. Upon completion, talk about what was learned in the process, what you would do differently in the future, and the benefits and challenges you encountered. Look seriously at the practical implications of radical analysis.

Epilogue

A S WE NEAR the end of this long discussion of multiple ways to systematically interrogate policies, it is our hope that you have become convinced of the benefits of stepping back from personal preferences with the help of an appropriately targeted approach to policy analysis. Now that you have witnessed a variety of ways to engage in policy analysis based on several widely differing perspectives on how the world is and how we can come to know it, we hope we have demonstrated the advantages of using multiple perspectives in researching a particular policy. It has been our intention to show that there is no perfect form of policy analysis, just as there is no perfect question to guide research.

We hope that you have been able to see that each approach has something to offer and that all approaches together provide the opportunity to understand complicated social policy in all its complexity. We are not necessarily advocating that every time an analyst engages in policy analysis research it should be undertaken from all possible perspectives. Most times the resources are not available for that, even if it would provide important comparative information. We do, however, advocate for conscious decision making and articulation of the exact purpose of the policy analysis and the research question guiding the analysis before a particular analytic approach is selected. We believe useful results depend on this, and we believe that this sort of analysis will and should be ongoing throughout one's life as a policy practitioner.

We agree with what Teddy Kennedy once said, "One of the great lessons I've learned from a life in politics is that no reform is ever truly complete. We must constantly keep moving forward, seeking ways to create the more perfect union." (Kennedy, 2009, p. 506). Embracing policy analysis as research may just be a reasonable way of constantly moving forward—at least we hope so.

This epilogue was developed as a final confirmation that the material in the text makes sense to you. You may have noticed that there was one model or approach in each of the paired sections that was not applied to the case study. We wanted to devise an experience of comparative analysis for readers as a final exercise of integration and skill development. So that is precisely what follows.

Below you will find a policy in the form of an agreement between a service fraternity at a university and Big Brothers Big Sisters of America (BBBSA). In Boxes E.1, E.2, and E.3, you will also find one policy research resource from each of the paradigmatic perspectives we have covered in this text. Your challenge is to engage in comparative policy analysis by replicating the way we have handled each of the models or approaches that were discussed in Chapters 4, 6, and 8.

Box E.1 Hofferbert's Model for Comparative Study of Policy Formation

What were the politically relevant incidents related to?

- Historic and geographic conditions?
- Socioeconomic composition?
- Mass political behavior?
- Governmental institutions?
- Elite behavior?

What became the formal policy conversion?

What is the policy output?

Source: Adapted from *The Study of Public Policy* (p. 228), by R. Hofferbert, 1974, Indianapolis, IN: Bobbs-Merrill.

Box E.2 Schuerich's Dimensions of Policy Analysis Following a Policy Archaeology Approach

Arena I—social problem: How did the social problem come to be constructed as it is?

Arena II—social regularities: What are the dimensions of the network that constitute the social regularities of the social problem as constructed?

Arena III—policy solutions: How did the range of acceptable policy solutions become constructed?

Arena IV—policy studies: How does the policy analysis itself influence how the problem is addressed?

Source: Adapted from "Public Archaeology," by J. J. Schuerich, 1994, *Journal of Education Policy, 9*(4), 297-316.

Box E.3 McPhail's The Feminist Policy Framework: Through a Gendered Lens

A. Values
   1. Do feminist values undergird the policy? Which feminism, which values?
   2. Are value conflicts involved in the problem representations either between different feminist perspectives or between feminist and mainstream values?
B. State and market control
   1. Are women's unpaid labor and work of caring considered and valued or taken for granted?
   2. Does the policy contain elements of social control of women?
   3. Does the policy replace the patriarchal male with the patriarchal state?
   4. How does the policy mediate gender relationships between the state, market, and family? For instance, does the policy increase women's dependence upon the state or men?
C. Multiple identities
   1. How does gender in this policy interact with race or ethnicity, sexual identity, class, religion, national origin, disability, or other identity categories?
   2. Are white, middle-class, heterosexual women the assumed standard for all women?
   3. Does the policy address the multiple identities of women? The multiple oppressions a single woman may face?
D. Equality
   1. Does the policy achieve gender equality? Is there equality of results or disparate impacts?
   2. Does the policy treat people differently in order to treat them equally well? Does the policy consider gender differences in order to create more equality?
   3. If the positions of women and men were reversed, would this policy be acceptable to men?
E. Special treatment and protection
   1. Does any special treatment of women cause unintended or restrictive consequences?
   2. Is there an implicit or explicit double standard?
   3. Does being labeled different and special cause a backlash that can be used to constrain rather than to liberate women?
F. Gender neutrality
   1. Does presumed gender neutrality hide the reality of the gendered nature of the problem or solution?

(continued)

(*continued*)

G. Context

   1. Are women clearly visible in the policy? Does the policy take into account the historical, legal, social, cultural, and political context of women's lives and lived experiences, both now and in the past?

   2. Is the policy defined as a traditional "women's issue" (i.e., "pink policy")? How is a policy that is not traditionally defined as a "women's issue" still a "women's issue"?

   3. Is the male experience used as a standard? Are results extrapolated from male experience and then applied to women?

   4. Have the programs, policies, methodologies, assumptions, and theories been examined for male bias?

   5. Is women's biology treated as normal rather than as an exception to a male-defined norm?

H. Language

   1. Does the language infer male dominance or female invisibility?

   2. Are gendered expectations and language encoded in the policy?

I. Equality and rights and care and responsibility:

   1. Is there a balance of rights and responsibilities for women and men in this policy?

   2. Does the policy sustain the pattern of men being viewed as public actors and women as private actors, or does the policy challenge this dichotomization?

   3. Does the policy bring men, corporations, and the government into caring and responsible roles? Is responsibility pushed uphill and redistributed?

   4. Does the policy pit the needs of women against the needs of their fetus or children?

   5. Are women penalized for either their roles as wives, mothers or caregivers or their refusal to adopt these roles?

J. Material or symbolic reforms

   1. Is the policy merely symbolic or does it come with teeth? Are the provisions for funding, enforcement, and evaluation?

   2. Are interest groups involved in overseeing the policy implementation?

   3. Is litigation possible to refine and expand the law's interpretation?

   4. What is the strength of authority of the agency administering the policy?

   5. Is there room to transform a symbolic reform into a material reform? How?

K. Role change and role equity

   1. Is the goal of the policy role equity or role change?

   2. Does the type of change proposed affect the chance of successful passage?

L. Power analysis

   1. Are women involved in making, shaping, and implementation of the policy? In which ways were they involved? How were they included or excluded? Were the representatives of women selected by women?

2. Does the policy work to empower women?
3. Who has the power to define the problem? What are competing representations?
4. How does this policy affect the balance of power? Are there winners and losers? Is a win-win solution a possibility?

M. Other

1. Is the social construction of the problem recognized? What are alternate representations of the problem?
2. Does this policy constitute backlash for previous women's policy gains?
3. How does feminist scholarship inform the issue?
4. What women's organizations were involved in the policy formulation and implementation? Was there consensus or disagreement?
5. Where are the policy silences? What are the problems for women that are denied the status of problem of others? What policy is *not* being proposed, discussed, and implemented?
6. How does the policy compare to similar policies transnationally? Are there alternative models that we can both learn from and borrow from?
7. Does the policy blame, stigmatize, regulate, or punish women?

Source: "A Feminist Policy Analysis Framework: Through a Gendered Lens," by B. A. McPhail, 2003, *The Social Policy Journal* 2(2/3), pp. 39–61. Used with permission.

Begin with the ways we have suggested in targeting the policy research:

- Develop an appropriate research question that could be handled by the analytic approach.
- Determine the form, level, and focus of the analysis given the policy that has been presented.
- Justify the use of the approach, including some evaluation of feasibility, related to data availability and risk assessment, when necessary.
- Then apply the model or approach at least at the level of determining what data would be necessary to respond to the questions and where those data might be located.

UNIVERSITY SERVICE LEARNING POLICY WITH BIG BROTHERS BIG SISTERS OF AMERICA

PREAMBLE

The men of the XYZ Fraternity, Inc. and Big Brothers Big Sisters of America (BBBSA) have partnered nationally since 19XX to promote the importance of African American adult men mentoring African American young men. The AB chapter of XYZ Fraternity, Inc. and the Big Brothers Big Sisters Services (BBBS), Inc., Tri-Cities Office are spearheading the effort to increase awareness and develop a dynamic relationship between State University and BBBSA.

The goal of this initiative in the long term is to make State University a pioneer among all historically black colleges and universities, in the likeness of its very own chapter of the XYZ Fraternity, Inc. AB chapter has gained national attention from the fraternity (including a letter of commendation from its immediate past general president and selection as Chapter of the Year). A potential partnership between State University and BBBSA is a win-win situation; BBBS has the potential to meet the criteria of 15 objectives outlined in the 2020 vision plan, including student engagement and faculty scholarship, research, communication and marketing, work with the police department, involvement in community development, and, most notably, serving community needs. BBBS is actively participating in the State University Service Learning Program, which will offer an incentive for students to engage the community, to provide more "Bigs" in BBBS, and to serve the youth in the area. The children of the area will greatly benefit from consistent and enthusiastic mentoring designed to enhance academic achievement, with college entrance being the goal. Overall, the "biggest" winners of this program will be both the children who are influenced by the college students and the "Bigs" who are inspired to continue as engaged citizens in their communities as human services/nonprofit world professionals or as lifelong volunteers.

This partnership is a reality. Some of the largest organizations on campus have already become involved with BBBS. The number of organizations that have already answered the call to mentor speaks loudly to the potential of what the university and the State University community can accomplish by engaging in this union with BBBS.

VISION

State University (SU) Will

1. Establish and sustain a relationship between the local XYZ chapter leadership and the local BBBS leadership.
2. Learn about Big Brothers Big Sisters' history and current program service delivery philosophy.
3. Appoint a point of contact from the institution to work with the liaisons to the BBBS agency.

4. Support and build connections to and within established fraternity and student organization service projects and programs dealing with BBBS.
5. Set a goal for the number of Bigs from the school to participate, monitor progress, and meet and revise the goal.
6. Recruit volunteers to be Bigs by
   - Supporting members to become Bigs.
   - Reaching out to friends, family, coworkers, and members of their faith community.
   - Hosting Big recruitment events in the African American community, their workplace, and the religious community.
   - Involving BBBS in the service learning program.
7. Work with BBBS to develop resources to support the partnership by participating in the agency's fund development efforts.
8. Support BBBS's search for high-quality talent to serve as agency staff and to serve on the agency's board of directors as well as regional and national leadership boards.
9. Share photographs of Bigs and Littles, particularly photographs with the Bigs wearing the organization's insignia.
10. Report on successful relationships between the Bigs and Littles and successful Big recruitment strategies.
11. Support a relationship between BBBS and alumni services to promote the program, SU's success within it, and expose BBBSA to more potential mentors nationally.

XYZ Fraternity, Inc. Will

1. Serve as primary liaisons between BBBSA, BBBS, and SU.
2. Build relationships between the national leaders of all interested parties.
3. Work to further establish and expand BBBS to the entire SU National Pan-Hellenic Council.
4. Feature members of the Pan-Hellenic organization and all other student organizations serving as Bigs in marketing and communications material.
5. Foster a lasting, life-long commitment of one-to-one mentoring, beginning at the undergraduate level.
6. Allow BBBS personnel to work with members at national and regional conventions.
7. Provide information on each organization's heritage and aspirations for the future.

8. Promote the creation of this historic partnership in
   ○ Media communications.
   ○ Public service announcements.
   ○ Linkage between respective Web sites.
   ○ Internal communications.
   ○ Providing assistance in reaching out to other organizations.

Big Brothers Big Sisters of America and BBBS Services, Inc. Tri-Cities Office Will

1. Establish and sustain a relationship between the university and local BBBS leadership.
2. Learn about the fraternities, sororities, and student organizations and the University's overall contribution to the local community and to the nation.
3. Set a goal for the number of Bigs from the chapter, monitor progress, and meet to revise the goal.
4. Assign staff to ensure that the chapters, its members, and University representatives receive excellent customer service from the agency.
5. Work with the student organizations, University departments, and the administration to develop resources to support the partnership.
6. Use its brand and public relations capacity to promote and celebrate SU and its constituents' contributions to youth development.
7. Report to SU the number, quality, and outcomes of the matches.
8. Report on successful relationships between the Bigs and Littles and on successful Big recruitment strategies.
9. Provide national and local leadership opportunities for the Bigs and Littles, thereby furthering the holistic education of the mentees and mentors.
10. Publicize and highlight the partnership and all related events and accomplishments nationally, regionally, and locally with media, potential donors, and agency and government leadership.

IN WITNESS WHEREOF, Big Brothers Big Sisters and State University hereby launch a partnership with the execution of the Memorandum on March XX, 20XX.

Once you have worked through each of the approaches, step back and analyze what was produced.

- What sorts of information did you gain and what did you give up when applying each approach?
- What were the challenges of each approach?
- Taken together what might you be able to accomplish?
- Finally, what are the costs and challenges of this sort of comparative policy research?

References

Adam, S., & Kriesi, H. (2007). The network approach. In P. A. Sabatier (Ed.), *Theories of the policy process* (2nd ed., pp. 129–154). Boulder, CO: Westview Press.

Agger, B. (1998). *Critical social theories: An introduction.* Boulder, CO: Westview Press.

American Association of Retired Persons (AARP). (2004). Baby boomers envision retirement II: Survey of boomers' expectations for retirement. Washington, DC: AARP.

American Society on Aging (ASA). (2009). ASA's civic engagement program. Retrieved July 7, 2009, from http://www.asaging.orgv2/civiceng/reports.cfm.

Appelbaum, P. (1992). Involuntary commitment from a systems perspective. *Law and Human Behavior, 16,* 61–74.

Ashcraft, K. L., & Mumby, D. K. (2004). *Reworking gender: A feminist communicology of organization.* Newbury Park, CA: Sage.

Baars, J. (1991). The challenge of critical studies. *Journal of Aging Studies, 5,* 219–243.

Bardach, E. (2005). *A practical guide for policy analysis: The eightfold path to more effective problem solving* (2nd ed.). Washington, DC: CQ Press.

Belenky, M. F., Bond, L. A., & Weinstock, J. S. (1997). *A tradition that has no name: Nurturing the development of people, families, and communities.* New York, NY: Basic Books.

Berger, P., & Luckmann, T. (1976). *The social construction of reality.* Harmondsworth, Middlesex, England: Penguin Books.

Blau, J. (with M. Abramovitz). (2007). *The dynamics of social welfare policy* (2nd ed.). New York, NY: Oxford University Press.

Blau, P. (1964). *Exchange and power in social life.* New York, NY: John Wiley & Sons, Inc.

Blomquist, W. (2007). The policy process and large-N comparative studies. In P. A. Sabatier (Ed.). *Theories of the policy process* (2nd ed., pp. 261–289). Boulder, CO: Westview Press.

Bordt, Rebecca L. (1997). *The structure of women's nonprofit organizations.* Bloomington, IN: Indiana University Press.

Brewer, G. (1973). *Politicians, bureaucrats, and the consultant: A critique of urban problem solving.* New York, NY: Basic Books.

Burrell, G. (1997). *Pandemonium toward a retro-organization theory*. London, England: Sage.

Burrell, G., & Morgan, G. (1979). *Sociological paradigms and organizational analysis*. London, England: Heinemann.

Calasanti, T. (2004). New directions in feminist gerontology: An introduction. *Journal of Aging Studies, 28*, 1–8.

Chambers, D. E., & Wedel, K. R. (2009). *Social policy and social programs: A method for the practical public policy analyst* (5th ed.). Boston, MA: Pearson.

Chambers, D. E., Wedel, K.R., & Rodwell, M. K. (1992). *Evaluating social programs*. New York, NY: Allyn and Bacon.

Chow, J. C-C., & Austin, M. J. (2008). The culturally responsive social service agency: An application of an evolving definition to a case study. *Administration in Social Work, 32*(4), 39–64.

Cohen, M., March, J., & Olsen, J. (1972). A garbage can model of organizational choice. *Administrative Science Quarterly, 17* (March), 1–15.

Dean, R. (1989). Ways of knowing in clinical practice. *Clinical Social Work Journal, 17*(2), 116–127.

Department of Mental Health Mental Retardation and Substance Abuse Services. (2008, April 23). *2008 General Assembly MH Omnibus Bill Chapter 850*. Department of Mental Health Mental Retardation and Substance Abuse Services. Retrieved July 7, 2008, from http://leg1.state.va.us/cgi-bin/legp504.exe?081+ful+CHAP0850

Dilthey, W. (1976). *Selected writings*. H. P. Rickman (Ed.). London, England: Cambridge University Press.

Dolgoff, R., & Feldstein, D. (2009). *Understanding social welfare: A search for social justice* (8th ed.). Boston, MA: Allyn & Bacon.

Estrada, R., & Marksamer, J. (2006). The legal rights of LGBT youth in state custody: What child welfare and juvenile justice professionals need to know. *Child Welfare, LXXXV*(2), 171–194.

Farmer, S. M., & Fedor, D. B. (1999). Volunteer participation and withdrawal: A psychological contract perspective on the role of expectations and organizational support. *Nonprofit Management and Leadership, 9*(4), 349–367.

Fauri, D. P., Netting, F. E., & O'Connor, M. K. (2005). *Social work macro practice: Exercises and activities for policy, community, and organization interventions*. Pacific Grove, CA: Brooks/Cole.

Fay, B. (1987). *Critical social science*. Ithaca, NY: Cornell University Press.

Ferree, M. M., & Martin, P. Y. (Eds.). (1995). *Feminist organizations: Harvest of the new women's movement*. Philadelphia, PA: Temple University Press.

Flynn, J. P. (1992). *Social agency policy: Analysis and presentation for community practice* (2nd ed.). Chicago, IL: Nelson-Hall Publishers.

Foucault, M. (1972). *Archaeology of knowledge and the discourse on language*. New York, NY: Pantheon.

Fraser, M., Taylor, M., Jackson, R., & O'Jack, J. (1991). Social work and science: Many ways of knowing? *Social Work Research and Abstracts, 27*(4), 5–15.

Gambrill, E. (2006). *Social work practice: A critical thinker's guide*. London, England: Oxford.

Gambrill, E. (2005). *Critical thinking in clinical practice: Improving the quality of judgments and decisions* (2nd ed.). Hoboken, NJ: John Wiley & Sons, Inc.

Gambrill, E., & Gibbs, L. (2009). *Critical thinking for helping professionals: A skills-based workbook* (3rd ed.). New York, NY: Oxford University Press.

Gergen, K., & Davis, K. (Eds.) (1985). *The social construction of the person*. New York, NY: Springer.

Gibbs, L. (2003). *Evidence-based practice for the helping professions*. Pacific Grove, CA: Brooks/Cole.

Gilbert, N., & Terrell, P. (2010). *Dimensions of social welfare policy* (7th ed.). Boston, MA: Allyn & Bacon.

Gilligan, C. (1982). *In a different voice: Psychological theory and women's development*. Cambridge, MA: Harvard University Press.

Gottschalk, S., & Witkin, S. (1991). Rationality in social work: A critical examination. *Journal of Sociology and Social Welfare, 18*, 121–136.

Guba, E. G. (1990). The alternative paradigm dialog. In E. G. Guba (Ed.), *The paradigm dialog* (pp. 17–27). Newbury Park, CA: Sage.

Guba, E. G. (1984). The effect of definitions of policy on the nature and outcomes of policy analysis. *Educational Leadership, 42*, 63–70.

Guba, E. G. (Ed.) (1999). *The paradigm dialog*. Newbury Park, CA: Sage.

Gupta, D. K. (2001). *Analyzing public policy: Concepts, tools, and techniques*. Washington, DC: CQ Press.

Hall, C. J. (2008). A practitioner's application and deconstruction of evidence-based practice. *Families in Society, 89*(3), 385–393.

Hardina, D. (2002). *Analytical skills for community organization practice*. New York, NY: Columbia University Press.

Hartman, A. (1990). Many ways of knowing. *Social Work, 35*, 3–4.

Heineman, R. A., Bluhm, W. T., Peterson, S. A., & Kearney, E. N. (2002). *The world of the policy analyst: Rationality, values, & politics* (3rd ed.). New York, NY: Chatham House Publishers.

Heron, J. (1981). Philosophical basis for a new paradigm. In P. Reason & J. Rowan (Eds.). *Human inquiry: A sourcebook of new paradigm research* (pp. 19–35). New York, NY: John Wiley & Sons, Inc.

Hick, S., Fook, J., & Pozzuto, R. (Eds.). (2005). *Social work: A critical turn*. Toronto, Canada: Thompson.

Hofferbert, R. (1974). *The study of public policy*. Indianapolis, IN: Bobbs-Merrill.

Holcomb, P. A., & Nightingale, D. S. (2003). Conceptual underpinnings of implementation analysis. In M. C. Lennon & T. Corbett (Eds.), *Policy into action: Implementation research and welfare reform* (pp. 39–55). Washington, DC: The Urban Institute Press.

Huttman, Elizabeth (1981). *Introduction to social policy*. New York, NY: McGraw-Hill.

Imhof, S., & Kaskie, B. (2008). How can we make the pain go away? Public policies to manage pain at the end of life. *The Gerontologist, 48*(4), 423–431.

Imre, R. (1985). Tacit knowledge in social work research practice. *Smith College Studies in Social Work, 55*(2), 137–148.

Imre, R. (1984). The nature of knowledge in social work. *Social Work, 29*(1), 41–45.

Ingram, H., Schneider, A., & deLeon, P. (2007). Social construction and policy design. In P. A. Sabatier (Ed.), *Theories of the policy process* (2nd ed., pp. 93–126). Boulder, CO: Westview Press.

Jansson, B. S. (2008). *Becoming an effective policy advocate: From policy practice to social justice* (5th ed.). Belmont, CA: Thomson Brooks/Cole.

Jansson, B. S. (2000). Policy analysis. In J. Midgley, M. B. Tracy, & M. Livermore (Eds.), *The handbook of social policy* (pp. 41–52). Newbury Park, CA: Sage.

Jenkins-Smith, H. C., & Sabatier, P. A. (1994). Evaluating the advocacy coalition framework. *Journal of Public Policy, 14*(2), 175–203.

Jenkins-Smith, H., & Weimer, D. (1986). Analysis as retrograde action: The case of strategic petroleum reserves. *Public Administration Review, 45*(4), 485–494.

Karger, H. J., & Stoesz, D. (2009). *American social welfare policy: A pluralist approach* (6th ed.). Boston, MA: Allyn & Bacon.

Kaskie, B., Imhof, S., Cavanaugh, J., & Culp, K. (2008). Civic engagement as a retirement role for aging Americans. *The Gerontologist, 48*(3), 368–377.

Keeney, B. (1983). *Aesthetics of change*. New York, NY: Guilford.

Kellner, D. (1989). *Critical theory, Marxism, and modernity*. Baltimore, MD: Johns Hopkins University Press.

Kennedy, E. M. (2009). *True compass*. New York, NY: Twelve.

Kingdon, J. W. (1984). *Agendas, alternatives, and public policies*. Boston, MA: Little, Brown.

Kingdon, J. W. (1995). *Agendas, alternatives, and public policies* (2nd ed.). New York, NY: Longman.

Kravetz, D. (2004). *Tales from the trenches: Politics and practice in feminist service organizations*. Dallas, TX: University Press of America.

Kroeger, O., & Thuesen, J. M. (1998). *Type talk: The 16 personality types that determine how we live, love, and work*. New York, NY: Dell.

Lather, P. (1986). Research as praxis. *Harvard Educational Review 56* (3), 257–277.

Lejano, R. P. (2006). *Frameworks for policy analysis: Merging text and context*. New York, NY: Routledge.

Lennon, M. C., & Corbett, T. (Eds.). (2003). *Policy into action: Implementation research and welfare reform*. Washington, DC: The Urban Institute Press.

Leonard, S. T. (1990). *Critical theory in political practice*. Princeton, NJ: Princeton University Press.

Lincoln, Y. S., & Guba, E. G. (1985). *Naturalistic inquiry*. Newbury Park, CA: Sage.

Lincoln, Y. S., & Guba, E. G. (1986). Research, evaluation, and policy analysis: Heuristics for disciplined inquiry. *Policy Studies Review, 5*(3), 546–565.

Lipsky, M. (1980). *Street level bureaucracy.* New York, NY: Russell Sage Foundation.

Macduff, N., Netting, F. E., & O'Connor, M. K. (2009) Multiple ways of coordinating volunteers with differing styles of service. *Journal of Community Practice, 17*(4), 400–423.

Mancini, M. A., & Lawson, H. A. (2009). Facilitating positive emotional labor in peer-providers of mental health services. *Administration in Social Work, 33,* 3–22.

March, C., Smyth, I., & Mukhopadhyay, M. (2003). *A guide to gender-analysis frameworks.* London, England: Oxfam.

Margolin, L. (1997). *Under the cover of kindness: The invention of social work.* Charlottesville, VA: University of Virginia Press.

Martinson, M., & Minkler, M. (2006). Civic engagement and older adults: A critical perspective. *The Gerontologist, 46*(3), 318–324.

Marx, K. (1977). *A contribution to the critique of political economy.* Moscow, Russia: Progress Publishers: notes by R. Rojas.

Marx, K. (1887). *Capital (Das Kapital).* Moscow, Russia: Progress Publishers.

Marx, K., & Engels, F. (1998). *The communist manifesto,* introduction by Martin Malia. New York, NY: Penguin Group.

Maturana, H. (1988). Reality: The search for objectivity or the quest for a compelling argument. *Irish Journal of Psychology 9,* 25–82.

McKnight, J. (1995). *The careless society: community and its counterfeits.* New York, NY: Basic Books.

McPhail, B. A. (2003). A feminist policy analysis framework: Through a gendered lens. *The Social Policy Journal, 2*(2/3), 39–61.

Metzendorf, D. (2005). *The evolution of feminist organizations: An organizational study.* Lanham, MD: University Press of America.

Minkler, M., & Holstein, M. B. (2008). From civil rights to . . . civil engagement? Concerns of two older critical gerontologists about a "new social movement" and what it portends. *Journal of Aging Studies, 22,* 196–204.

Mollica, R. L. (2008). Trends in state regulation of assisted living. *Generations, 31*(3), 67–70.

Morris, P. M. (2002). The capabilities perspective: A framework for social justice. *Families in Society: The Journal of Contemporary Human Services, 83*(4), 365–372.

Morrow-Howell, N., Hinterlong, J., Rozario, P., & Tang, F. (2003). The effects of volunteering on the well-being of older adults. *Journal of Gerontology, 58B,* S137–146.

Moser, C. (1993). *Gender planning and development. Theory, practice and training.* London, England: Routledge.

Mullaly, B. (2007). *The new structural social work: Ideology, theory, and practice* (3rd ed.). Ontario, Canada: Oxford University Press.

Nelson, B. J. (1984). *Making an issue of child abuse: Political agenda setting for social problems*. Chicago, IL: University of Chicago Press.

Netting, F. E., Kettner, P. M., & McMurtry, S. M. (2008). *Social work macro practice* (4th ed.). Boston, MA: Allyn & Bacon.

Netting, F. E., & O'Connor, M. K. (2008). Recognizing the need for evidence-based practices in organizational and community settings. *Journal of Evidence-Based Social Work*, 4(3/4), 473–496.

Netting, F. E., O'Connor, M. K., & Fauri, D. P. (2008). *Comparative approaches to program planning*. Hoboken, NJ: John Wiley & Sons, Inc.

Newman, T. (2002). Promoting resilience: A review of effective strategies for child care services. Exeter, England: Center for Evidence Based Social Sciences.

Nussbaum, M. C. (2006). *Frontiers of justice*. Cambridge, MA: The Belknap Press of Harvard University.

O'Connor, M. K., & Netting, F. E. (2009). *Organization practice: A guide to understanding human service organizations*. Hoboken, NJ: John Wiley & Sons, Inc.

O'Connor, M. K., & Netting, F. E. (2008). Teaching policy analysis as research: Consideration and extension of options. *Journal of Social Work Education*, 44(3), 159–172.

Ostrom, E. (2007). Institutional rational choice: An assessment of the institutional analysis and development framework. In P. A. Sabatier (Ed.), *Theories of the policy process* (2nd ed., pp. 21–64). Boulder, CO: Westview Press.

Pascall, G. (1986). *Social policy: A feminist analysis*. London, England: Tavistock Publications.

Patton, C. V., & Sawicki, D. S. (1993). *Basic methods of policy analysis and planning*. Englewood Cliffs: NJ: Prentice Hall.

Paul, R. W. (1993). *Critical thinking: What every person needs to know to survive in a rapidly changing world*. Santa Rosa, CA: Foundation for Critical Thinking.

Paul, R. W., & Elder, L. (2002). *Critical thinking: Tools for taking charge of your professional life*. Upper Saddle River, NJ: Pearson Education, Inc.

Paul, R. W., & Elder, L. (2009). *The miniature guide to critical thinking concepts and tools*. Dillon Beach, CA: The Foundation for Critical Thinking.

Pew Research Center (2005). Baby Boomers Approach Age 60: From the Age of Aquarius to the Age of Responsibility. Retrieved July 6, 2009, from http://pewsocialtrends.org/assets/pdf/socialtrends-boomers120805.pdf.

Polanyi, M. (1962). *Personal knowledge: Toward a post-critical philosophy*. Chicago, IL: University of Chicago Press.

Polanyi, M. (1966). *The tacit dimension*. Garden City, NY: Doubleday.

Popkewitz, T. (1984). *Paradigm and ideology in educational research; The social functions of the intellectual*. London, England: Falmer Press.

Popple, P. R., & Leighninger, L. (2008). *The policy-based profession: An introduction to social welfare policy analysis for social workers*. Boston, MA: Allyn & Bacon.

Prigmore, C. S., & Atherton, C. R. (1986). *Social welfare policy: Analysis and formulation* (2nd ed.). Lexington, MA: Heath.

Rawls, J. (1971). *A theory of justice*. Cambridge, MA: Harvard University Press.

Reamer, F. G. (1993). *The philosophical foundations of social work*. New York, NY: Columbia University Press.

Rehner, J. (1994). *Practical strategies for critical thinking*. Boston, MA: Houghton Mifflin.

Roby, J. L., & Shaw, S. A. (2006). The African orphan crisis and international adoption. *Social Work, 51*(3), 199–210.

Ross, D. (2006). Game theory. Stanford Encyclopedia of Philosophy, pp. 68. Retrieved July 26, 2009, from http://plato.stanford.edu/entries/game-theory/.

Ruggiero, V. (2001). *Thinking critically about ethical issues* (5th ed.). Boston, MA: McGraw-Hill.

Sabatier, P. A. (Ed.) (2007). *Theories of the policy process* (2nd ed.). Boulder, CO: Westview Press.

Sabatier, P. A. (1986). Top-down and bottom-up models of policy implementation: A critical analysis and suggested synthesis. *Journal of Public Policy, 6* (January), 21–48.

Sabatier, P. A., & Weible, C. M. (2007). The advocacy coalition framework: Innovations and clarifications. In P. A. Sabatier (Ed.), *Theories of the policy process* (2nd ed., pp. 189–220). Boulder, CO: Westview Press.

Scheurich, J. J. (1994). Policy archaeology: A new policy studies methodology. *Journal of Education Policy, 9*(4), 297–316.

Schiele, J. H. (2000). *Human services and the Afrocentric paradigm*. New York, NY: The Haworth Press.

Schlager, E. (2007). A comparison of frameworks, theories, and models of policy processes. In P. A. Sabatier (Ed.), *Theories of the policy process* (2nd ed., pp. 293–319). Boulder, CO: Westview Press.

Schlager, E., & Blomquist, W. (1996). A comparison of three emerging theories of the policy process. *Political Research Quarterly, 49*(3), 651–672.

Segal, E., & Bruzuzy, S. (1998). *Social welfare policy, programs, and practice*. Itasca, IL: F. E. Peacock.

Sen, A. (1992). *Inequality reexamined*. New York, NY: Russell Sage Foundation.

Shafritz, J., & Ott, J. S. (2001). *Classics of organization theory* (5th ed.). Fort Worth, TX: Harcourt College Publishers.

Shannon, C. S. (2009). An uptapped resource: Understanding volunteers aged 8 to 12. *Nonprofit Voluntary Sector Quarterly, 38*(5), 828–845.

Simon, H. (1957). *Models of man*. New York, NY: John Wiley & Sons, Inc.

Specht, H., & Courtney, M. (1994). *Unfaithful angels: How social work abandoned its mission*. New York, NY: The Free Press.

Stone, D. (2002). *Policy paradox: The art of political decision making* (revised ed.). New York, NY: Norton.

Tang, F., & Morrow-Howell, N. (2008). Involvement in voluntary organizations: How older adults access volunteer roles. *Journal of Gerontological Social Work, 51*(3–4), 210–227.

Tang, F., Morrow-Howell, N., & Hong, S. (2009). Inclusion of diverse older populations in volunteering: The importance of institutional facilitation. *Nonprofit Voluntary Sector Quarterly, 38*(5), 810–827.

Tanner, M. (2008). The grass is not always greener: A look at national health care systems. *Policy Analysis, 613,* 1–48.

Taylor, J. B. (2008). *My stroke of insight: A brain scientist's personal journey.* New York, NY: Viking.

Thomas, R. L., & Medina, C. K. (2008). Leveraging social capital among organizations to secure employment for welfare clients. *Journal of Community Practice, 16*(3), 271–291.

True, J. L., Jones, B. D., & Baumgartner, F. R. (2007). Punctuated-equilibrium theory: Explaining stability and change in public policymaking. In P. A. Sabatier (Ed.), *Theories of the policy process* (2nd ed., pp. 155–187). Boulder, CO: Westview Press.

Tyson, K. (1995). A new approach to relevant scientific research for practitioners: The heuristic paradigm. *Social Work, 37,* 541–556.

Van Parijs, P. (2000). The ground floor of the world: On the socio-economic consequences of linguistic globalization. *International Political Science Review, 21*(2), 217–233.

Varela, F. (1989). Reflections on the circulation of concepts between the biology of cognition and systemic family therapy. *Family Process, 28,* 15–24.

Watzlawick, P. (1984). *The invented reality.* New York, NY: Norton.

Weick, K. E. (1979). *The social psychology of organizing* (2nd ed.). New York, NY: Random House.

Wittgenstein, L. (1889–1961). Tractatus logico-philosophicus suivi de investigations philosophiques. Paris, France: Librairie Gallimard.

Wollebaek, D., & Selle, P. (2002). Does participation in voluntary associations contribute to social capital? The impact of intensity, scope, and type. *Nonprofit and Voluntary Sector Quarterly, 32*(1), 32–61.

Zahariadis, N. (2007). The multiple streams framework: Structure, limitations, prospects. In P. A. Sabatier (Ed.), *Theories of the policy process* (2nd ed., pp. 65–92). Boulder, CO: Westview Press.

About the Authors

Mary Katherine O'Connor is a professor in the School of Social Work at Virginia Commonwealth University, where she has taught in the MSW and PhD programs for 23 years. She received a BS in Art from Immaculate Heart College, Hollywood, CA, and MSW and PhD degrees from the University of Kansas. Prior to entering academia, Dr. O'Connor was a member of the Peace Corps in Brazil, and she has extensive direct and administrative practice experience in child welfare in both the governmental and the nonprofit sectors. She was a Fulbright Scholar in Brazil, where she taught constructivist research and conducted research with street children. She was the director of a child welfare stipend program that prepares BSW and MSW students for careers in public child welfare practice. Her present research with Dr. Netting involves investigating the organizational practices of 100-year-old agencies in Richmond, VA. She is a member of the National Association of Social Workers and the Council on Social Work Education, where she served a term as member of the Women's Commission (now Council). She is the coauthor of *Evaluating Social Programs* with Drs. Donald Chambers and Kenneth Wedel, coauthor of *Organization Practice* with Dr. Netting (now in its second edition), coauthor of *Social Work Macro Practice Workbook* and *Comparative Approaches to Program Planning* with Drs. Netting and David Fauri, and is the sole author of *Social Work Constructivist Research*. She has written numerous book chapters and journal articles with a particular focus on organization practice, child welfare issues, or constructivist research methods. She is the School of Social Work faculty nominee for the Virginia Commonwealth University 2010 Distinguished Teaching Award. She is a consulting editor for *Health and Social Work* and serves on the editorial boards of the *Journal of Progressive Human Services, Child Abuse and Neglect*, the *International Journal*, the *Journal of Qualitative Social Work Research and Practice*, and the *Journal of Social Work Education*. In addition, she reviews articles for several other journals in the areas of family violence, child welfare, and qualitative methodology.

F. Ellen Netting is professor of Social Work and holds the Samuel S. Wurtzel Endowed Chair at Virginia Commonwealth University, where she has taught in the BSW, MSW, and PhD programs for 17 years, having previously taught for 10 years at Arizona State University. She received her BA from Duke University, her MSW from the University of Tennessee at Knoxville, and her PhD from the University of Chicago. She continues to collaborate with Dr. Peter M. Kettner and Dr. Steven L. McMurtry on *Social Work Macro Practice*, published by Allyn & Bacon, now in its fourth edition (2008). She is the coauthor of 10 other books and has published more than 175 book chapters and refereed journal articles. She received the VCU Distinguished Scholar Award in 1997, was elected to the National Academy of Social Work Practice as a Distinguished Scholar in 1998, and received the Recent Contributions to Scholarship award at the Council on Social Work Education's Annual Program Meeting in February 2005. Her scholarship has focused on health and human service delivery issues for frail elders, as well as on nonprofit management concerns, primarily in religiously affiliated agencies. She was coinvestigator for the John A. Hartford Foundation Primary Care Physician Initiative, a national demonstration on primary care physician practice in geriatrics, in conjunction with an interdisciplinary team of researchers. She serves on the editorial boards of *Nonprofit Management and Leadership*, the *Journal of Community Practice*, the *Journal of Applied Gerontology*, the *Journal of Gerontological Social Work*, and the *Journal of Religious Gerontology*. She is consulting editor for the *Journal of Social Work Education* and *Social Work* and reviews articles for numerous journals in the areas of social work, nonprofit management, and aging.

Author Index

Foucault, M., 153, 155
Fraser, M., 138

Gambrill, E., 3, 37, 207
Gergen, K., 145
Gibbs, L., 3, 37, 207
Gilbert, N., xvii, 11, 47, 49, 50, 51
Gilligan, C., 211
Gottschalk, S., 138
Guba, E. G., xvi, xvii, 10, 38, 47,
    48, 50, 51, 52, 55, 56, 57, 91, 139,
    140, 157, 161, 162, 163, 165, 193,
    195, 197, 208
Gupta, D. K., 1

Hall, C. J., 37
Hardina, D., 216, 264
Hartman, A., 138
Heineman, R. A., 1
Heron, J., 138
Hick, S., 246
Hinterlong, J., 120
Hofferbert, R., 89, 90, 276
Holcomb, P. A., 95, 96, 123, 124,
    125, 126, 127
Hong, S., 268
Huttman, E., 92, 94, 115, 117, 118,
    119, 123

Imhof, S., 50, 54, 120
Imre, R., 138, 140
Ingram, H., 146, 147

Jackson, R., 138
Jansson, B. S., xvii, 12, 13,
    14, 37, 38, 48, 91, 111, 112,
    114, 115
Jenkins-Smith, H., 206
Jenkins-Smith, H. C., 148,
    156
Jones, B. D., 216

Karger, H. J., xvii
Kaskie, B., 50, 54, 120
Kearney, E. N., 1
Keeney, B., 145
Kellner, D., 211
Kennedy, E. M., 275
Kettner, P. M., 29
Kingdon, J. W., 30, 143, 144, 157,
    158, 159, 182, 183, 184, 185,
    187, 188
Kravetz, D., 264
Kriesi, H., 215, 216
Kroeger, O., 207

Lather, P., 209
Lawson, H. A., 21
Leighninger, L., xvii, 1, 2, 37
Lejano, R. P., 1, 55, 57, 59, 77, 83,
    85, 137, 138, 207, 211, 226,
    227, 228, 235, 254, 255, 257,
    260
Lennon, M. C., 38
Leonard, S. T., 212
Lincoln, Y. S., 38, 139, 140
Lipsky, M., 161
Luckmann, T., 145

Macduff, N., 258
Mancini, M. A., 21
March, J., 30, 144
Margolin, L., 246
Marksamer, J., 53, 54
Martin, P. Y., 264
Martinson, M., 48, 54, 259
Marx, K., 5, 211, 218, 220
Maturana, H., 145
McKnight, J., 246
McMurtry, S. M., 29
McPhail, B. A., 220, 221, 223, 279
Medina, C. K., 51, 52, 54
Metzendorf, D., 264

Subject Index